MOVINGBODIES

Studies in Rhetoric/Communication   Thomas W. Benson, Series Editor

MOVING BODIES

KENNETH BURKE AT THE EDGES OF LANGUAGE

DEBRA HAWHEE

The University of South Carolina Press

© 2009 University of South Carolina

Published by the University of South Carolina Press
Columbia, South Carolina 29208

www.sc.edu/uscpress

Manufactured in the United States of America

21 20 19 18 17 16 15 14   10 9 8 7 6 5 4 3 2

Library of Congress Cataloging-in-Publication Data

Hawhee, Debra.
   Moving bodies : Kenneth Burke at the edges of language / Debra Hawhee.
     p. cm. — (Studies in rhetoric/communication)
   Includes bibliographical references and index.
   ISBN 978-1-57003-809-9 (cloth : alk. paper)
 1. Burke, Kenneth, 1897–1993. I. Title.
   B945.B774H39 2009
   191—dc22
                             2009003453

ISBN 978-1-61117-090-0 (pbk.)

CONTENTS

Series Editor's Preface vii
Acknowledgments ix
Abbreviations xi

    Introduction: An "Excursion" 1
1 Bodies as Equipment for Moving (from Artist
    to Audience) 12
2 Burke's Mystical Method 30
3 Burke on Drugs: Efficiency and the Valuation of Habits 55
4 From the Rhetoric of Science to the Science of Rhetoric:
    The Case of Endocrinology 75
5 Seeing "Deviance" as Inclination: Kretschmerian
    Constitutions and Bodily Occupations 92
6 Body Language: Paget and Gesture-Speech Theory 106
7 Welcome to the Beauty Clinic 125
    Conclusion: Action in Motion 156

Notes 169
Works Cited 189
Index 205
About the Author 217

SERIES EDITOR'S PREFACE

Debra Hawhee's *Moving Bodies: Kenneth Burke at the Edges of Language* suggests that Kenneth Burke did not conceive of the body as "reason's binary other." The famous Burkean distinction between motion and action, she argues, is not a simple binary. Properly understood, it complicates the relationships of body and action, body and mind, body and culture, and body and language. Hawhee reconfigures the narrative of Burke's turn from aesthetics to rhetoric by finding in his early short fiction and his music criticism an interest in bodies—both the artist's body and the responding body of the audience—thus setting Burke in his early aesthetic work already on a rhetorical path. Hawhee discovers in Burke's early stories, collected in *The White Oxen* (1924), the body as "a generator of belief." Burke's music criticism rejected what he described as the common critical preferences toward either "secular mysticism" or technical accomplishment, inventing instead a critical language to describe the incipient or actual responses of listeners to the musical experience. The rhythmic and harmonic features of the music are acted out in the bodies of the audience. At the end of the 1920s, Burke wrote a passage in *Counter-Statement* (1931) for which his early fiction and music criticism had prepared him: "A rhythm is a promise which the poet makes to the reader—and in proportion as the reader comes to rely upon this promise, he falls into a state of general surrender which makes him more likely to accept without resistance the rest of the poet's material. In becoming receptive to so much, he becomes receptive to still more. The varied rhythms of prose also have their 'motor' analogies. . . . We mean that in all rhythmic experiences one's 'muscular imagination' is touched." Hawhee notes with appreciation the observation of her former teacher Jack Selzer that in *Counter-Statement*, "Burke hatches what Selzer calls his 'tremendous innovation,' which is the theory of form as eloquence (*Kenneth Burke in Greenwich Village* 143)—of art as rhetorical" and goes on to note that the triggering passage in Burke is about physical bodies.

Burke's thinking about bodies and rhetoric was shaped, Hawhee argues, by his early encounter with mysticism, especially as expressed in the mystical dance performances brought to America by G. I. Gurdjieff and in the philosophical and psychological writings of William James. In a discussion of James, Burke offers his notion of "frames of acceptance": "By 'frames of acceptance' we mean the more or less organized system of meanings by which a thinking man gauges the historical situation and adopts a role with relation to it."

Professor Hawhee follows Burke's interest in human bodies and their relations to language and rhetoric through his reflections on drugs, the rhetoric of science, deviance, body language, and the "cloacal" imagination. Hawhee depicts Burke in the 1950s not as simply purifying his work into his "Symbolic of Motives" but also as experiencing and trying to come to terms with physical decline and his diminishing powers as a writer. She examines the "productive work of breakdown," and how "two bodies—the body of theory and Burke's own ailing body—both sculpted and stultified his writing in this period." In *Moving Bodies* Debra Hawhee offers a challenging new reading of Kenneth Burke and, through him, a fresh and original investigation of body criticism, language, and rhetoric.

THOMAS W. BENSON

ACKNOWLEDGMENTS

This book is the result of seven years' work and the efforts of scores of people. Foremost on the list of people I would like to thank is Jack Selzer, whose capacious knowledge, catchy enthusiasm, and unremitting generosity are really unmatchable. Selzer is the reason so many scholars have pursued Burke studies beyond their seminar papers. Thanks too to my other mentors—Janet Atwill, Sharon Crowley, Cheryl Glenn, Peter Mortensen, and Jeffrey Walker—whom I tried to shield from doing too much with this book but whose encouragement nevertheless kept me on task. Thanks too to members of the Burke family, especially Elspeth Hart, Anthony Burke, Michael Burke, and Julie Whitaker for their generous hospitality and for their thoughtful engagement on this book in particular.

A number of archivists, trustees, and rights holders were helpful and responsive to my requests to reuse material. For the cover image, I thank the Oskar Schlemmer Theatre Estate and Archive, Secretariat: 28824 Oggebblo (VB), Italy, for permission to reproduce "The Symbol in Man (Dematerialization)" ©2008; photograph courtesy of Archive C. Raman Schlemmer, IT–28824 (VB), Italy. Thanks to Sarah Cannon Holden, granddaughter of W. B. Cannon, for allowing me to reproduce "Walter B. Cannon's autonomic nervous system" from his *Bodily Changes in Pain, Hunger, Fear, and Rage* (1915). Mr. Robert Cowley gave me permission to quote from the Malcolm Cowley Papers at the Newberry Library. Mr. Anthony Burke, of the Kenneth Burke Literary Trust, granted me permission to quote from the Kenneth Burke Papers. The Rare Books and Manuscripts Section, Special Collections of the Pennsylvania State University Libraries gave me permission to quote from the Kenneth Burke Papers, and the Manuscripts Division of the Department of Rare Books and Special Collections, Princeton University Library, permitted me to quote from an August 1933 letter from Kenneth Burke in the Allen Tate Papers. Taylor and Francis granted permission to reprint in chapter 3 portions of my article "Burke on Drugs," which appeared in *Rhetoric Society Quarterly* 31, no. 1 (2004): 5–28, and to include in chapter 6 my article "Language as Sensuous Action: Kenneth Burke, Sir Richard Paget, and Gesture-Speech Theory," which appeared in *Quarterly Journal of Speech* 92 (2006): 331–54.

The members of Jack Selzer's spring 2000 seminar on Kenneth Burke—especially Dana Anderson, Jessica Enoch, Jodie Nicotra, and Dan Smith—put up with the interloper who had taken the course four or five years earlier and were the first to discuss with me Burke's curious interest in biology. Thanks also to David Bartholomae, Martin Camargo, and Barbara Wilson, who provided release time from teaching, and to the University of Illinois and the University of Pittsburgh for research grants. Special collections librarians at Penn State University, Vanderbilt University, and the Newberry Library have also been most helpful, especially Sandra Stelts at Penn State. For their invaluable assistance with the unwieldy research, I thank Kim Hensley Owens, Jon Stone, Nicole Walls, and Amy Wan. Thanks also to Kassie Lamp and Christa Olson, who helped with all-important "end-game" matters, including the index. I am grateful to Barbara Biesecker, Celeste Condit, Ann George, and Ellen Quandahl for showing that women need to be in the Burke mix as well. I'm ever grateful to those kindhearted souls who read early drafts of my work, including Dana Anderson, the late Wayne Booth, Gregory Clark, Cara Finnegan, Ann George, Joshua Gunn, Cory Holding, Jordynn Jack, David Kaufer, Melissa Littlefield, Steven Mailloux, Elizabeth Mazzolini, Ned O'Gorman, Catherine Prendergast, Jack Selzer (again), Spencer Schaffner, and Julia Walker. Michael Rothberg and Jack Selzer each kindly gave the mysticism material a large venue. Other important sounding boards include the members of my summer seminar: Elizabeth Baldridge, Melissa Girard, Robin Jensen, and Keguro Macharia; participants in the Unit for Criticism and Interpretive Theory's affect seminar and conference, especially Samantha Frost; scholars in rhetorical studies: Michael Bernard-Donals, David Blakesley, Don Bialostosky, Deborah Brandt, Collin Brooke, Dan Brouwer, Celeste Condit, Diane Davis, Richard Graff, Stephen Hartnett, Gordon Hutner, Jenell Johnson, Jay Kastely, Michele Kennerly, Andrew King, John Lucaites, Dennis Lynch, John Lyne, Robert Markley, John Murphy, Cary Nelson, Martin Nystrand, Christa Olson, Jeremy Packer, Phaedra Pezzullo, Alisse Portnoy, John Poulakos, Jim Seitz, Melissa Tombro, Martha Webber, Robert Wess, Mike Witmore, and Anne Wysocki; close colleagues: Stephanie Foote, Marah Gubar, and Kellie Robertson. Readers of blogos also provided important feedback on the occasional scholarly post. Members of the English Department at the University of Michigan unwittingly pushed me to write chapter 7, where it all falls together. Gregory Clark and David Henry published early versions of two chapters in the journals they edited. Deborah Holdstein published a short piece derived from the conclusion in *College Composition and Communication*'s "Re/Visions" feature. Project Chicago and a sabbatical granted by my university helped me finish things when I did.

No doubt my largest debt of gratitude is owed to John Marsh, the toughest, most attuned, and sharpest-eyed reader I know. He read—and wrote on—every page of this book, some more than once, as well as those pages that didn't end up here.

ABBREVIATIONS

ATH = *Attitudes toward History* (1937)
CS = *Counter-Statement* (1931)
GM = *A Grammar of Motives* (1945)
PC = *Permanence and Change: An Anatomy of Purpose* (1935)
PLF = "The Philosophy of Literary Form" (1941)

Introduction | An "Excursion"

The July 1920 issue of the *Dial* features a two-page piece called simply "The Excursion." The piece, a story written by Kenneth Duva Burke, then twenty-three years old, is, according to Jack Selzer, one among a set of Burke's stories that "gloss over hard distinctions between art and criticism in a way that anticipates the criticism-as-art in [his 1931 book] *Counter-Statement* and in much of Burke's other work not only in the 1920s but after" (*Kenneth Burke in Greenwich Village* 90). As Selzer claims, the fable/character sketch operates as a "relentless exploration of a characteristically modernist theme that deeply interested him [Burke] during the 1920s . . . : the place of the artist in society, the tension between artistic temperament and the commercial, technological, and material imperatives of the age" (90). All of these thematic currents indeed run through "The Excursion," which features a despairing narrator plotting to destroy an anthill.

"Do Ants Talk?" A Language of Bodies

Yet to focus strictly on broad-stroke modernist themes risks missing two crucial points about the story: (1) that it connects thought with materiality and mobility, and (2) that it posits sensuousness as communication. Here is the opening paragraph: "Having nothing to do, and having searched in vain among the notes of a piano for something to think on, I started off on a walk, trusting that I might scent a scandal on the breeze, or see God's toe peep through the sky. I passed a barber shop, a grocery store, a little Italian girl, a chicken coop, a road-house, an abandoned quarry, a field of nervous wheat. All this distance I had walked under God's blue sky, and still without a thought. But at last, after trudging on for hours, I came upon a thought. Miles upon miles I had walked for a thought, and at last I came upon an ant hill" (27).

Noteworthy in this passage is the narrator's quest for thought through movement—first in the rhythmic, tinkly notes of the piano, and then on a meandering walk. That the "swarming mass" (27) of an anthill finally counts as "a thought" for the questing narrator further underscores the importance of both movement and material for thought. Moreover, the hill itself, presumably the product of the toiling ants, might be read as an instance of what political theorist Jane Bennett calls "thing power," whereby matter pulses with energy, revealing a "world where the line between inert matter and vital energy, between animate, and inanimate, is permeable" (352). Such permeability in fact becomes the story's focus when Burke's narrator destroys the anthill and then erupts into a wailing meditation on death and suffering.

Just before the destructive act, however, as the narrator inspects the anthill, he observes two ants approaching and touching each other. Wondering what that could "mean," he asks himself, "Do ants talk?" (28). "The Excursion," then, not only sounds what would become signature modernist themes in modernist tones of despair, but the story also shows Burke working very early on with the force of matter, and concomitantly with a rhythmic, sensuous, material notion of communication and, indeed, of thought itself. Burke's story, that is, presents an account of thought and communication that depends not on cognition—an extensive movement of mind—but on physical, responsive movement and external, sensuous connection, even in the instances of the character's fingers on piano keys, of his feet on the ground, and of the ants on each other. However momentarily, Burke's "Excursion" figures communication as haptic and bodily.

These notions of vitality, energy, and bodily communication would form the swarming mass of concepts that Burke never stopped contemplating, that he at times mangled, but out of which he ultimately fashioned the theories of language and rhetoric that would become signposts for rhetorical studies and, to a lesser degree but still significantly, literary studies. At the center of that swarming mass, as with both the ants and the narrator of "The Excursion," is the thinking, sensing, moving body. Bodies, for Burke, enable critical reflection on meaning-making from an anti-Cartesian, noncognitive, nonrational perspective—that is, from a perspective that does not begin by privileging reason or conscious thought. It would be a mistake, however, to believe (as I did when I began writing this book) that Burke moves to the body as reason's binary other, the sole answer to a Cartesianism that privileges mind and reason. Instead a focus on the body as more than just the obverse of the mind can enable a productive theoretical move to the thought-work of rhythm, energy, material, and movement. Such a move to the body thereby complicates an easy separation between mind and body, body and culture, and, as this book will show, body and language. At its most broadly productive, a move to the body also engages the multiple scientific, musical, or religious perspectives that most carefully contemplate bodies, rhythms, and movements, none of which can or need be easily disentangled from sociocultural or economic forces, but all of which bear importantly on meaning making, language use, and, yes, thought itself. Such a move, that is, calls for transdisciplinarity.

Trans- or Inter-? Studies for the Twenty-first Century

Transdisciplinarity has become a focus of late in response to the rapid proliferation of disciplines, what French-Romanian particle physicist Basarab Nicolescu refers to in his *Manifesto of Transdisciplinarity* as a "disciplinary big bang" (34). This proliferation has not been limited to the cluster of fields Nicolescu knows best—the physical sciences—but in, and importantly, across, the social sciences and humanities as well. According to feminist social scientists Irene Dölling and Sabine Hark, transdisciplinarity both functions "as an epistemological and methodological strategy" and reconfigures disciplines as "multiple interconnections shot through by cross-disciplinary pathways" (1195). At stake in transdisciplinarity are the limits of knowledge itself, and most transdisciplinary work simultaneously respects disciplinary knowledge and acknowledges the limitations of working within the framework of a single discipline.[1]

What distinguishes transdisciplinarity from interdisciplinarity is its effort to suspend—however temporarily—one's own disciplinary terms and values in favor of a broad, open, multilevel inquiry. As Nicolescu puts it, "interdisciplinarity overflows the disciplines, but its goal still remains within the framework of disciplinary research" (43). That is, interdisciplinarity is marked by disciplinary affinity—closely allied fields such as history and literary studies or gender studies and rhetorical studies sharing methods and cross-listing courses—whereas transdisciplinarity is marked by shared interest in a particular matter or problem but often draws together radically different approaches. The difference is a matter of sharing methodologies (something interdisciplinarity does quite well) versus broadening perspective, one of the main goals of transdisciplinarity. Such an effort requires a suspension of disbelief in the values of other fields, an intellectual leap of faith. As Dölling and Hark argue, transdisciplinarity calls for "continual reexamination of artificially drawn and contingent boundaries and that which they exclude" (1197). Too often a signal of disciplinary boundaries has to do with watchwords. When such words as *origin* or *biology* or even *biography* appear before well-trained critical theorists in literary, rhetorical, or cultural studies, those words are met with at best skeptical looks, at worst whistle-blowing dismissal. Often such suspicion owes to solid philosophical commitments, but such disciplinary dismissal also effectively polices boundaries and stultifies the expansion of perspectives.

Transdisciplinarity, Incongruity

From an early point in his career and however unwittingly, Kenneth Burke became something of a spokesperson for transdisciplinarity. This is largely because he never toed any disciplinary line but was interested instead in thinking as broadly as possible about language, meaning making, rhetoric, and, as this book will show, bodies. In many ways twenty-first-century transdisciplinarity captures the spirit of Burkean inquiry, especially as manifest in Burke's early critical method, which he called "perspective by incongruity." At base, perspective by incongruity calls for balancing a particular interpretive perspective with another perspective that sees things differently—often radically so. Burke poses the question this way: "Out of all this overlapping, conflicting, and supplementing of interpretive frames, what arises as a *totality*? The only thing that all this seems to make for is a reinforcement of the *interpretive attitude* itself" (*Permanence and Change* [PC] 3e 118). These lines, written more than seventy years ago, may speak to our transdisciplinary moment, for if *discipline* is substituted for *interpretive attitudes*, Burke's lines pose a crucial question about the limits of disciplinary knowledge: at what point do disciplines exhaust their perspectives and begin to exist simply as reinforcers of themselves? Such a question assumes a discipline that is insular, and thanks to decades of interdisciplinary work, insularity is fairly rare these days. And yet the basic divisions—sciences and the humanities—still more often than not hold firm.

Burke's perspective by incongruity grows out of an attempt to "see around the edges of the orientation in which a . . . thinker lives" (*PC* 3e 117), and it involves changing what and how we study. Burke's second book, *Permanence and Change* (1935), features a long meditation on perspective by incongruity during which Burke offers that perhaps "one should study one's dog for his *Napoleonic* qualities, or observe mosquitoes for signs of wisdom to which we are forever closed. One should discuss sneezing in the terms heretofore reserved for the analysis of a brilliant invention, as if it were a creative act, a vast synthesis uniting in its simple self a multitude of prior factors" (3e 119–20). This passage hearkens back to the "thought" Burke's excursive narrator happens upon at the foot of the anthill. Burke goes on to employ a "hypothetical" research problem: "Imagine, then, setting out to study mankind, with whose system of speech you are largely familiar. Imagine beginning your course of study *precisely by depriving yourself of this familiarity*, attempting to understand motives and purposes by avoiding as much as possible the clues handed you ready-made in the texture of the language itself. In this you will have deliberately discarded available data in the interests of a fresh point of view, the heuristic or perspective value of a planned incongruity" (3e 121).

Here we have one of the most distilled accounts of Burke's own intellectual mission and its basic method. It is a method that learns through suspension, through a deliberate forgetting of what one already "knows." This book therefore offers Burke's planned incongruity, his deliberate forgetting, as a useful tactic, a transdisciplinary tactic, for approaching the body and new materialisms. Such deliberate forgetting is, I offer, crucial to a transdisciplinary moment. To flip over the tactic of deliberate forgetting would most likely reveal a kind of radical, obsessive openness. Such openness allowed Burke's ruminative writings to radiate multiply, as he puts it in his essay "The Philosophy of Literary Form" (PLF), "The main ideal of criticism, as I conceive it, is to use all that is there to use" (PLF 23). To use all that is there to use, to exhaust all available investigative resources, names exactly the spirit of transdisciplinarity this book finds in Burke's work. As a result of his exhaustive, radiating, transdisciplinary approach, Burke was able to incorporate into his work unflinchingly and at times audaciously such seemingly opposed perspectives as mysticism, endocrinology, and constitutional medicine in order to take up repeatedly questions about bodies and language: What do we talk about when we talk about bodies? How is it that (as Cicero says) our bodies talk? How does what the body says alter how it sees and is seen? By considering in turn bodies stultified through mystical experience, illness, or anaesthesia; animated by adrenaline or ideas; poked and prodded by psychiatrists and physicians, Burke developed a transdisciplinary perspective on bodies and the fascinating and sometimes peculiar ways that clenching bodies, deformed bodies, recalcitrant bodies, or dancing bodies all sneak up on language.

Body Clusters

Lest culling a transdisciplinary perspective from Burke seem somehow anachronistic, I want to offer as a historical warrant Burke's clustering approach, which is tropically indebted to synecdoche. He discusses this particular approach in his long 1941 essay "The Philosophy of Literary Form": "It should be understandable by now why we consider synecdoche to be the basic process of representation, as approached from the standpoint of 'equations' or 'clusters of what goes with what.' To say that one can substitute part for whole, whole for part, container for thing contained, thing contained for the container, cause for effect, or effect for cause, is simply to say that both members of these pairs belong in the same associational cluster" (77).

Burke's synecdochic, cluster approach to criticism writ large favors what Eve Kosofsky Sedgwick in *Touching Feeling* terms "the ambition of thinking other than dualistically" (1); it aims for something besides what Burke calls "polar otherness" (PLF 78). For Burke polar otherness names that which "unites things that are [deemed] *opposite to* one another" while "synecdochic otherness . . . unites things that are simply *different* from one another" (78). In terms of bodies a Burkean synecdochic approach would have us suspend the question "What distinguishes body from mind or language?" in favor of the question "What (else) do we talk about when we talk about bodies (or mind, or language)?" These days, a clustering of terms would be the best place to begin answering that question. When we talk about bodies, that is, we talk about sensation, touch, texture, affect, materiality, performativity, movement, gesture, habits, entrainment, biology, physiology, rhythm, and performance, for starters. Such clustering can—and likely will—persist.

That this conceptual clustering can persist suggests that the main focus of this book—bodies—is a question that has not yet been exhausted. Nowhere is the need for transdisciplinary perspectives more obvious than in a consideration of bodies and materiality. In this context the observations made by economist Manfred Max-Neef become salient. Max-Neef offers transdisciplinarity as "a different manner of seeing the world, more systemic and holistic" (14), and suggests that such an approach would be most usefully imagined around big, broad, thematic areas—his suggestion is water—rather than specific disciplines. Other such thematic areas might include food, animals, language, climate, and—by now it should come as no surprise—bodies. Kenneth Burke, I argue, offers a productive foray into a transdisciplinary perspective on bodies.

Transdisciplinarity is often especially useful when a particular framework gets stuck in the mud of its own binaries. The case in point of this book is that of body theory in the humanities and social sciences. Judith Butler's work, along with an important set of feminist scholars (Joan Scott, Susan Bordo, Londa Schiebinger, and Elizabeth Grosz among them), combined with the increasing attention paid to Foucault in recent decades, created the conditions for what Fredric Jameson calls "the proliferation of theories of the body nowadays" ("The End" 713). Jameson ascribes this proliferation to what he characterizes as the "deeper tendency of the socioeconomic order": a "reduction to the present," or temporality's end, which he claims happens when "experience" is rendered nominalistically, thereby evacuating history (712–13). On balance, according to Jameson, body theory produces "the valorization of the body and its experience as the only authentic form of materialism" (713). For the most part I find Jameson's view of the recent turn to the body as a corollary to temporality's end or a radical "reduction to the present" to be itself rather reductive, and it ignores the possibility of a body historiography, an approach to historical work that keeps its eyes trained on materiality.[2]

Furthermore, Jameson's point about a broader tendency to nominalize—in the case of body theory, to organize research according to the noun *body* (and a problematically singular noun at that)—also tends toward holding bodies still and ignores those scholars who focus on moving bodies. Jameson casts the problem in this way: "The problem with the body as a positive slogan is that the body itself, as a unified entity, is . . . an empty totality that organizes the world without participating in it" (713). So when, for example, performance theorist Julia Walker invokes dance theorist Randy Martin to offer up the material performing body as a "kinetic force of political resistance" (171), she offers the body as nothing if not participatory and also, crucially, as mobile. In doing so Walker also aligns with cultural theorist Brian Massumi in his intimation that bodies both are and are not the problem.

The bind for body theorists is that bodies become a problem when they come to "stand in" for subject positions—what Jameson calls the tendency to nominalize. Such nominal positionality does little to shift the conversations (or change the subject, as it were). And what is more, such positioning undoes exactly what makes bodies bodies: as Massumi puts it in *Parables for the Virtual*, "the idea of positionality begins by subtracting movement from the picture" (3). Contemporary theory thus has a tendency to freeze bodies, to analyze them for their symbolic properties, thereby evacuating and ignoring their capacity to sense and to move through time.

Part of the problem, Massumi intimates, is our vocabulary for talking about bodies, and extrapolating from Jameson, we might add grammatical number to the list. Working with Burke's body theories, I have, like Massumi, come up against the limits of humanistic approaches to the body, especially with the available categories of essentialism and constructivism. That the Burkean Robert Wess fingers the Burke of *Permanence and Change* as a biological essentialist is a case in point (*Kenneth Burke* 66). Burke's engagement with bodies from a variety of disciplinary vantage points foregrounds the body as a vital, connective, mobile, and transformational force, a force that exceeds—even as it bends and bends with—discourse. And yet if we suspend our discipline-induced fear of essentializing, we might see things differently. Attention to Burke's early theories of the body reveals what Massumi might call a "productivist" approach to the body, a term that refuses the usually available—and somewhat anemic—terms *constructivist* and *essentialist* and, as Massumi suggests, would emphasize interactivity, intensities, and emergence (12). Such an approach might need to go beyond the humanistic enterprise for other ways to discuss bodily movement and change in time. For Burke mystics, with their clairvoyance, their attempts to "see around the corner," as he puts it in *Permanence and Change* (3e 222), model a kind of productivist approach. Mystical bodies, drugged bodies, hormonal bodies, bodies theorized through evolution or examined through 1920s constitutional morphology are about neither authenticity nor experience, they do not come into focus through a kind of myopia, and they do not make it easy to settle for the language of positionality. Instead, these bodies strain toward transformative capacity, what we might term affectability.

Burke, then, may be brought in line with contemporary body theories in a way that subtly refutes recent examinations of Burkean bodies. In other words, now that scholars such as Elizabeth A. Wilson, Teresa Brennan, Leslie Paul Thiele, William E. Connolly, Celeste M. Condit ("Materiality"), and Elizabeth Grosz (*Nick of Time*) have ventured into discourses of biology, neuroscience, and biological evolution, essentialism is no longer the name of the "gotcha" game, and as Jane Bennett helpfully suggests, social constitution is no longer the "punchline"

(358). And they never were for Burke. A transdisciplinary approach to the question of bodies allows us to set aside—however temporarily—such disciplinary hang-ups in order to, as Wilson puts it, "generate more vibrant, biologically attuned accounts of the body" (14). A biological perspective cannot so easily be placed in reductivist, determinist, or even essentialist brackets, because biologists and their allied scientists—endocrinologists and even neurologists, as Brennan's work helpfully demonstrates—track processes that bear closely on meaning making and communicative processes. As political theorist Leslie Paul Thiele argues, the emergence of fields such as neuroeconomics, neuropolitics, neuropsychology, and neuroethics signals the possibility of fruitful cross-disciplinary alliances that offer "tantalizing glimpses of a more holistic approach to the human condition" (ix). In a similar spirit, rhetorical theorist Celeste M. Condit offers what she terms a "program of transilience" to help humanists and social scientists coalesce around questions of the relationships between biology and what Burke called "symbolicity" (*How Should We Study the Symbolizing Animal?* 10–11, 13). For Condit, Burke is front and center in these efforts. Such syncretic approaches, too, allow a consideration of the nonhuman condition of humans, in other words, the importance of things—"natural" as well as synthetic (Jane Bennett 347–350). At stake in the drawing together of multiple disciplinary perspectives is a thoroughgoing view of meaning making itself, and as theorist William Paulson sees it, scientific knowledge bears crucially on meaning: "Cultural anthropologists did well to assert that we humans live in a world of humanly created meanings, but we also live in a material world of terrain, weather, and bodies—of things that we have not made and that act in ways that impinge upon the cultural and symbolic orders through which they take on meaning for us. For a long time it may have seemed possible to keep these worlds fairly separate, and thus to divide our intellectual labors between natural and human sciences. No more" (101). Paulson, Bennett, Condit, and Thiele therefore all point out how Jameson is both right and decidedly wrong. He is right that it would be a problem to allow "the body" to stand in for individual, singular experience (or as Massumi puts it, to hold bodies still), but Jameson is wrong in accusing all work on bodies of doing so and even in deeming experience so easily dismissed—legions of phenomenologists would certainly protest. And yet as I have been suggesting, and as Burke along with a host of contemporary theorists in multiple fields suggest, when we talk about bodies, we are often talking about so much more. We are talking about affect and nature and language; about movement and pain and environment. As literary theorist Cary Wolfe has pointed out, Burke's refusal to "condemn 'biologism' wholesale'" makes him a more "socially responsible critic" in that he "neatly walks the tightrope between the natural and social realms in what he calls his 'Metabiology'" (73). As Wolfe and scholars in ecocriticism show, we have skirted past the time when jettisoning terms such as *biology* and *nature* is worthwhile or even desirable.³ This book serves as an extended instance of where—and how—the question of bodies has taken one thinker. As it happens, that thinker has always been figured as multiple himself (Rueckert, *Encounters;* Hawhee, "Burke on Drugs").

This book, that is, offers a transdisciplinary excursion through Burke's writings on, about, and through bodies. Such an excursion cannot solely take the form of close readings of Burke's writings, but instead must move between his writings and all the discourses—scientific and otherwise—Burke turned to in order to navigate his thought about bodies. As such, aside from the explicit discussion of transdisciplinarity above, the remaining chapters in this book show Burke *performing* transdisciplinarity and consider inductively, by example, what such a view offers contemporary body theories. The book therefore comments beyond Burkean studies or even rhetorical and literary studies and shows, with Burke's writings as a backdrop, the ways multiple discourses on the body in the twentieth century differently constitute bodies and, more pointedly, how language, meaning, and communication both emerge from and help constitute bodies. In doing so, the book also offers Burke as one of that century's first rhetoricians of science, and by this I do not just mean someone who examined the rhetorical force of science, but someone who strategically and regularly engaged with that force and with scientific knowledge itself, always with an interest in how new sciences such as neurology, endocrinology, and morphology could inform his own consideration of rhetorical, symbolic processes.

But Burke was thinking about bodies long before he wandered into discourses of science and religion, so it makes sense to examine his earliest published writings—in this case his early-1920s foray into short fiction and his music criticism—where there is ample evidence that bodies (sick bodies, charged bodies, rhythmic bodies) served as important guides for Burke from the beginning. As chapter 1, "Bodies as Equipment for Moving (from Artist to Audience)," argues, Burke's early musings on bodily matters guided him right into questions of rhetoric and communication for what would become his lifelong excursion. Chapter 2, "Burke's Mystical Method," examines the importance of mysticism for Burke's transdisciplinary approach to bodies. From the Russian mystic G. I. Gurdjieff and his students' mystical dance performances, Burke drew a respect for the transformational capacity of bodies. For Burke, Gurdjieff's bodily mysticism joined nicely with William James's intellectual mysticism, which was marked by a radical openness and what Burke calls meliorism. That meliorism, a conviction that things can be better, involved, as the chapter discusses, eschewing that which is "rationally finished"—gleaming polished conclusions—in favor of the muddy gunk of materiality.

And what could be more gunky than scientific experimentation? Chapters 3, 4, 5, and 6 show Burke incorporating into his theories of bodies and language findings from four different domains of scientific (or in some cases pseudoscientific) knowledge—drug research, endocrinology, constitutional medicine, and a peculiar evolutionary theory of language called gesture-speech, which holds that the human capacity for language found its evolutionary beginnings in bodily gesture. With very few exceptions, these discourses have been ignored by scholars working on Burke, in part because they are wound so tightly with discourses such as psychoanalysis, discourses more familiar to scholars in the humanities and social sciences. Burke's more "sciency" passages frequently spill into his notoriously rambling footnotes or end up on the editing block in subsequent editions. And yet following these discourses out into the footnotes and beyond the chopping block nevertheless helps build a vital account of language and bodies edging closer together. That account is not wholly celebratory, but at times it serves to remind us why the terms *essentialism* and *social construction* took hold in the first place. Such is the case in Burke's engagement with constitutional medicine, which held that body measurements are sure indexes of psychiatric inclinations. Still, even in such a roundly dismissed science, Burke manages to cull, however imperfect, an account of bodily deviance as other than deviance.

Deviance, pain, and illness frequently crop up in talk of bodies, and Burke's contributions are no exception. Chapter 7, "Welcome to the Beauty Clinic," works in the mode of what I call "body biography" to examine Burke's return to bodily matters in the 1950s. During that decade bodies seeped into Burke's critical and fictional writings, despite his at-times resolute efforts to bracket the question of physicality while he labored over his "Symbolic of Motives," which was to be the third and final installment of the "motives" trilogy. When considered alongside his strained and pained published work from that decade, Burke's letters show that he grappled with his own aging, ailing body just as much as he did with the body in theory. His letters help document an emerging theory of body-thinking, which later becomes manifest in his cloacal criticism, criticism that focuses on the otherwise repulsive underbelly of humanity: excrement, vomit, pollution. This mode of criticism, puzzling to most Burke scholars, overtly resists what Burke calls the "Beauty Clinic," the tendency to clean ourselves up in thought and body, and to ignore offscourings. And yet for Burke the rotten stench of excrement and dirty bathwater is the basis of life.

Burke's cloacal criticism therefore clarifies Burke's ecocritical legacy, and this chapter works to show the inseparability of bodies and language, of bodies and ecology, of bodies and politics, of bodies and life. Burke's 1958 quasi-fictional essay "The Anaesthetic Revelation of Herone Liddell" dramatizes this turn to bodies and ecology as indispensable for a theory of language, the import of which makes isolating a theory of symbolic motives an empty, futile exercise.

My research for this book has shown me—much to my surprise—that an examination of Burke's bodily theories cannot possibly be confined to a single monograph. I have therefore sacrificed exhaustiveness in favor of depth and have focused on the fields that bear most notably (or in some cases surprisingly) on rhetoric and language theory in the hopes that other scholars will augment accordingly.[4] At times my treks through the various discourses Burke engages to think about bodies track closely with Burke's own theoretical interventions, offering, for example, a somatic genealogy of dramatism, arguably Burke's most widely known critical concept. At other times this book becomes immersed in biographical details, but only when there is a theoretical payoff, as with the method of "body biography" performed in the book's final chapter. At still other times, Burke and his writings become more of a backdrop, a humanistic stage for drawing together scientific, social scientific, and humanistic ways of thinking about language, the body, and more. Given that Burke wrote for a solid seven decades during the twentieth century, the historical stage he provides is vast.

One point of this book, then, is that despite the dismissiveness of critics such as Jameson and Terry Eagleton, humanistic, cultural studies of the body are neither all that new nor newly passé (Eagleton, *After Theory* 2–3). Instead, they have formed a crucial cluster of concepts that helps us get beyond the distinctly Jamesonian "rational polish" of his 2003 intervention, thereby helping us see anew an impasse Jameson reached with Burke himself in the late 1970s in the pages of *Critical Inquiry*, an impasse that led Burke, once again (and once and for all), back to bodily matters. I will discuss that era in the conclusion, focusing primarily on a little-known review Burke wrote of the second edition of J. L. Austin's monumental study of performative language, *How to Do Things with Words*.

In that review Burke uses Austin's speech-act theory to elaborate dramatism vis-à-vis action and motion, the categories that Burke settles on to theorize language and bodies respectively. The conclusion, then, shows how accounts by thinkers such as Jameson, with their insistence on language as always and only an epistemological tool, pin themselves to rationality and ideology, eschewing materiality, attitudes, affect, rhythm, bodies, and movement—the stuff of life. As I hope this excursion through Burke's most bodily theories will show, music and mysticism have as much to teach us about bodies as do medicine and morphology, and the links Burke finds to language are at times rather surprising. The task remains to learn to listen.

Bodies as Equipment for Moving (from Artist to Audience)

One-third insomnia
One-third art
One-third The Man
With the Cardiac Heart.
    Kenneth Burke, "Know Thyself"

These epigraphic—even oddly epitaphic—Burkean lines provide a tidy glimpse of Burke's relation to his own body, a relation he obsessed about throughout his life, culminating in a peculiarly revelatory surgical episode considered in this book's final chapter. Sandwiched between the bodily maladies of Burke's chronic insomnia and his tendency toward "coronary spasms" is the tiny little word *art*.[1] This positioning of art as the middle third, a condition among conditions, is more, I contend, than a formal convenience allowing a rhyme with *heart*. The self-knowledge commanded by the poem's oracular title returns Burke not just to bodily ailments, but also to bodily rhythms. That is, both of Burke's chronic maladies—his well-known insomnia and an odd condition he referred to as his "gulpo-gaggo-gaspo," which was finally diagnosed in 1952 as "coronary spasms"—can best be characterized as different sorts of arrhythmia, with the inability to sleep disrupting "normal" circadian rhythms, and with the skipping, palpitating heart disrupting the "regular" pulse sequence.[2] Metrically even the rhythm of the first three lines is offset by the differently metered last line.[3] For Burke, as this chapter will show, art too shares this disruptive, arrhythmic capacity.

From a very early point in Burke's long career, the category of art was intimately bound up with the body, its rhythms and irruptions. In this opening chapter I want to begin my investigation of Burke's bodily theories and their persistence in his theories of language and rhetoric by examining two genres that have so far received little critical attention but that nonetheless document the beginnings of Burke's interest in rhythmic and arrhythmic bodies and their connection to art: his short fiction and his music criticism.

For most, Burke's first book, *Counter-Statement* (1931), sufficiently charts his "turn" from aesthetics to rhetoric, or in the case of Jack Selzer's argument, the development of Burke's rhetorical aesthetics. And yet a look at some of Burke's other writings from the 1920s differently amplifies this crucial moment in his career, revealing that moment as neither a turn away from aesthetics to rhetoric nor even a Hegelian-style synthesis of the two. Rather, Burke's other artistic experiments mark a shift in focus from one set of bodies (the bodies of artists) to another (the bodies in an audience) that helps to locate more precisely an incipient Burkean rhetoric. Such an examination troubles the usual treatment of Burke's turn to rhetoric as something of a "conversion," a turn away from questions of aesthetics and art that formed his early commitments. Even two of the most nuanced readings of Burke's engagements with aesthetics—those offered by William Rueckert and Robert Wess—still, however subtly, oppose aesthetics and rhetoric and lean toward a separation of Burke's "aesthetic humanism" (Wess's term) found most notably in *Counter-Statement* (CS) and his move to more rhetorical-sociological concerns in the books that followed.[4] Selzer's reading of *Counter-Statement* most thoroughly situates the book within the culture of modernist literary movements generally and Greenwich Village specifically and begins to lay the groundwork for a slightly different account of Burke's "turn" to rhetoric. Still Selzer's account focuses (understandably) on a distinctly *literary* aesthetic and therefore finds itself grappling with the same tensions found in Rueckert and Wess: those between Burke's rhetorical leanings and what Selzer calls his "aesthete sensibility" (137). Such a move, however subtly, retroactively posits a disciplinary split between the literary and the rhetorical that may well have persisted in modernist thought but did not necessarily matter so much for Burke. And it also risks ignoring the centrality of bodies to aesthetics, for as Terry Eagleton asserts in *Ideology of the Aesthetic*: "Aesthetics is born as a discourse of the body" (1).

Burke's short fiction features as many musical as it does literary artists and critics and offers tantalizing glimpses of Burke's engagement with a broader category of aesthetics, one that encompasses multiple artistic media. Music, as a medium that more or less brackets signification in favor of rhythmic transformations, introduces Burke to a view that aligns with Gregory Clark's recent conclusion—also reached through a joint consideration of music and Burkean theory—that the aesthetic and rhetorical are not so easily distinguishable ("Virtuosos" 45). A look at Burke's music criticism, therefore, suggests that the music scene, by which I mean the live scene of musical performance, offers a powerful instance of aesthetic activity writ large as always and everywhere rhetorical—that is, productive of effects—and crucially, these effects are produced on and through the live and lively bodies in the audience.

In this chapter and in this book as a whole, I want to make a case for a less dramatic transition *from* aesthetics *to* rhetoric by emphasizing Burke's early commitments to phenomenology and materiality. In brief this chapter's argument goes something like this: Burke's interest in bodies, manifest early on in his short fiction (which focuses on artists' decidedly arrhythmic bodies) and later in his music criticism (which focuses on the polyrhythmic effects of artistic form on bodies in the audience), sets up a strong and distinctive if incipient rhetoric. It is his inclination toward bodies, I contend, that first sets Burke to investigate rhetoric, communication, meaning making, and language. Moreover that inclination toward bodies leads Burke to investigate all manner of bodily knowledge and ultimately urges a transdisciplinary view of the body, one that would help Burke—and by extension us—better understand the at times impossibly complicated relations among language, rhetoric, and the body.

And so this chapter offers two new points of entry into Burke's rhetorical theories, two bodily "beginnings." First, it joins only a handful of others (most recently Selzer) in writing about Burke's short fiction, this time to consider the way his stories and sketches grapple with relations between art and the body, especially sick or ailing bodies, bodies out of sync with "normal" societal rhythms. Artists' bodies, in Burke's fiction, are particularly "indisposed" to societal trends, and that, for Burke, is a good thing. The second crucial beginning, then, is Burke's music criticism, which I contend documents his turn to audiences in that he approaches ticket holders in terms of receptivity, inclination, and disposition, all formulations that take him through bodies and their rhythms and, ultimately, to rhetoric. Still, as Henri Lefebvre contends in *Rhythmanalysis,* the mundaneness, repetitiveness, and sheer physicalness of everyday rhythms become most noticeable through their disruption (67–69). And so disruption marks Burke's—and this book's—first beginning.

Beginnings I: Case Studies in Arrhythmia

The bulk of Burke's short fiction features bodies with aesthetic inclinations, inclinations that frequently accompany *dis*inclinations. That is, so many of Burke's aesthetically inclined characters are in some way indisposed, even to the point of pathology. This emphasis on inclinations and their concomitant *in*dispositions brings with it a noticeable, if seemingly peculiar, suspicion of healthy, humming bodies, a suspicion that drives the three stories I will examine here, "Mrs. Maecenas," "The White Oxen," and "David Wassermann."

In *Kenneth Burke in Greenwich Village,* Jack Selzer offers one of the few extended treatments of Burke's short fiction, describing how Burke composed fiction almost anywhere *but* Greenwich Village. Selzer writes eloquently about a young Burke eagerly seeking ways to enjoy "healthy summers away from city heat and impurity and contagion" (85), noting that during these periods of rural respite—namely the summers of 1919, 1920, and 1921—Burke wrote a good deal of short fiction. In the summer of 1919, according to Selzer, while staying at a remote cottage in Candor, New York, Burke wrote, among other stories and sketches, "The Olympians," "The Excursion" (see introduction), and "Mrs. Maecenas." The following year, during an extended summer stay in Asheville, North Carolina, he wrote "David Wassermann," composed a draft of "My Dear Mrs. Wurtelbach," and revised "The White Oxen" (Selzer 88). And during the summer of 1921, during what Selzer calls "Burke's most ambitious and extensive retreat" (88), he wrote "The Death of Tragedy," "The Book of Yul," "A Progression," "In Quest of Olympus," and "After Hours" (89). Selzer's lively descriptions capture Burke's near-euphoria during these rural stretches, during which he swam, canoed, fished, hiked, climbed, and chopped wood. These were, it seems, healthy, robust times for Burke, who even marveled in a letter to Malcolm Cowley from Maine that "there is not a spot on my body that I can't make as hard as a skullbone" (September 12, 1921; Jay 101).

It is perhaps surprising, then, that much of the fiction Burke produced during these strong, "healthy," outdoorsy periods has a literary soft spot for unhealthy, weak-bodied characters. Among the sick in Burke's very early fiction are Mr. Beck, the rheumatoid, palpitating music teacher in "The Olympians"; the gawky, pasty, headachy young Siegfried in "Mrs. Maecenas"; and the title character of "The Soul of Kajn Tafha," who has had the lobes of his ears torn off. David Wassermann, the protagonist in the story of the same name, is a keyed-up recovering neurasthenic who spouts off at his therapist, his bar buddies, and his ex-lover. These characters, with their various nervous and physical ailments, are best read as Selzer reads them, as sensitive youth set against insensitive society (95), but something even more elaborate seems to be going on with these unhealthy characters and their shaky, achy bodies. The trope of health and particularly healthiness in Burke's fiction, it turns out, is not as positive as it seemed to be in his own summer excursions at the time. Indeed the few healthy bodies in Burke's fiction are regarded with suspicion; they are oblivious to art and incapable of critique—in short, they are miserably status quo.

The strongest hints that healthy bodies are perhaps suspect appear in Burke's story "Mrs. Maecenas." Here the title character, a recent widow of a former university president and, as indicated by her name, a devoted patron of the arts (especially literature and music) who "maintained her former connections with the university" (346) in order to feed her peculiar "weakness for genius-hunting" (348), is growing "weary" of the "vigorous" university and its predictable lot of healthy, happy students: "Everywhere, everywhere, typical young Americans were springing up, sturdy tough daisy-minds that were cheerful, healthy, and banal. How could art thrive here, she asked herself, in a land so unfavorable to the artist's temper!" (347). Early on in the story, then, the robust, seemingly lively campus works against all that Mrs. Maecenas cares about: art, literature, and most particularly, the "artist's temper," a mercurial, dissatisfied, even puny constitution that runs counter to the "miserably sane and normal" constitutions best exemplified by the school's football star, "big Dick Halloway, handsome blond-haired Dick, the hero of the university" (348). Students like Dick epitomize, for Mrs. Maecenas, all that is embarrassing about the university, "that great machine," which "could dump its annual output of standardized 'leaders of America,' could ship them off every commencement day labeled 'with all the advantages of a college education'" (348). To Mrs. Maecenas, Dick and his daisy-minded cohort are products of an efficient system of citizen production, a tax- and tuition-supported assembly line for hearty, happy, robust, and—importantly—dull Americans: "The university became healthier, and she quietly blushed for the future of America" (348). In the face of predictably spirited campus activity, Mrs. Maecenas pleaded ill health and retreated "nearer to her books and her piano" (348).

From the outset the story scenically aligns healthy bodies and the 1920s university, where "the engineering and agricultural schools"—subject areas that are distinctly American and decidedly "practical"—"grew steadily more *vigorous*" (347; emphasis added). That scene, "a land so unfavorable to the artist's temper," is of course deemed unfavorable to art also; as Mrs. Maecenas puts it, invoking de Gourmont, "Art was once loved; then it was tolerated; and now it will soon be prohibited, so that we must express our devotion to it in secret, deep in the catacombs" (350). Instead, art and artistic "genius," as the story continues, become associated with alcohol (in the story art, like alcohol in the 1920s, becomes "prohibited"), and the artist with maladaptive tendencies.

When in the midst of her wallowing Mrs. Maecenas spots among the daisies a young Siegfried, "a rather gawkily formed young man" with a love for French novels and nips of whiskey, she "knew she had found her genius" (348). Siegfried begins to visit her, seeking deliverance "from this American captivity" (349), and after several visits, and in the middle of a conversation about Aristotle's "massive sanity," it is revealed that he suffers from headaches (352). Later, while critiquing Siegfried's recitation of his rendition of the Bible, Mrs. Maecenas cinches the close relation between ill health and artistic capacity when she observes excitedly that his "mind is so gloriously unhealthy, so à la Baudelaire" (354). Their relationship—and the story—comes to an abrupt close, however, when Mrs. Maecenas discovers Siegfried's dreadfully normal acne:

> "But, Siegfried," she cried out in sudden horror, "what is the matter with your face?"
>
> He looked up in astonishment. Then he thought he understood: she was pampering him, no doubt. "The paleness? Am I unusually pale tonight? I was smoking a lot today."

"Uh . . . y—yes. Why, yes, the pallor." Then she seemed to recover. "But that is not unusual, I suppose. The artist's temper . . . nervosity . . . pallor would be natural."

Siegfried understood now. It was not the *pallor*, then, but the *redness*. *Nemo mundus a sorde*; nature is such a tyrant. Yesterday they had broken out, and today they were all over his chin. But how annoying that she should react so to pimples! (358)

This passage, in addition to confusing the previously stark difference between Siegfried and all the other students à la his change in complexion, reveals distinct characteristics associated with the "artist's temper," namely "nervosity" and "pallor." Sensitive, certainly, but even more than that, the artist's temper registers in this story—à la the revolutionary poet, Baudelaire—as a propensity for headaches, nervousness (Baudelaire too is well known to have suffered from an acute nervous condition), wanness, and for overall ill health. The artist's temper and body inseparably and inexorably register protest against the standardized constitutions of others, in this case the decidedly American students. Burke's artist, when it comes to cultural norms, are particularly indisposed. And when, as in Siegfried's case, the body does not maintain its maladjustments—if the complexion for some reason changes—that body may all too easily be cast back into the university assembly line.

Those of Burke's characters who end up with restored health—as well as a secure place among the status quo—follow various paths, and the path of the title character in the story "David Wassermann" is perhaps the one of most resistance. The story, which Selzer rightly reads as "a ritual portrait of a would-be bohemian torn by a bourgeois desire for sex and safety" (97), opens with the recollected words of Wassermann's psychoanalyst followed by Wassermann's wildly questioning reflection: "'You have it all,' Wright had said. 'To begin with, you are a neurasthenic, or at least, you have just recovered from neurasthenia. You are a Jew. You have the memory of sex, although at present you are continent; also, you are in love. And the twenties is naturally a restless period anyhow.' Was Wright being decent for once? Did he mean that just as he had said it? The bastard!" (24). Despite the claim that Wassermann has "just recovered from neurasthenia," one of his symptoms shows itself in the next paragraph: "Cynthia must be watching how his hands trembled. That was the neurasthenia. . . . if the neurasthenia was there, why clamp it in a vise? Let them tremble, and perhaps even encourage them a little" (24). Wassermann's neurasthenia, invoked at the story's outset, puts forth most compellingly the role of the ailing, nervous body in Burke's fiction. Wassermann himself bespeaks a pointed theory of innovation, enabled by maladjustment and forestalled only by "healthy" adjustments that emulate dominant dispositions, mundane rhythms. Embedded in this theory of artistic creation is a critique of body-numbing, "healthy," efficient rationality.

A multisymptom nervous disorder described by the term's originator, G. M. Beard, as a depleted nerve force caused by "civilization," neurasthenia came to be known as the "disorder of modernity" (Hofstra 1) and was also frequently associated with artists and elites.[5] According to Amelia Jones, whose *Irrational Modernism* situates neurasthenia in the context of Dadaism, neurasthenia is a "complex network of bodily/psychic symptoms that rupture the subject's smooth functioning, propelling her into a heightened state of irrationality." "To be a neurasthenic," Jones continues, "is to experience every stimulus of one's surroundings acutely as an attack on one's emotional and corporeal integrity" (28). In other words, modern neurasthenia was thought to function as a capacity to experience multiple senses and perspectives at once, causing the neurasthenic to be intensely affected on a neural level by one's surroundings—noises, smells, and even, as instanced in Burke's story, silent pauses. Burke's Wassermann is keyed up, and it shows. It shows in his trembling hands; it shows in his sensitivity to street noise—"Why, Cynthia," Wassermann pleads to his former lover, "must you insist on walking on these noisy streets?" (31). It shows in his relations to objects in the world, which he characterizes with prophetic certainty as relations of fear and pain, as he explains to his therapist, the appropriately named Dr. Wright: "Everything in the world's one little devil's tongue for me to bleed on. If it's a chair, I'll stove my shins on it in the dark; if it's a razor, the relation between us is an immediate possibility of my hurling it out the window; if it's a person, it'll say 'How are you,' and I'll nearly pass out apoplectic with pounding sentences. Don't you ever get that?" (28). But Wright does not get it, which draws Wassermann's ire both toward Wright and the "blunt" edge of his psychoanalytic method, of which Wassermann says,

> It gets on a man's nerves, especially a man like me. It would be highly admirable, if it weren't so easy to apply. Another trouble with it is that it is inclined to become too pat. It fits roughly in too many cases to be nicely adapted to any of them. And in time it blunts a man, since it gets him into making a broad division of his sensations: this thing I recognize, this thing I am being silent about. With the final result that you become inarticulate. You forget how to carve neat slices off a big steaming idea. You become no better than an amoeba, approaching what is pleasant, and retreating from what is unpleasant, without intelligent observations. (27)

For Wassermann the edges of psychoanalysis are too dull, its techniques too deliberately simple to be able to "penetrate" (27) the complexity of his symptoms. While Selzer argues that Burke's story resists the choice between bourgeois and bohemian lifestyles (*Kenneth Burke in Greenwich Village* 94), I would contend that the one sympathetic "character" is Wassermann's highly discerning neurasthenic body, which can be intellectualized not through psychoanalysis but through a more finely tuned diagnosis, as he says later on in the story: "There's always some satisfaction in a precise diagnosis. So long as I can chart my defections, I at least have the intellectuality of the chart to encourage me" (30).[6] Embedded in this snippet as well as his long screed against psychoanalysis is a subtle alliance between the intellectual art of making fine distinctions—such as that involved in carving "neat slices off a big steaming idea"—and the multiple quivering sensations his body permits. Neurasthenia in effect sharpens Wassermann's senses, thus enabling such a precise carving up of the world. As Wassermann's turn toward "health" occurs—signified by marriage and a job at his father's clothing firm—he begins to condemn the discerning intelligence the story otherwise upholds. The shift in perspective is marked by a shift in metaphors. No longer a sharp-edged blade, intelligence becomes a disease. "Intelligence," he tells his wide-eyed bar friends, "is a parasitic growth, and saps the body like a cancer. It endangers the silver medium. The brain was once a mere implement of the body, functioning solely to add to the body's welfare, like the kidneys. But now it is threatening to usurp an entity of its own. . . . And so, I have stuffed my brain with rich, oozy clarity, with the consequence that I can see every pore in every nose, and catch the smell of every armpit" (30–31).

The story/sketch of Wassermann creates a strong sense that his bodily symptoms—what Selzer would rightly characterize as extreme sensitivities—stand as a form of protest against the passive acceptance he sees all around: Cynthia's ability to shut out the traffic noise; Wright's inability to wield anything but the flat, dull statements of psychoanalysis; and ultimately Wassermann's own capitulation to marriage and a business partnership with his father.

Just as in "Mrs. Maecenas," the unhealthy body in "David Wassermann" is the body with the capacity to discern, to invent, to make sharp distinctions; it is the body with inclinations to "sharpness" itself—represented variously as art, as reading, as critical acumen. The healthy body, conversely, is one not "sapped" by intelligence ("Wassermann" 30). Unhealthy bodies in these stories are "ill disposed" to the current surroundings—be they university, office, or city streets. Any form of "recovery" or, in the case of Siegfried, a covering over of the symptoms of ill health, leads the characters back to the numb dullness of a status quo existence. Treatment and recovery—especially in the form of psychoanalysis—are therefore called into question, even railed against, as ailing bodies are exalted for their clarity and their surprising capacities.

The idea of a sickly artist is by no means new with Burke, of course, though Burke, by providing distinctive settings (a sports-minded university; a Manhattan therapist's office) arguably gives such characters modern American flavor. A number of romantic poets whom Burke wrote about—namely Coleridge and Keats—exhibited similar maladaptive tendencies. His sickly characters also allude to those found in works by European authors Thomas Mann and André Gide, from whom Burke culls a stance toward art that is both "conscientious" and "corrupt" (*CS* 106), one that disrupts the body's staunch dogma. "Since the body is dogmatic, a generator of belief," he observes, "society might well be benefited by the corrective of a disintegrating art, which converts each simplicity into a complexity, which ruins the possibility of ready hierarchies, which concerns itself with the problematical, the experimental, and thus by implication works corrosively upon those expansionistic certainties preparing the way for our social cataclysms. An art may be of value purely through preventing a society from becoming too assertively, too hopelessly, itself" (105). Burke arrives at this conclusion after a lengthy consideration of the characters in writings of Mann and Gide, characters he describes as "deviations from type," with Mann's tendency toward characters "who are physically extravagant" (92) and Gide's recurring theme of sickness (95). Both tendencies, according to Burke, stem from a "constant preoccupation with conformity" (93). Such a preoccupation also runs through Burke's fiction, and of all the hierarchies whose possibilities get "ruined," perhaps the most notable, in these stories at least, is the one of health over illness, particularly that which, according to Sander Gilman's thorough analysis of early-twentieth-century medical art, aligns health with beauty and goodness and illness with ugliness and evil (10–13). The story that perhaps most notably disrupts these hierarchical associations through its undercurrent of worry about aspirations to the status quo is Burke's 1924 "The White Oxen," which became the title story of his short fiction collection.

In "The White Oxen," a bildungsroman with surprisingly little development, the twin clichés "strong as an ox" and "healthy as an ox" become playfully literal. The well-fed colorless oxen, the protagonist's favorite of the zoo animals, stand as the most content of all the animals.[7] The story sets the oxen against other animals, such as the caged birds, which are "in a state of continued agitation, hopping about, trying their wings, jerking their heads, dipping for a grain of corn, peeping" (11), or the out-of-element polar bear, who "was restless, nervous like the ill-tempered lion, or the slinking hyenas" (12). The oxen, by contrast, "were chewing in deliberate contentment. At times they would move their heads to look in another direction; at such times they ceased their chewing, as though disapproving of too many simultaneous motions. But once their head was firmly established in this new direction, their chewing would be resumed. Calm, harmless, sleepy, they lolled about their cage. Each movement of their body went through a graded progression: it was prepared for by an unhurried tautening of the flesh, executed with absolute assurance of the result, after which the oxen easily and imperceptibly settled down again into a state of relaxation" (12).

The oxen, here depicted as methodically simple creatures incapable of or at least uninterested in complex movements and happy to be fed and cared for, are noticeably like the healthy and content university students in "Mrs. Maecenas"—

banal, "unambitious as the dead" (22). The adolescent Matthew Carr, the story's main character, comforted by and attached to the oxen, visits them at the zoo regularly for a time and then begins to exhibit oxenlike qualities himself. He becomes reluctant to "devote much extra time to dull and mysterious books" and after high school does not seek to move beyond his guardian relatives' home until necessity and his uncle urge him to. In his first roommate, Gabriel, Matthew thrills at "the sudden rediscovery that here was one of his white oxen, harmless and kindly" (52). After suffering swift disappointment in the face of Gabriel's un-oxenlike qualities—Gabriel, after all, reads too much and ends up stealing money from Matthew—Matthew himself becomes even more like the white oxen, especially at work: "Of good health, he came to the office regularly, and discharged his duties with a gratifying rigidity of scruple. The important thing was that he was steady, a quality which was much more valuable in routine work than wide-awake business acumen. Given something to do, and told how to do it, Matthew was sure to do it satisfactorily" (57).

Matthew, comfortable and content in his office job, has, by the end of the story, in his desire to share the oxen's "blissful sloth of semi-sensation" become "the purest of his white oxen" (62). Noteworthy too is the first line's explicit association of Matthew's sturdy reliability with his "good health." When set against "Mrs. Maecenas" and "David Wassermann," and read alongside Burke's essay on Mann and Gide, "The White Oxen" explores the tendency of a "healthy," "adjusted" body to fall into mundane, routinized rhythms. The story, that is, effectively flips the equation found in Mann's *Buddenbrooks*, wherein, according to Burke, "What is lost in health and moral certitude is gained in questioning and conscientiousness, in social and aesthetic sensitiveness, until we arrive at little Hanno the musician, who, like [Mann's] Aschenbach, finally mingles inspiration with disease, as we watch his improvisations become the first symptoms of the typhoid fever that is to result in his death" (96).

If for Mann's Hanno, much as for Burke's Wassermann, such "inspiration" is at home with—or even leads to—sickness, then for Matthew Carr simple, uninspiring routines maintain a modicum of health and comfort. Such a reading of Carr departs from Selzer, who, conversely, aligns Carr with characters like Wassermann in that he is "set apart" from society. A focus on the tropes of unhealthiness and an ability to make fine distinctions calls such a reading into question even as it offers a way for the story to "fit" with a larger concern about artist and society. More to the point of this book, such a focus also shows Burke working very early on with bodily shapes, movements, and rhythms to offer the body as a "generator of belief."

As the rest of this book will demonstrate, this early concern with bodies and their rhythmic/arrhythmic capacities carries over into Burke's criticism and ultimately into his theories of language, rhetoric, and communication. And yet the turn to criticism marks a subtle but important shift for Burke's bodily theories. Whereas the early short fiction concerns itself with symbolizing bodies and works to distinguish the ailing bodies of artists from the healthy bodies of nonartists, figuring both kinds of bodies as sets of inclinations and even exploring the possibilities of bodily protest, the bodies in his criticism are not as much symbolic as they are dogmatic. In other words, if Burke's fiction dramatizes the body's capacity to be more or less inclined toward simple or complex movements, then his music criticism pursues the question of belief and inclination more pointedly. He also follows more carefully a notion of rhythm, asking what possibilities bodily rhythms and inclinations might hold for the ability of art—music or literature—to incite change. Which brings me to Burke's second beginning.

Beginnings II: Rhythms

In his debut piece as author of the *Dial*'s "Musical Chronicle" column (December 1927), Burke introduces himself to readers—with humble "misgivings"—as a "docent," offering his criticism as something of a "*non-sequitur*" (535).[8] He then proceeds to "inventory" (read: consider and then reject) the available modes of music criticism, beginning with what might be read as a question of scale: that is, treating music as the equivalent of the sublime itself on the one (grand) hand, or on the other (more minuscule) hand as attending to the minutiae of technical composition. As Burke phrases the two distinct approaches, "Music as a substitute for religion, a secular mysticism, belief without theology (which incidentally it has been ever since the founding of the Church); or music as the individuation of certain harmonic principles, to be discussed in terms of modulation, cadence, augmented fifths, and as many of the newer clusters as one could find names for" (535).

In short, for Burke, those approaches boil down to "music as orgy—or music as a mechanism" (535), grand and small scales, neither of which he finds appealing or even particularly helpful. In the former Burke locates the "vocabulary of heroism," wherein the composers pompously describe the "inspiration of their works"; if engaging in the latter, what Burke dubs the "anti-orgy," or the focus on technical composition and performance, one would, according to Burke, "(a) become quickly aware of one's own lacunae in musical knowledge, and (b) attempt a task in which ignominy would be in direct proportion to efficiency" (536). Perhaps unsurprisingly after bracketing these two critical approaches, Burke then goes on to "choose what is left." In turning away from both the genius of the composer and the technical merits of the composition, Burke's perspective swivels inevitably to the other side of the performance: the side that features the ticketed seats. Burke, that is, wants to offer a "useful" (536), investigative (537) kind of music criticism, one that considers performances in multiple registers and takes seriously the varied effects of musical performances. He writes, "We recognize, perhaps too readily, that even the sublime can be cheapened by the multitude—and here enters the wedge whereby criticism may force itself out of the class of parasites into the class of the useful; for at those wayward and unpredictable times when a composer's eloquence is happening outside of us rather than within us, much can still be made arresting to the prying eye and we be rescued from sloth, by substituting investigation for sympathy. In five hours of Wagner, are not at least three of them best salvaged by 'study'? Relaxing from the attempt to vibrate avec, one watches 'what he does with the horns'?" (537). Burke seems to want to become the layperson's music critic, which may well be why his stint lasted no longer than two years. And while his musical criticism might not be considered all that impressive among music historians, it nevertheless offers an important window on the development of Burke's rhetorical aesthetic. As a member of an audience trying to imagine what he will write about as music critic, Burke, lacking somewhat in technical expertise, cannot help but focus on the musical performance's multiple rhetorical effects.

To imagine that audience members are able to sustain mystical or sublime engagement through the entirety of a four- or five-hour performance is to overestimate the audience, or rather to underestimate the audience's ability to switch registers multiple times in the course of a single performance, a point Burke makes in the passage above with the line about watching what a particular musician "does with the horns," as well as in a reflection on varieties of emotion: "One could hold that musicians must keep the pot a-boiling with pedantry, and that to expect of an audience a sustained emotional tension is to ask for nothing short of pathology" (537). He extends the pathologizing claim by a representative anecdote: "I know an individual who, the first time he heard the Sacre, wept, choked, and suffered acute convulsions of the chest muscles at each irruption of the rhythm. On second hearing he was an old man, and sat motionless, stonily suffering the concert like an Indian scanning the horizon" (537). Two things are noteworthy about Burke's anecdote. First, Burke seems keenly aware of music's ability to enliven multiple bodily senses,[9] and secondly, the example points to the possibility of varied effects, depending on the audience member's capacities—bodily and otherwise.

Such a focus on audience bodies leads Burke the music critic to statements such as "aesthetic enjoyment involves some spirit of barter on the part of the audience" (February 1928, 174–78), and ultimately to a more communicative and rhetorical view of music. His music reviews therefore frequently move quickly from technical to effective analysis, as in his April 1928 review of the Hall Johnson Jubilee Singers, about whom Burke writes that "the zest, the unction, the physical undulations, the naïve Epicureanism of these singers overwhelmed us, like a revelation" (358). The following month Burke's review of Stravinsky's *Oedipus Rex* remains focused almost exclusively on audience bodies, particularly in his comparison of the music to a particular type of torture:

> There is a mode of torment, most often accredited to China, whereby the victim is kept from relapsing into sleep by an incessant goading. Presumably, by even the subtlest and most economical of movements, one could come to induce in his man a state of fiendish exasperation, until the slightest tickle might cause him to thrash about, like some happily captured fish thrown up on the sand. The Strawinsky [sic] method of appeal was somewhat similar. The obsessive element of the music was continuous, maintained by an extreme shrewdness and parsimony in both repetition and variation. The power was not derived from the multiplication of the voices, nor from the bulk of the instruments; it was a thing of texture and form. The rhythmic effects were subtilized beyond perception—the great orchestral hiccoughs of the Sacre were gone, rhythmic changes residing not in the upheaval of the total mass, but in internal adjustments and timings. (May 1928, 445)

These lines, written at about the time Burke was still drafting parts of *Counter-Statement,* focus on the performance's shrewd use of repetition and variation, producing rhythmic effects so subtle as to be "beyond perception," but instead somehow located "internally," in the relation between particular instruments, between the "pugnacious and rousing" brasses and the "odd and unnerving" woodwinds (445). These rhythmic features, which become effects, are cast, interestingly, in the distinctly rhetorical language of appeal.

Framing these various discussions about musical appeals—that is, rhythms and their capacities to affect or even violate bodies—is a larger concern about what to make of the new music, and whether it is the job of the musician to train the audience to hear its "new idiom" (December 1927, 538–39). As Burke argues in his first chronicle entry, the reading of music as "universal" is an "error" (538); music is instead beholden to its moment and is also, he seems to suggest, rhetorical in the traditional Roman sense—with the trifold task of instructing, delighting, and moving. Burke writes that the artist must ask "first that the audience divine his idiom and then, divining it, be influenced by it and obey its exhortations" (538). Burke's model of musical rhetoric involves a certain giving over of oneself on the part of the audience member, and that giving over seems to happen at the level of bodily perception. For Burke music is timely, and with all the modernist experiments with repetition and variation, subtle (as with Stravinsky) or not (as with Stokowski), is the notion that musical agitations pose questions (January 1928, 85), push the accepted limits of what music can do, create new idioms, and expose the point of intolerance (May 1928, 446), all by "tapping" senses of touch, sight, and sound. In short music works rhetorically, and it does so through the body.

As Burke settles into his role as "official" musical chronicler, he also settles more comfortably into a bodily rhetorical view of music that takes him deeper into questions of how exactly music achieves its sensuous, bodily effects. In June 1929 he begins his entry with a comment on the form of opera: "Opera is naturally a semaphoric thing—its plot should be signalled to the audience, whose participation is not constant, but momentarily overcomes their sense of aloofness" (538). By invoking the metaphor of a semaphore, Burke marks the ability of an operatic performance to signal strongly—even to oversignal—and to do so in a stiff, exaggerated way, as with flags on sticks. It is a method of signaling that produces the audience as distant analysts who remain aloof because they can.

Still, other contemporary performances help Burke to theorize more subtle modes of "signaling": "Perhaps," he continues, "Debussy went much farther than Wagner in eliminating this tragic distance, for despite the exceptional emotions which he invokes, his effects are intimate" (538). Burke accounts for Debussy's unusual operatic intimacy in this way: "He does not confront us, he surrounds or permeates us, utilizing for his appeal a fluctuant method which relies more upon our sensibility than upon analysis" (538). At work in this entry are several distinctions and assumptions, most notably the commonplace association of analysis with distance, set against the pair sensibility and intimacy. Sensuous rather than analytic feelers are activated through the operatic performance's ability to—in Burke's words—surround or even permeate, to produce opera watchers' bodies as sensuous, sensitive membranes and to deplete effectively if slowly any distance between performance and audience. Debussy's method, Burke avers, is "fluctuant" and takes opera to what might be its "logical conclusion": "the progression from wooden conventionalizations to fluidity, from the stressing of aesthetic propriety to the stressing of emotional effectiveness" (538). With the final distinction between aesthetic propriety and emotional effectiveness, Burke reveals his own Debussy-inspired move to focus not on generic aesthetic or even technical conventions but rather on particular effects of combined rhythms and tones, especially the work of variation to draw attention to those rhythms and tones, producing a somewhat jarring effect. After describing two sequential but sharply distinct musical performances, one eloquent in its sparseness and the next displaying a "fury of rhythms" (538), Burke observes how "the experience was an uncertain commingling of monotony and change, wherein the melodic lines could quickly engrave themselves upon us" (539). This particular chronicle entry once again reveals Burke's peculiarly rhetorical approach to music criticism, an approach that attends to movement and manipulation of rhythms and their effects on audience bodies. It also anticipates his later observation in one of *The Philosophy of Literary Form*'s lesser-known essays, that melody "lays us open" (345).[10]

Burke's rhetorical stance toward art is of course fleshed out before *The Philosophy of Literary Form*, most notably in the essays of *Counter-Statement*. Yet it is important, too, to consider how Burke's role as music critic gave him a chance to contemplate dispositional effects and even, as evidenced in *Counter-Statement*, to meditate on the differences between musical and discursive repetition. During his two-year tenure as the *Dial*'s music critic, Burke trains his attention on rhythm and repetition, perhaps for reasons outlined in the essay "Psychology and Form": "One reason why music can stand repetition so much more sturdily than correspondingly good prose is that music, of all the arts, is by its nature least suited to the psychology of information, and has remained closer to the psychology of form" (CS 34). Here Burke hearkens back to a view expressed in a very early letter to Cowley, wherein he vows to Cowley that, faced with the "limited range of expression" in writing, he is "going for certain to take up exclusively the study of music" (May 1, 1916; Jay 24). "Think of it, Mal," the not quite nineteen-year-old Burke writes excitedly, "to have two mediums!" He goes on: "Music awakens more reactions in us" (May 1, 1916; Jay 24). Some years later, in "Psychology and Form," he suggested that with music "form cannot atrophy"; that "every dissonant chord cries for its solution, and whether the musician resolves or refuses to resolve this dissonance into the chord which the body cries for, he is dealing in human appetites" (CS 34). He continues by contrasting "good prose," which, according to Burke, is "more prone to the temptations of pure information" and so "cannot so much bear repetition since the aesthetic value of information is lost once that information is imparted" (35). Such a view develops most explicitly in his music criticism, where everywhere there appear meditations on music vis-à-vis literature.

In December 1928, at the opening of the new concert season, Burke writes what he calls a "sociological preface to our present season" (530) in which he reflects broadly on "that vast enterprise of music" (529). Music, for Burke, is "that art which has charms to make the soothed breast savage, and which tends as naturally towards the grandiloquent as literature tends towards laundry lists" (529). Here Burke registers his remorse at what he would later characterize as literature's capitulation to information—that is, effectively detaching from eloquence. As his "preface" culminates, Burke locates in musical aesthetics the potential for arrhythmia that he located in the pathologies of his fictional characters: "Not the least service of art," he writes in this music entry, "lies in its ability to make action more difficult. And one particular brand of art may, by its specific message, still further strengthen this questioning attitude. What, it may be asked, was ever discovered without certainty of the most rabid and unbalanced sort? And what, it may be answered, was ever preserved without the agency of sleepless distrust?" (530). These anticipatory musings, if read in the context of the decidedly out-of-sync bodies in Burke's short fiction, suggest that musical irruption, with its ability to pose the most "unbalanced" and "distrustful" of rhythms, has the capacity to disrupt regular rhythms of the status quo, a point that for Burke distills music to sheer rhetorical force, unencumbered by information. Meditation on the contemporary musical aesthetic allows Burke to theorize in a new but critical milieu principles that would bear importantly on the literary aesthetics he explores in the early *Counter-Statement* essay "The Adepts of Pure Literature," in which he celebrates, among others, the feverish de Gourmont and the nauseating Flaubert (8). Music, as sheer sound and rhythm, therefore enables Burke to theorize the rhythmic, poetic qualities—and by extension, the disruptive, interventive capacities—of language as well, a point I will elaborate more fully in chapter 6.[11]

Indeed, music—and Burke's "makeshift" post as the *Dial*'s music critic—draws Burke's attention so sharply to the audience that it must be given at least partial credit for Burke's move into rhetoric, a move that I contend was in the works well before *Counter-Statement*.[12] Two passages in *Counter-Statement*, one early and one late, show how the music-body-rhetoric cluster persisted for Burke. First, in "Psychology and Form," music and a discussion of lullaby open a paragraph in which Burke critiques the assumption of psychoanalysis that art is the result of an artist's "waking dream" (35). "It is, rather, the audience which dreams, while the artist oversees the conditions which determine this dream. He is the manipulator of blood, brains, heart, and bowels" (36). Here, Burke hatches what Selzer calls his "tremendous innovation," which is the theory of form as eloquence (*Kenneth Burke in Greenwich Village* 143)—of art as rhetorical. But Burke develops that theory with direct reference to physical bodies. Music, "fitted less than any other art for imparting information" (*CS* 36), thus stands as rhetorical force par excellence, and thereby the most effective medium for accessing and affecting bodies. Music, therefore, gets him there.

The music-body-rhetoric cluster becomes ever more prominent a bit later in *Counter-Statement*'s "Lexicon Rhetoricae," when Burke draws together the appeal of form, rhythm, and the body. The movements of the passage are crucial for my argument, so I quote it in its entirety:

> The appeal of form as exemplified in rhythm enjoys a special advantage in that rhythm is more closely allied with "bodily" processes. Systole and diastole, alternation of the feet in walking, inhalation and exhalation, up and down, in and out, back and forth, such are the types of distinctly motor experiences "tapped" by rhythm. Rhythm is so natural to the organism that even a succession of uniform beats will be interpreted as a succession of accented and unaccented beats. The rhythm of a page, in setting up a corresponding rhythm in the body, creates marked degrees of expectancy, or acquiescence. A rhythm is a promise which the poet makes to the reader—and in proportion as the reader comes to rely upon this promise, he falls

into a state of general surrender which makes him more likely to accept without resistance the rest of the poet's material. In becoming receptive to so much, he becomes receptive to still more. The varied rhythms of prose also have their "motor" analogies. A reader sensitive to prose rhythms is like a man hurrying through a crowd; at one time he must halt, at another time he can leap forward; he darts perilously between saunterers; he guards himself in turning sharp corners. We mean that in all rhythmic experiences one's "muscular imagination" is touched. Similarly with sounds, there is some analogy to actual movement, since sounds may rise and fall, and in a remote way one rises and falls with them. (140–41)

This particular passage, which I will return to in chapter 3 in a slightly different vein, can here be read as the critical counterpart to Burke's "Excursion," discussed in the preface. Here bodies are presented as metronomes, pulsing, moving, vibrating "processes," what the "rhythmanalyst" Henri Lefebvre calls "bundles of rhythms" (104), and what Eagleton figures as a rigorous logic of pulses (*Ideology* 17). Such a conception of bodies helps draw attention, in the passage above, to the sheer number of ways that bodies move throughout the section—from the steady thumping pulse to the multiple, sometimes erratic ways of walking, to the regularities of breathing. Bodily rhythms—the fact that bodies are constituted by such regular intervals of motion—also "set up" bodies as *moveable by* rhythms, be they soothingly melodious or even jarringly prosaic.

In a study of metaphors of musical motion, Mark L. Johnson and Steve Larson note that rhythm and the body mark an important point of convergence between music and language. "Music," they write, "is meaningful in specific ways that some language cannot be, but it shares in the general embodiment of meaning that underlies all forms of symbolic expression, including gesture, body language, ritual, spoken words, visual communication, and so on. Thinking about how music moves us is not going to explain everything we need to know about language, but it is an excellent place to begin to understand how all meaning emerges in the flesh, blood, and bone of our embodied experience" (81).

At stake for Johnson and Larson is the body's role in meaning making, a concern shared by Burke and inevitably encountered by those who consider bodies these days in relation to language in any number of media, be it literature, music, cinema, or informatics. And yet Burke would not settle for merely pointing out the importance of the body and moving on. Instead his inquiry into music's effects on bodies takes him to the edges of language, particularly language as rhythm, wherein rhythm becomes not merely an aesthetic feature but an enlivening force—sheer energy—with a unique capacity to mingle with and transform bodily energies and rhythms already churning, humming, and moving. And so it is that Burke's move from symbolizing the arrhythmic bodies of artists to tuning in to polyrhythmic bodies in an audience, a move enabled by his early and continuing work with music, helps to account more fully for his ultimate move to things rhetorical.

Burke's early allegiance to the related formulations of bodies-as-inclinations and bodies-as-movement therefore guides his own movement through various religious and scientific discourses that would help him develop his theories of language, meaning making, and communication, and music's isolation of rhetorical energy and rhythm extends to Burke's intense interest in mysticism, an interest that, as the next chapter shows, grew out of his regard for things bodily.

2

Burke's Mystical Method

> Mysticism is no rare thing. True, the attaining of it in its pure state is rare. And its secular analogues, in grand or gracious symbolism, are rare. But the need for it, the itch, is everywhere.
>
> Kenneth Burke, *A Rhetoric of Motives*

Burke's 1935 book, *Permanence and Change: An Anatomy of Purpose*, ends with a famously resounding cry. Nietzschean as much for its aphoristic drama as for its swipe at "purely human boasts of grandeur" and its quiveringly staunch assertion that humans "build their cultures by huddling together, nervously loquacious, at the edge of an abyss" (272), this final line may well be one of Burke's most frequently quoted.[1] And yet the line's mystical cast—with its dizzying vantage point and its reference to the dwarfing force of the unknown—has gone largely unremarked. In adopting this line epigraphically, scholars of culture, language, and rhetoric have perhaps unwittingly adopted a mantra of mysticism. That is, the line—and even, I will hazard, *Permanence and Change* as a book—only makes sense in the context of mysticism, for only in mysticism, Burke writes earlier in the book, does "there so often recur the compelling image of the *abyss*, some aweful [sic] internal chasm . . . a sense of distance, division, or vertigo which has at times been verbalized by reference to a 'geographical' place, the bottomless pit of hell" (146; emphasis in original).

In *A Grammar of Motives* (*GM*), too, mysticism figures prominently as the tradition that features Burke's pentadic "purpose" (128). There, Burke draws from his trusty Baldwin dictionary to offer a two-part definition of sorts.[2] "Mysticism," Burke writes, leading up to the quotation of Baldwin, "embraces 'those forms of speculative and religious thought which profess to attain an immediate apprehension of the divine essence or the ultimate ground of existence.' And: 'Penetrated by the thought of the ultimate of all experience, and impatient of even a seeming separation from the creative source of things, mysticism succumbs to a species of metaphysical fascination'" (*GM* 287). The Baldwin entry invokes some key components of the mysticisms Burke engages in *Permanence and Change* and its companion volume, *Attitudes toward History* (*ATH*)—namely creativity, immediacy, and perspective—and therefore offers a good starting point for charting his mystical tendencies. And yet the Baldwin definition places a barely perceptible emphasis on the supernatural side, and thereby anticipates Burke's stance in *The Rhetoric of Religion*, which Joshua Gunn rightly points out overemphasizes the spiritual and supernatural (xxi–xxii). Such an emphasis leaves behind the decidedly nonsupernatural (at one point Burke even calls it "secular") cast of mysticism as it figures in Burke's early critical methods, most notably *Permanence and Change* and *Attitudes toward History*. The mysticism in those two books, in locating in the body the "ultimate ground of existence," falls in step with the notions of bodily rhythm discussed in the previous chapter.[3] Radically open, doggedly perspectival, at home with confusion (PC 194), and curiously, distinctly physical, mysticism served as Burke's fusive device.

Take, for example, *Permanence and Change*'s "ultimate" line. This line manages to capture simultaneously two perspectives: (1) the up-close, zoomed-in perspective of the "nervously loquacious" in the thick of "rhetoric and traffic" (272); and (2) the faraway, zoomed-out perspective that turns skyscrapers into toothpicks and cars into so many crawling ants. For just beyond the tangled cities, Burke writes, "there lies the eternally unsolvable Enigma . . . right on the edges of our metropolitan bickerings, stretching outward to interstellar infinity and inward to the depths of the mind" (272). The quickness of this almost cinematic pullback, which allows these contradictory perspectives to persist at once, has a vertiginous effect and effectively shakes things up. What's more, if read as a mystical limn itself stretching between *Permanence and Change* and *Attitudes toward History*, the famous line renders these two as markedly mystical books.

Together these companion volumes offer mysticism as a poetic, intensely corporeal method similar in some respects to a particularly modernist occult poetics elaborated by Gunn in *Modern Occult Rhetoric* but also notably distinctive, especially with its bodily beginnings.[4] If *Permanence and Change* ponders mysticism as a corporeal style of engagement, *Attitudes toward History* converts mysticism into a critical method, one based on the "mystical . . . hankerings" of, most notably, William James.[5]

Burke among the Mystics

To chart Burke's engagements with mysticism is itself a daunting, vertiginous task, but his letters help locate his earliest encounters with mysticism in the mid-1920s.[6]

That he was at least in mysticism's proximity by that time is certain, for in a 1924 letter to Burke, Cowley claims to have learned secondhand, through Allen Tate, that their mutual friends "Frank, Munson, and Crane have gone much deeper into [the prominent mystical thinkers of the day] Gurdjieff, Ouspensky, etc. than we ever suspected, and that any reference to mysticism outrages not an idea but a cult" (November 16, 1924; Jay 165). Cowley continues, grumbling, "it is forbidden to say a word against mysticism." At the time Burke responded resolutely, "I do openly and avowedly, of course, share your distrust of this parlor mysticism," and then elaborated: "These mystics feed too well for me to take them seriously" (November 20, 1924; Jay 166). Burke's charge is deliberately restricted to Waldo Frank and his circle, though; in fact he goes on to offer W. B. Yeats as a more "sincere" mystic figure: "Yeats got religion. Yeats lived the life of a mystic, disorbited, tootle-voiced, among cranks and horrors" (November 20, 1924, Jay 166). Here, the word *disorbited* suggests a certain irregularity of movement, while *tootle-voiced* evokes the uneven ambling of a flute. Yeats, that is, effectively counters Frank's version of mysticism, which seems to Burke a bit too orbited, its "voice" unwavering. In other words, a sincere mystic, in not following a predetermined path, gives oneself over to a radical, unknowable otherness, while Frank's version of mysticism seems to Burke utterly self-directed, self-certain, and superficial. As Burke emphatically phrases it in that same letter to Cowley, again writing of Frank and his circle, "Of all the attitudes toward life, mysticism most demands denials and suicidal liberties. *I have never, in word or act, seen their mysticism*" (November 20, 1924, Jay 166; emphasis in original).

The point is that Burke not only knew of mysticism by 1924, but he was very much in the process of forming a stance toward it, even explicitly formulating it as an attitude toward life, a formulation that persisted in his writings for decades. Even at his most skeptical moment, Burke maintains a certain respect for mysticism. He does not "distrust" all mystics, just those "parlor" ones who remained on the surface of mysticism without fully inhabiting it. And while his own strong commitment to mysticism does not become evident until later, his early respect for Yeats suggests the possibility for a percolating sort of relation in the 1920s.

By the early 1930s Burke seems to have edged closer to mysticism, appending the following postscript to a 1931 letter to William Carlos Williams: "Am reading Ouspensky's New Model of the Universe. It is, I gather, the primer of mysticism, the introduction to wisdom-of-the-East wisdom" (July 20, 1931; East 52). Next, playfully invoking the crisp image of the Arrow Collar Man, then the rage in men's fashion and a bourgeois symbol of uprightness and respectability, Burke adds somewhat speculatively, "So who knows—perhaps I shall become an Arrow Collar Mystic after all?"[7] Burke follows this bemused, playful question with another hedge: "The chapter on the five Yogas made me want, just a little bit, to learn Sanskrit" (July 20, 1931; East 52).

If mysticism had been percolating for Burke in the 1920s, then his reading of Ouspensky's "primer" seems crucial for the next phase of Burke's mysticism in the 1930s, one that emerges in various letters and reviews and culminates in his open exploration of mysticism and the body in *Permanence and Change, Attitudes toward History*, and other 1930s writings.[8]

This chapter sketches the two kinds of mysticism Burke engaged during those dozen-plus years between 1924 and 1937. On the one hand there is the bodily Gurdjieffian mysticism espoused by Frank and his circle and written about by P. D. Ouspensky, and on the other hand, there is a mystic attitude Burke later culls from William James, who like Yeats, Burke believes, "got" mysticism. In G. I. Gurdjieff, Burke found a mystic who shared his regard for the rhythmic, communicative body, and in James he found an intellectual mystic whose writings made available the kind of "attitudinal" mysticism he had grown to admire in Gurdjieff and his followers, Ouspensky and A. R. Orage. Together these two strands of mysticism most closely approximated the open, rhythmic variation Burke valued early on in Yeats.

The result of Burke's engagement with mysticism, I will suggest, is a critical method that foregrounds the body as a vital, connective, transformational force, thereby expanding on the "tappable" rhythmic body he had found in his engagements with music considered in the previous chapter. What follows will examine just what qualities Burke gleaned from mystic thinkers such as Gurdjieff and James, and then consider how these mystical approaches formed Burke's views on the body in particular. The final part of the chapter will examine how Burke's engagement with James keeps the body in mind while moving into James's mysticism and consequently into mysticism's symbols and language. The body thus stands as Burke's foray into the crucial discourse of mysticism, a discourse he would not soon abandon. But since the connection between mysticism and bodies is not immediately obvious, I want to begin by establishing exactly how Burke connected mysticism and the body in the first place. The answers—perhaps surprisingly—come from Burke's decidedly political "antics of refusal."

"A Minute Ear to the Body": Burke's Mystical Purpose

In 1933 Burke sent a long, gut-spilling letter to the southern Agrarian poet and literary critic Allen Tate defending his *Counter-Statement* against Tate's "public" charges of "madness" and "bitterness" and enumerating the reasons behind what Burke reformulates as his "antics of refusal."[9] The letter is an intensely political screed, offering twenty-six axioms, each marked by letters of the alphabet. Axioms A through G lament the current economy and what Burke calls the "genius of machinery." H and I propose that "the only way of combating [sic] this trend . . . is by the discovery and stressing of a point of reference outside the circle of values arising out of the machine." Axioms J through S reach an almost feverish pitch, predicting, in turn, "a terrific lot of blowing-up," Burke's own death, and then maybe, finally, revolt. Burke then tempers his sorrow by returning in axiom T to "the point of reference outside the system," which he identifies as "the genius of the body itself" (emphasis in original).[10] The next few axioms are crucial for framing Burke's "way in" to mysticism, so I offer them in their entirety:

"(u) I thus come to believe that one should 'hold a minute ear to the body'; (v) in so doing, I begin to find that, at other periods of human history, when other systems of ethics were coming into disrepute as our commercial ethic now is, people were given to a similar habit of seeking in the body-processes the <u>undeniable</u> point of reference outside the system whereby sturdier and more accurate moral exhortations could be built up; (w) I discover that such people were called mystics; (x) I look longingly and respectfully into their works" (August 19, 1933).[11] On one level this passage has an incredibly logical, cumulative structure. Burke professes a newfound belief in the body, a belief he sees himself sharing with mystics of the past and for the same reasons: a certain disenchantment with the prevailing system of ethics.

And yet on another level, the syllogistic movement of the axioms remains somewhat surprising. Why, in the midst of the Depression, in a period portending "a terrific lot of blowing-up," would Kenneth Burke, a leftist, turn to the body, and why, more specifically, to mysticism? And further, where did Burke learn to link mysticism and the body?

Permanence and Change, the book Burke was working on when he sent this letter to Tate, mentions mysticism and mystics frequently, though it does so in mostly general terms without naming specific strands of mysticism. Still, in that book Burke helpfully describes mysticism as "the farthest reach of the search for new perspectives" (223) and notes that such mystical reaching "may be expected to flourish at periods when traditional ways of seeing and doing (with their accompanying verbalizations) have begun to lose their authority" (223). "The mystic," he writes, "seeks a sounder basis of certainty than those provided by the flux of history" (222). Paradoxically these sounder bases frequently reside in "occult" activities, that is, activities that turn on a kind of hidden or esoteric knowledge.[12]

Echoes of Burke's point about "the flux of history" can be found in Gauri Viswanathan's *Critical Inquiry* article on occultism and, with a slightly different emphasis, in Joshua Gunn's *Modern Occult Rhetoric*, the only extant consideration of occultism's rhetoric. Viswanathan uses Max Weber to argue that the otherworldliness of occultism is often a response to "fragmentariness," or to a kind of alienation. "Alienated from structured forms of bureaucratic life, otherworldliness (which often takes the form of occultism)," writes Viswanathan, "is an attempt to recuperate meaning from a suppressed past, which in being suppressed leads to a fragmentary view of history" (19). As an alienated and thus alternative way of seeing, occultism (in Viswanathan's case, nineteenth-century Theosophy) provides a new set of nonrational rationalizations, a new way to imagine what Viswanathan calls "an alternative cultural governance" (20), or what Gunn, following Theosophy's Helena Petrovna Blavatsky, figures as "The Middle Way." Gunn too offers Theosophy as a "reactive discourse" (58), only he focuses less on fragmentariness produced by bureaucracy and more on the conflict between Darwinism and spiritualism (58 ff), and Theosophy's role in drawing together these seemingly incommensurable views.

Like the Theosophists described by Viswanathan, Burke was feeling alienated from his own aesthetic and political culture, as evident throughout the letter to Tate, most palpably in axiom R: "I hold it thus to be a hideous inefficiency that I, who am to live but once, must pass my time in so assinine [sic] an era; wherein precisely the resources which could make us joyous are allowed to mark the centre of our disasters" (August 19, 1933). Perhaps in emulation of former Theosophists Yeats and D. H. Lawrence, whose mystic tendencies he admired,[13] Burke looked elsewhere. Indeed he developed an intense interest in a particular strand of mysticism that had in the 1920s taken hold of his immediate literary and intellectual cohort—that professed by G. I. Gurdjieff, an internationally known Russian mystic. Gurdjieff's famously difficult mysticism became known to the literati of Greenwich Village through translations and expansions offered by two of his followers, the English editor of the *New Age*, A. R. Orage, and Russian mathematician and mystic P. D. Ouspensky, and perhaps most relevantly, through dance movements performed in New York by students from Gurdjieff's Institute for the Harmonious Development of Man, located near Paris.[14]

Mysticism's Body: Gurdjieff in New York

At Gurdjieff's institute, pupils underwent intensive and restorative training in the form of dance movements, regular mindful labor, and sustained, reflective study of Eastern philosophy. In January 1924 Gurdjieff brought these performances, referred to simply as "movements," to New York and caused something of a sensation.

The "circles of intelligentsia," so called by Burke's friend the literary critic Gorham Munson, had to be readied as an audience for these unfamiliar performances. While Gurdjieff's student Louise Welch claims that regular Americans were remarkably unprepared for such innovative, sacred performances (4), their literary and artistic counterparts in Greenwich Village were at least intellectually prepared. Their intellectual preparation owed to the work of Gurdjieff's followers Ouspensky and Orage.

Ouspensky's book *Tertium Organum*, the title of which is Latin for "third instrument," had been translated into English in 1920, and almost immediately reached Burke's circles. The book's aim is indicated by its title: to think between the Organon of Aristotle, which deals with how the subject thinks, and Francis Bacon's *Novum Organum*, which is concerned with how objects are known (Bragdon 1). The hoped-for effect is a synthetic suspension of subject and object that places both on an even plane. The book, influenced by Ouspensky's study of Gurdjieff, draws together philosophies of all stripes—notably Buddhist philosophy, along with Dostoyevsky, Kant, William James, and Henri Bergson. This synthesis of East and West produced a renewed focus on perception and a solid commitment to the body's capacity to open itself up to different orders of perception. Throughout the book Ouspensky uses the language of vision, such as when he suggests "the sensation of motion in time arises in us because we are looking at the world as if through a narrow slit" (39). He compares a mystical attainment of higher consciousness to "ascending a mountain or going up in a balloon," an act through which one "begins to see *simultaneously* and *at once* many things which it is impossible to see simultaneously and at once from below" (41; emphasis in original)—space and time in Ouspensky's book expand together, exposing their inseparability, and as he puts it, "the angle of vision will enlarge during such an ascent, the *moment* will expand" (41; emphasis in original).

For Ouspensky, as for Gurdjieff, this capacity to seek and attain broader perspectives already exists in and happens through the body: "Eastern philosophy," Ouspensky writes, "regards the physical body as something *impermanent* which is in a condition of perpetual interchange with its surroundings. The particles come and go. *After one* second the body is already not absolutely the same as it was one second before" (46; emphasis in original). The body's ontology of variation thus makes possible the multiple planes of awareness Gurdjieffian mysticism seeks. Put most starkly, Ouspensky uses Western philosophy to discuss limitations of the current instrument of perception—organum—and turns to Eastern philosophy to move past these limitations. Gurdjieff's mysticism therefore entails copious attention to bodily movement—in everyday activity such as household chores, walking, and sitting, as well as in cultivated, practiced postures drawn from yoga and ancient dance. Ouspensky's version offers an important domain for exploring the body's capacity for variation—and the domain for that exploration is art.

It is no wonder, then, that Ouspensky's book caught on in Burke's circles. Burke himself characterizes the moment of *Tertium Organum* in a 1931 *New Republic* review of Ouspensky's followup book, *A New Model of the Universe*. The review opens with a brief discussion of the impact Ouspensky's earlier book made during a moment when the "intellectual and emotional" conditions were just right "for a turn to other attitudes" ("In Quest of the Way" 104). In such moments, Burke continues, "there are signs that the positivistic West would gladly renounce its positivism in favor of a mystical guidance, though men of intelligence and emotional decency have, for the most part, been denied much opportunity in this direction unless they were content to piece together little religions of their own." Church-related "dogmatists," he then suggests, were of little help in the matter, "enlisted" as they were "more in the cause of institutionalism than of insight" (104). "Accordingly," Burke writes, "when Mr. Ouspensky came forward some years ago with his 'Tertium Organum: A Key to the Enigmas of the

World,' the situation was considerably improved. In him mysticism found an apologist of distinction" (104). He could confidently state that Ouspensky's book had arrived at a propitious moment since most of his friends eagerly devoured it.

According to Gorham Munson, for example, Hart Crane obtained a copy of *Tertium Organum* in 1922, and it was soon dog-eared and full of marked-up passages, such as this one: "Thus in art we have already the first experiments in *a language of the future*. Art anticipates a psychic evolution and divines its future forms" (quoted in Munson 196; emphasis in original). Crane, Munson, and Frank, all enamored with the notion of the artist as clairvoyant and art as the future, seized on such passages in *Tertium Organum,* and others like them: "In art it is necessary to study 'occultism'—the hidden side of life. The artist must be a clairvoyant: he must see that which others do not see: he must be a magician: must possess the power to make others see that which they do not themselves see, but which he does see" (quoted in Munson, 197).

Ouspensky's book thus held sway over the group that Crane recalls to Munson in a somewhat nostalgic letter as the "Munson-Burke-Toomer-etc. engagements" (HC to GM, 7–9–1924; Munson 210). This line of Crane's likely led literary scholar Robert Bone to name Burke as one of the primary members of "a semi-mystical literary group" whose members, Bone claims, also included Jean Toomer, Hart Crane, Waldo Frank, and Gorham Munson (81). As Crane's letters testify, the Ouspensky-Gurdjieff version of mysticism had a transformative effect on these figures, most notably Toomer, who followed Gurdjieff to Paris in July 1924 (Byrd 72).[15] One of Crane's biographers even writes of a sort of secret society, complete with "pass-words and 'countersigns' with which Ouspensky said those with the 'higher consciousness' were to greet one another" (Unterecker 249).

While Ouspensky's book provided an occasion to study and discuss and, importantly, intellectualize Gurdjieff, A. R. Orage made it possible to witness him. While in London, Orage, the socialist-Nietzschean editor of the *New Age,* spent years studying Gurdjieff's system, attended lectures by Ouspensky alongside T. S. Eliot (Taylor 18), and corresponded with Ezra Pound. In December 1923, though, Orage set out for New York to help "prepare the way" for Gurdjieff, and immediately upon his arrival Orage went straight to the offices of the *Little Review* to visit the editors Margaret Anderson and Jane Heap, already devotees of Gurdjieff.[16] Anderson and Heap organized regular meetings at their apartment on East Eleventh Street (Munson 258). Just after the new year, on January 9, Orage delivered his first lecture at the Sunwise Turn Book Shop, introducing the audience to Gurdjieff's life and teaching and "emphasizing," according to one account, "the conception that contemporary individuals have little control over their own intellectual, emotional, and physical possibilities, and so live largely in a state of sleep" (Taylor 43). He spoke of Gurdjieffian movements and their capacity to produce "a new quality of concentration and attention and a new direction of the mind" (Munson 254). He laid out a new conception of consciousness that reconciles subjectivism and objectivism, a notion of consciousness that sounded familiar to readers of Ouspensky; yet hearing about it from a man whose words, as Munson puts it, "seemed tipped with light" (258) was even more powerful for many in attendance.

There is much more to say about mysticism's effects on this literary group, but since my aim is to follow Burke's engagements with mysticism, and since Burke's interactions with Frank and Munson (and their mysticism) were, like Cowley's, strained at best, suffice it to say that whether or not Burke read *Tertium Organum* in the early 1920s, it is certain that he was exposed to it—in the pages of the *Dial*[17] and from the typewriters and mouths of his friends Frank, Crane, Munson, and Toomer. And yet because all the buzz about Ouspensky focused on quests for higher consciousness achieved through art, the importance of the body for Ouspensky's—and especially Gurdjieff's—method seems to have received little emphasis from Burke's group.[18] But the arrival of Gurdjieff himself along with a troupe of students to perform the dances and bodily gestures so central to his mysticism would remedy such an oversight. Ouspensky's and Orage's preparatory work helped Greenwich Villagers begin to grasp the body's importance for achieving mystical insight in Gurdjieff's system. And though such a view can be written about and lectured on, it is perhaps most aptly danced.

Dancing Ideas

And dance Gurdjieff's pupils did. According to Munson's memoir, which offers a thorough account of Gurdjieff in the village, "the program of ancient dances and movements" was "the indisputable triumph of the tour" (257). As Munson's and other extant descriptions of the Gurdjieffian performances attest, the dances contained two sets of six "obligatory exercises." Munson lists them as follows: "the Initiation of a Priestess, several Dervish dances, a pilgrimage movement called 'measuring the way by one's length,' several women's dances, the Big Seven or enneagram dance, the 'stop exercise,' and a number of folk and manual labor dances" (Munson 209).

Margaret Anderson recalls that "these dances were taken from, or based upon, sacred temple dances which Gurdjieff had seen in the monasteries of Tibet, and their mathematics were said to contain exact esoteric knowledge" (79). Dance thus functioned, as Orage's introductory lectures explained, as a sacred art of communication. The dancers were arranged in three rows and wore billowing white tunics cinched at the waist with sashes tied on the left side, over white trousers that were gathered at the ankle (Welch 4–5). Gorham Munson recalls the strong emphasis Orage placed on the significance of dance in the East and

West and his discussion of ancient times, when "dance was a branch of real art, and served the purposes of higher knowledge and religion. A person who specialized in a subject communicated his knowledge through works of art, particularly dances, as we spread knowledge through books. . . . The ancient sacred dance is not only a medium for aesthetic experience, but a book, as it were, or script, containing a definite piece of knowledge" (Munson 254–55).

Louise Welch records Orage's explanation of the dances in this way: "The farthest possible limits of one's strength are known through the combination of unnatural movements in the individual gymnastics, which help to obtain certain qualities of sensation, various degrees of concentration, and the requisite directing of thought and the senses" (5). Gurdjieff's dancers sought to expand the body's limits through rigorous training in precise movements. On February 19, 1924, the *New York Times* printed a lengthy description of the dances taught at Gurdjieff's institute. The description itself captures the performances' energy and grace:

> The movements are not only bewildering in their complexity, and amazing in the precision of their execution, but rich in diversity, harmonious in rhythm, and exceedingly beautiful in the gracefulness of the postures, which are quite unknown to Europe. To the accompaniment of mystical and inspiring music, handed down from remote antiquity, the sacred dances are executed with deeply religious dignity, which is profoundly impressive. . . . The demonstrations . . . consist of movements which include the sacred gymnastics of the esoteric schools, the religious ceremonies of the antique Orient and the ritual movements of monks and dervishes—besides the folk dances of many a remote community. (Hoffman)

One dance exercise in particular helps illustrate how such knowledge is simultaneously learned and performed. In a 1924 *Century Magazine* article, C. H. Bechhofer describes the "stop exercises," in which dancers perform a series of dance steps. In Bechhofer's words, "In the middle of a complicated movement, Gurjiev suddenly shouts 'Stop!' Instantly every one becomes still in the attitude he or she is in, however uncomfortable it may be; and so they stop until he releases them" (74). As Jean Toomer, writing about his training at Gurdjieff's institute, recalls, the command to stop means one "must not merely suspend all movement, but also maintain the tension of his muscles, his facial expression . . . in the same state as it was at the word of the command, keeping his gaze fixed at the point at which its directed when the command is uttered."[19] Such exercises, Bechhofer observes, are "designed to help them contemplate themselves in action" (74), to attend to bodily movements at any (and thus every) moment. As the stop exercises suggest, all the movements were part of a larger system based on what Hoffman, writing for the *Times*, called a principle of "irregularity." Orage's explanation is elegant in its simplicity: "Since the body is made to stop in quite unplanned positions, the dancer cannot help but observe himself in a new situation—between postures, as it were" (Welch 6). As Welch explains it, such exaggerated attention to motion through stillness was "one way to break the vicious circle of . . . automatism" (6). By introducing intensive awareness at any (or every) moment, the training and performances draw one's attention to the body's mechanical sense of habit, and new kinds of movements, new modes of communication, become possible.

Bechhofer, reporting from a visit to Gurdjieff's institute near Paris, writes that Gurdjieff's system works "by showing you your particular habits and making you aware of them" (71). The piece continues: "A newfound harmony is achieved through manual labor, physical exercises, and dance. One exercise asks students to perform physical exercises while doing math problems," all with the aim of helping them "to contemplate themselves in action" (74). The desired effect on the practitioner and observer of Gurdjieffian movement is a new kind of knowledge, a vital, transformative knowledge learned in and communicated through minute attention to bodies. As the *Times* article puts it, Gurdjieff's school "is a place where habits are changed, fixed ideas are broken up, mechanical routines do not exist, and adaptability to ever-changing forms and modes of life is practiced." Such goals are in line with Gurdjieff's writings, which Gunn characterizes as full of "neologisms and long torturous sentences . . . deliberately designed to 'dismay automatic thinking' and expand consciousness to higher levels of reading" (42). The aim, in short, of Gurdjieff's mystic philosophy is to make the normal and everyday seem very, very strange.

By all accounts, then, the training and resulting performances aimed to alter existing habits radically, to revitalize bodies, and to communicate sacred and vital knowledge through those bodies. As Welch's description suggests, the movements effected a shift in emphasis from habitual self-expression to a broad awareness of the body's capacity to learn and change. "If the spectators watched carefully," Welch writes, "they could recognize the changes in state brought about by the movements and the dancers' attentiveness to them" (7). The stop exercise, according to Toomer's firsthand account, "enables us to see and feel our body in postures and positions totally . . . unnatural to it."[20] Welch recalls that the exercise "shocked" onlookers "into the vision of a new possibility." Some even recalled later that the dancers, having been ordered to stop midmovement at the very edge of the stage, even fell into the orchestra pit (6). For the most part, though, the exercises enact the larger point of Gurdjieff's mysticism: to suspend all physical, mental, and emotional habits in order to allow for new possibilities of movement and thought.[21]

The students of mysticism therefore danced the belief professed by Gurdjieff, Ouspensky, and Orage that human life is conducted in dreams supported by mechanical habits that keep people in a perpetual state of "waking sleep." As Welch recorded Orage's words: "Not only do our bodies move mechanically, but we feel mechanically and we think mechanically" (10–11). This mechanical behavior and movement seals off "direct contact with life." The work of the dance performances therefore "was to participate in waking up, in arousing ourselves from this heavy but comfortable sleep and participate in the movement toward consciousness. Then we would see what was before our eyes, indeed all our senses, and be sensitive to the impact of what is" (11).

Witnessing the live performances, according to Munson, "had a strange impact that can only be described as awakening" (255). Indeed, he writes elsewhere in his memoir that he and his partner, Elizabeth Delza, were "sleepless for hours afterwards, such was its awakening effect" (208). And on February 3, 1924, Hart Crane described one performance in a letter to his mother: "Last night I was invited to witness some astonishing dances and psychic feats performed by a group of pupils belonging to the now famous mystic monastery founded by Gurdieff [sic] near Versailles, (Paris,) that is giving some private demonstrations of their training methods in New York now. . . . I can't possibly begin to describe the elaborate theories and plan of this institution, nor go into the details of this single demonstration, but it was very, very interesting—and things were done by amateurs which would stump the Russian ballet, I'm sure" (February 3, 1924; Crane 174).

Jean Toomer, who attended the same performance as Crane, describes how "the dancers caught hold of me, fascinated me, spoke to me in a language strange to my experience. . . . Though I could have listened to it again and again, I had a sense from the very first that the music had not been composed to be listened to, but to be enacted. . . . And so it moved me."[22]

Other, lesser-known attendees claimed that the dances "seemed to offer a new way of being alive" (Welch 8) and that they "vibrate to the shocks of real life" (John Cowper Powys to A. R. Orage, 1930; quoted in Welch 12). According to Munson, "people who had no use for the ideas of Gurdjieff excepted the dances from their censure; the dances, they said, were strange and wonderful" (257). These descriptions begin to render what was no doubt an energetic and energizing event, one that jolted the New York intelligentsia out of their seats, out of what Orage called the "mechanical functioning" of the mind and body and toward "a vital order" (Welch 8). In Toomer's phrasing, "It was a call to action in those very moments that were being performed on the stage, or in a march of men and women towards a destiny not even foreshadowed in the ordinary world" (quoted in Byrd 69). These astonishing, solemn bodily performances thus foregrounded communication, transformation, and, above all, vitality.

With their practices designed to thwart the body's—and the culture's—tendencies toward machinelike movements and to find through the body new ways of moving through and thus of seeing the world, Gurdjieff, Orage, Ouspensky, and the dancing pupils were the mystics whose work would, in his phrasing, garner Kenneth Burke's sincere respect and longing. Recall that in the letter to Tate Burke devotes several axioms to detailing the problems with what he calls the "genius of the machine" before offering the "genius of the body" as a necessary counterpoint, an antic of refusal. In doing so Burke, however tacitly, sets Gurdjieff, Orage, and Ouspensky, whose mystical philosophy enlivened and was enlivened by bodies, against the mechanical "automatism" of daily life.[23]

Burke recorded at least one instance of practicing Gurdjieffian bodily awareness in his daily movements. In a letter to Malcolm Cowley dated November 8, 1924, written after Gurdjieff's New York tour, he writes, "I note the solidity of my shoes as they thump over rocks and sod. I stop to observe perspective. At such times I always reflect that there is no anguish but physical pain, and that so far the good God has pretty well spared me that. I resolve again to bite hard and keep my muscles firm. . . . At such moments the psychophysical parallel becomes apparent" (Jay 164). The rest of the letter discusses a philosophical move to "things of the spirit" in relation to his own recent desolation. Without naming either Gurdjieff or Ouspensky in his self-diagnosis, Burke still invokes their teachings. He writes, "While what does this mean: that when my brain has been absent and I suddenly recall . . . that I have, by an elaborate system of overlapping strokes, been drawing in my mind the three letters, in capitals, ONE, each square, so that the O is composed of four straight lines and four right angles" (Jay 164). What Burke posits here is the tendency, described by Gurdjieff, to become so routinized as to create an illusion of solidness, of unity (one). As Burke puts it earlier in the letter: "There is nowhere I can go that my self does not go with me."

This self, this ONE created through "an elaborate system of overlapping strokes," has been made, machinelike, through continual repetition of habituated practice. Gurdjieff, calling such existence a state of "sleep," encourages an "awakening" through such attention as Burke gives to the soles of his shoes "as they thump over rocks and sod" and the careful observation of a moment—that is, through a new bodily awareness. In Burke's words, "I stop to observe perspective." The letter to Cowley serves as strong evidence that Burke was at least trying out some of the practices taught at Gurdjieff's institute.

If Burke sometimes experimented with mystical meditative practices, he would also explicitly engage mystical teaching in his writing. In addition to his review of Ouspensky's follow-up to *Tertium Organum*, an even more compelling indication of Burke's interest in Gurdjieff's performances appears in a 1935 review of the new American Ballet at the Adelphi Theater ("The Dance"). This review plainly shows how Gurdjieffian movements enlivened Burke's belief in the body, and specifically in the work of dance as a radical, mystical art of transformation.

The problem with the American Ballet, as Burke sees it, is that dance in American culture frequently does not seek to involve its onlookers. His criticism of both contemporary dance and contemporary culture becomes clear as he poses a series of wry questions and offers satirical answers:

> Are we physically sluggish after too many months of winter? Then let a few lithe experts on the stage be agile for us. Are we made poor in manners, through having dodged among traffic, pushed through subway crowds, and grabbed a bite on the run? Then let a dozen lovely young girls devote their entire day to modulations of the body, until they become miracles of gracefulness. Are we, who deal primarily with the *symbols* of production and distribution, inclined to lose our zest for muscular expression? Then let a special group be charged with the upholding of this function. Let them attain the acme of physical discipline, in behalf of our flaccidness. ("The Dance" 343)

The review proceeds to posit the ballet as "another world," a "decadent" world wherein "the decadence," he writes, "arises from the fact that the great disproportion between the exertions of the performer and the languishing of the audience makes naturally for the *spectacular* kind of art, the Roman circus" (343). In the first paragraph of the review Burke manages to offer a critique that is at base an economic one: the audience at the ballet, for the most part mired in the consumption of "symbols" rather than the means of production and distribution, have become so machinelike as to become physically "sluggish" and "flaccid." They have, in short, lost touch with bodily aspects of labor and simple movement—just as Gurdjieff's system teaches. American ballet thus suffers from a radical separation between the capable dancers and the incapable viewers—those who know how to move their bodies and those who merely buy a ticket and sit through a performance, waiting, as Burke puts it, "in comfort . . . withhold[ing] our sovereign approval" (343). He goes on to offer details of the evening's performances, noting the points at which the "audience registered its enthusiasm," couched in candid and sobering qualifications such as this one: "Yet I do not feel that the American Ballet has wholly solved its 'problems'" (344).

What follows this critique is the most explicit discussion of Gurdjieff's mystical dance in Burke's writings. Dance, he suggests, has lost its magic. And he means magic in the ancient, sacred, mystical sense. "The dance," he writes, "was originally religious": "In the era of primitive magic it was as 'practical' as medicine or chemistry; for in the savage schema of causality such benign events as the abundance of crops and victory in war could only be brought about by their symbolic enactment in dance form" (344). Burke goes on to lament the evacuation of magic from the performances by American ballet companies, to bemoan the empty spectacle that remains. In doing so he sets up an argument for a return of magical, mystical mimesis. His proposal, cast in the language of Orage and Gurdjieff, reads as follows: "The way in which the felicitous use of the body could most instruct us, it seems to me, would not be by the creation of abstract loveliness, for which we are too damned unfit, but by helping us build anew from the areas of mimetic expression in which we still have some spontaneous experience. It might help us regain the use of posture and gesture by ritualistically projecting the ways in which we do actually move and place ourselves. It must be very patient, and not get too far ahead of us who are mimetically ailing" (344).

Burke's request shares the same aims of Gurdjieff's stop exercises, their sudden freezing in midmovement to call attention to habitual motion, and their emphasis on vitality and transformation. In short Burke wants American Ballet of 1935 to function more like the Gurdjieffian performances did for Greenwich Villagers in 1924. Such an instructive, "felicitous use of the body" would, in Burke's view, jolt viewers out of their customary habit of ignoring bodily processes and movements, thus calling attention to the rituals of everyday life and offering ways to alter them.

Burke does not stop with this proposal, but instead moves on to explore dance and the body's relation to language. To do so he makes a seemingly base assertion that would likely turn off any devotees of ballet: "My dog," he writes, "is a dancer." He is a dancer, Burke continues, "in the surprising way he conjugates, let us say, the verb 'to eat.' For the present tense he uses, quite literally, the act of eating. But for the future tense, to say 'I will eat,' he sniffs at his plate, glances ill-naturedly at the cat, and salivates. And to express the perfect tense of this astoundingly irregular verb, to say 'I have eaten,' he picks himself a cool spot under the porch, curls up, and goes to sleep." "Dancing," Burke suggests, "may be linguistically as versatile as that" (344).

By tapping the versatility of gesture and movement, by reflecting on the strangeness of such mundane bodily habits as his dog's feeding rituals, Burke has taken dance—and with it its mystical commitments—to the edges of what would always concern him: language. In doing so he suggests that dance, with its precisely choreographed postures and movements, both meets and exceeds what he later called humans' capacity for symbol use. The exploration ends pointedly with the following conclusion, which finally casts the entire discussion explicitly in terms of mysticism: "Perhaps the dance can illuminatingly bewilder our linguistic habits of mind, and tends ultimately to become mystical, because it is thus always living in the 'eternal now,' making its pasts and futures by nonlogical leaps into the present tenses of other verbs. As such it is a most vital art" (344). With this sentence Burke reveals how the body, especially in the mystical context of dance, can enable transformation—to shake the audience participants out of their everyday bodily habits and to consider just how dancing bodies can communicate on such a radically different register from language, thereby making available a new mixture of tenses, even as they perform in the vital, all-present, "eternal now." Even more important, Burke marks how dance works on a "nonlogical" level, thus underscoring his notion of the body as productive and, just as Orage stipulated, of dance as a communicative art.

Mysticism, Mimesis, and Movement

All of these connections between the body, mysticism, and communication evidently fall together when Burke sits down to write *Permanence and Change*. Indeed it may well be that dance helped him to conceive of communication as he does in that work, that is, "in its broadest sense, not merely as the purveying of information, but also as the sharing of sympathies and purposes, the doing of acts in common" (PC 250). Yet, while Orage made dance analogous to a book as a communicative event, Burke, in *Permanence and Change*, places them in tandem. Communication cannot, he argues, "be confined to pages of a book" (253). He goes on to link "obvious symbolism of poetry on the page" with "symbolism of posture, gesture, and tonality," what he calls "a purely mimetic symbolism, such as we find not only in formal modes of expression like the dance, but also in our spontaneous mind-body correlations between mood and appearance" (253). This passage in *Permanence and Change*, when read alongside Burke's review of the American Ballet and in the context of Gurdjieffian mysticism, shows Burke doing exactly what he exhorted Tate they should all do: "turn a minute ear to the body."

Burke performs another such turn in *Permanence and Change*, where he contrasts the West's conquest-driven mentality, as seen, for instance, in the widespread respect for "climbing," which leads to Western religions asking adherents to pray in a crouching posture, what Burke calls "its deliberate mimetics of humiliation" (247). "In a society stressing advancement," he observes, "the mystic begins his rites by a symbolic self-abasement" (247). Burke notes that in the East, by contrast, "the corresponding initiatory stage seems to have been generally contrived by assuming the outward postures of complete calm, with particular emphasis on regularity of breathing. By reason of the deep correspondence between mind and body, these external conditions become the organic imagery that may be expected to call forth its psychic counterparts" (247). Here again Burke tacitly invokes Gurdjieff and his followers' amalgam of Eastern and Western practices, philosophies, and movements. On balance such a mysticism emphasizes bodily mimesis seen in the postures of prayer as well as the yogic belief in the body's capacity to "call forth" calmness and focus.

Burke then goes on to discuss how the "intensities of mystical experience" themselves counter the widespread notion that a mystical experience takes place in "complete passivity." The "deliberate techniques," as Burke calls them, of mysticism—the assuming and holding of exact postures as in yoga or in Gurdjieff's stop exercises—combine to produce "a kind of 'pure action.'" Burke then goes deeper into the body's neurological functioning to discuss how the movement of muscles is caused by nervous stimulation. The result, in Burke's phrasing, is that "any *directed* movement (such as a practical act) would involve the repression of some other nervous impulse. But," he continues, "if the nerves could be stimulated without the accompaniment of muscular movement, even conflicting nervous impulses could proclaim themselves simultaneously" (248). The upshot of Burke's quick detour through neurology is this: "It is at least a possibility that the pronounced sense of unity to which mystics habitually testify involves some neurological condition of 'pure action,' wherein a kind of dissociation between impulse and movement is established, and all the conflicting kinds of nervous impulse may 'glow' at once since they do not lead to overt muscular response. Such a possibility would explain why we could choose either the words *pure action* or *total passivity* to describe the state" (249).

By now it is probably clear that Burke was more than intrigued by mysticism, and moreover that he had investments in first exploring and then proving mysticism's potential for a kind of action. He goes on to discuss how this "virtue" of religion "was consciously or unconsciously manipulated" (249) and made into a dubious device. Such manipulation, however, does not for Burke detract from mysticism as a potential mode of active, vital transformation. And his brief excursus on the physiology of mysticism—a passage Burke himself excerpts for a lengthy discussion in *A Grammar of Motives*—follows Gurdjieff in its claim for the body's role in mystical redirection.

Moreover, as the subtitle of chapter 7, "The Mystic's Sterilization of Combat," suggests, the section on mystic action has a political edge as well, one that matches Burke's lamentations to Tate. He writes that "action in the realm of normal experience involves patterns of striving, competition, and conquest which reach their ultimate conclusion in war" (249). As promised in his letter to Tate, Burke looks to mystics for another model. Here he briefly "defends" D. H. Lawrence against "charges" leveled by I. A. Richards that he is guilty of "ethical universe building." The "qualified defense" begins just after Burke pauses to "pull a great many words together by showing their engagement in one another" (250). The words include the familiar key terms of the book: *action, poetry, ethics, occupation, preoccupation, orientation, cooperation,* and *communication*: "The ethical," he writes, "is thus linked with the communicative (particularly when we consider communication in its broadest sense, not merely as the purveying of information, but also as the sharing of sympathies and purposes, the doing of acts in common)" (250). After a lengthy engagement with Richards's critique of Lawrence wherein he disparages Lawrence's appeals to astronomy but praises his poetry, and after a long meditation on perspectives (253n), Burke hits on one of the refrains of *Permanence and Change*: that poetry extends beyond verse on a page, even if it begins there. "A man," he observes, "can extract courage from a poem by reading that he is captain of his soul; he can reinforce this same statement mimetically by walking down the street as vigorously as though he were the captain of his soul; or he can translate the mood into a more complex set of relationships by greeting an acquaintance as one captain-of-his-soul to another" (255). Here Burke, with a none-too-subtle allusion to Walt Whitman, whom his next book, *Attitudes toward History*, discusses as a mystical captain of sorts, analogically transfers the effects of Gurdjieffian dance to the effects of poetry, exploring poetry's ability to incite different movements, to suspend prevailing habits.

In the span of only eight pages, Burke has moved from broad observations about contemporary politics—the culture of combat, the seeming inevitability of war—to a close focus on one's everyday manner of walking. And mysticism bears importantly on both, with its demand for attention to habits large and small and its quest for transformation. The mysticism percolating for Burke in the mid-1920s had by 1931 thus become the site of intense curiosity; by 1933 a political effort; and by the mid-1930s a full-blown intellectual commitment. The subtle mysticism at work in *Permanence and Change* provides one important way for Burke to develop his theories about bodies, their affectability, and their role in calling attention to communicative processes. As he puts it in "The Search for Motives" chapter: "Mysticism may cover a variety of manifestations. But in the main it seems to be an attempt to define the ultimate motivation of human conduct by seeing around the corner of our accepted verbalizations" (222).

While Crane abandoned the mystical teachings of Gurdjieff five years before his death, and Munson and Frank moved on to something else, Burke shaped a kind of political, intellectual, and bodily mysticism more slowly but perhaps more surely than his contemporaries. The productive notion of bodies in *Permanence and Change* owes in part to Gurdjieff and his students. In other words, rather than positing a body made through discourse or—even more nebulous—culture, and rather than viewing the body as a strong, stable rock of certainty, Burke instead followed the Gurdjieffian mystics in figuring the body as a variable gathering of intensities, a site of movement and change.

And if Gurdjieff's intense devotion to bodies is what drew Burke into mysticism, the openness—indeed, the demand for—transformation that many "manifestations" of mysticism share is likely what kept him interested. *Attitudes toward History* documents Burke's move to another crucial philosophical mysticism, one that, like Gurdjieff's mysticism, privileges openness and radical transformation. Burke would find that such mysticism is best conveyed in the work of William James.

James's Mystical Attitude

The first chapter of Burke's 1937 book *Attitudes toward History* opens with the figure of William James. James is presented alongside Walt Whitman and Ralph

Waldo Emerson as one of three American luminaries, all possessing what Burke calls "mystical, or transcendental, hankerings" (5). These mystical tendencies, as the chapter makes clear, are rather central to their status, in Burke's view, as the holders of "the three most well-rounded . . . frames of acceptance in American literature" (*ATH* 3e 5). A closer look at James as a mystical figure of acceptance will help clarify just what Burke means by "frames of acceptance," how a mystically inflected acceptance connects with Burke's work on language and art and, importantly, how the physical version of mysticism funnels into Burke's method of incongruity. In other words, the mysticism in *Attitudes toward History* helps show how Burke's bodily theories so easily evolve into general theories of language and symbolic action.

I want to focus on James for several reasons. First, he holds a primary place in Burke's chapter on mystics, not only because he appears first in Burke's discussion, but also because James helps Burke set the terms of mysticism and because Burke devotes twice as much space to James as he devotes to Emerson and Whitman combined. Second, and perhaps this is why he receives such focus in Burke's opening chapter, James is frequently regarded, in G. William Barnard's words, as "one of the founding fathers of the academic study of mysticism" (1). James's most famous book, *The Varieties of Religious Experience*, culminates in what would become in the twentieth century the most cited discussion of mysticism. And third, the principles Burke gathers from James's "mystical hankerings" effectively structure his own mystical method, specifically the one alive in *Attitudes toward History*. James, modeling the kind of active, vital reception taught by Gurdjieff, helps Burke to take mysticism further into questions of language and perspective.

Many of the sections on James in that first chapter are culled from a review Burke published in a 1936 issue of *Science and Society* on Ralph Barton Perry's *The Thought and Character of William James*. James's work provides a handy way for Burke to establish what would be the main cluster of terms in *Attitudes toward History*—*language, action, frames of acceptance* and *rejection, attitudes*—and to cast them in the radiant light of mysticism. James, in fact, more than Burke, begins *Attitudes toward History*: "To 'accept the universe' or to 'protest against it.' William James puts them side by side, as '*voluntary* alternatives' between which 'in a given case of evil the mind seesaws.' And: 'The second not being resorted to till [sic] the first has failed, it would seem either that the second were an insincere *pis aller*, or the first a superfluous vanity.' Characteristically, James looks for a way of avoiding both" (3). Burke then offers the key phrase of the book's first section: "By 'frames of acceptance' we mean the more or less organized system of meanings by which a thinking man gauges the historical situation and adopts a role with relation to it" (5). Frames of acceptance, then, function as cultural-rhetorical hinges, and as the subsequent discussion of mysticism in *Attitudes toward History* suggests, mysticism swings those hinges wide open.

Such openness is discussed with frequent and explicit references to Perry's book—particularly the chapter that focuses on James's composition of the Gifford Lectures and the resulting *Varieties of Religious Experience*. *The Thought and Character of William James* documents James's commitment to mysticism by gathering notes and early drafts of his lectures and is especially noteworthy for the version of James Burke gleans from it. The book, for example, makes available notes James made on "Faith," which discuss a kind of primordial struggle when it comes to religion. The notes reveal that for James, "the struggle seems to be that of a less articulate and more profound part of our nature to hold out, and keep itself standing, against the attempts of a more superficial and explicit or loquacious part, to suppress it. The profounder part believes; but it can *say* so little. . . . Yet I must shape things and argue to the conclusion that a man's religion is the deepest and wisest thing in his life. I must frankly establish the breach between the life of articulate reason, and the push of the subconscious, the irrational instinctive part, which is more vital. In religion, the vital needs, the mystical overbeliefs, proceed from an ultrarational region. They are *gifts*" (258; emphasis in Perry).

What gets dramatized in these notes is a classic struggle between stammering, overly rational language and the sheer vitality of mystical beliefs. Mysticism for James thus paradoxically names the unnameable: the vital, "instinctive," ultrarational "push" involved in the mystical quest for new perspectives. In James's phrasing, "It is a question of *life*, of living in these gifts or not living" (258). No doubt Burke picked up on the conviction of James's associations, and he seems to find in James what he admired in Yeats's "disorbited, tootle-voiced" orientation. In his review of Perry, Burke quotes James's biographer to show how late in his life James forswore "his *Sturm und Drang* propensities forever in order that he might satisfy his intellectual scruples and the 'respectable academic minds' of his colleagues" (122), and then he quickly adds a point that Perry does not: "But having reached this decision," Burke observes of James, "he died" (6). He continues, "His biographer notes the coincidence without irony, though irony might be justified. Perhaps, having resolved to 'be good,' he had nothing more to live for" (6). While James's published writings on mysticism sketch his intellectual openness, Perry's account of James presents a more torturous relation to his work, but one guided by the kind of vitality and liveliness sought by Gurdjieff and his students—and that Burke hoped American ballet might achieve.

Burke also draws details from Perry's biography about the circles in which James grew up, particularly "his father and his father's friends, who were attracted to . . . spiritism" and who were, in Perry's words, "not likely to have any prejudices against mediumship, clairvoyance, mesmerism, automatic writing, and crystal gazing. From his youth James contemplated such 'phenomena' without repulsion and with an open mind" (9). This open receptivity becomes Burke's primary focus when working through James's frame of acceptance. As Burke puts it with snips of phrases from Perry, "He was not conditioned to 'know' in advance, once and for all, who the 'cranks' were. Without snobbery, he was 'one who welcomed light from any quarter'" (9).

The result is a particularly humble and open-minded philosopher. James's still-famous lectures, *The Varieties of Religious Experience*, exhibit this humility and openness in his stance toward mysticism: "Whether my treatment of mystical states will shed more light or darkness, I do not know, for my own constitution shuts me out from their enjoyment almost entirely, and I can speak of them only second hand" (281). And yet James's qualifying sentence, while humble and respectful, is not entirely honest (Gale 254). For all James's disclaimers in *Varieties* and elsewhere about not possessing the dispositional capacity to "taste" or "see" his mysticism, he nevertheless found ways to inhale it. According to James, that is, mystical states can be induced via alcohol or drugs. In his consideration of sobriety as the "ordinary consciousness," James notes, "sobriety diminishes, discriminates, and says no; drunkenness expands, unites, and says yes. . . . The drunken consciousness," James concludes, "is one bit of the mystic consciousness" (286–87). Another bit, of course, would be the drugged consciousness, and James discusses at length how substances such as nitrous oxide "stimulate the mystical consciousness in an extraordinary degree" (287). Such an observation is, in James's case, thoroughly empirical.

It is well known that James himself experimented with nitrous oxide after reading a pamphlet published by the New York mystic Benjamin Paul Blood, who, as Burke puts it, "had found God in a dentist chair" ("William James" 122). Combining his own experiment with those narrated by others, James concludes that "the keynote of the experience is the tremendously exciting sense of an intense metaphysical illumination. Truth lies open to the view in depth beneath depth of almost blinding evidence. The mind sees all logical relations of being with an apparent subtlety and instantaniety to which its normal consciousness offers no parallel" (206). While inhabiting the different order of consciousness introduced by nitrous oxide, James witnessed the obliteration of difference among common binaries. He took "sheet after sheet" of notes, mostly phrases, "the most coherent and articulate" of which was: "There are no differences but differences of degree between different degrees of difference and no difference" (207). Reading like a line from Gertrude Stein, this particular sentence revealed to James a radical diminution of difference approaching a "sense of unity," what he calls "indifferentism" (208). Such an achievement (as James calls it), which he claims enabled him to understand Hegel "better than ever before," ultimately ends "either in a laugh at the ultimate nothingness, or in a mood of vertiginous amazement at a meaningless infinity" (208). Laughter or awestruck wonder are, to James, perfectly appropriate mystical responses.

James's experimentation with nitrous oxide, along with his extensive study of mystical writings, led him to observe that "as a rule, mystical states merely add a supersensuous meaning to the ordinary outward data of consciousness" (317). In other words, mysticism does not contradict science or sober experience, but rather augments them. It is thus James's *incorporation* of mysticism that Burke labels his "meliorism" ("William James" 123; *ATH* 12), a term Burke uses to note James's penchant for perspectival fusion: "Distrusting absolutism (which is really the *superlative*, identifying the One and the Best)," Burke writes of James, "he thought in terms of *more* rather than *all*. Hence his dislike of monism, authority, the rationally finished" (12; emphasis in original). Not unlike Gurdjieff, that is, James resisted a singular, restrictive perspective; according to Burke he "felt that too much of vital importance might, by the nature of the method, necessarily be left out of the account" (14). This Jamesian meliorism helps account for what Burke elsewhere characterizes as James's "wayward manifestations that are, in their extreme aspects called 'mystical'" (11), and it also squares with the transdisciplinarity this book attributes to Burke.

Perry's book also usefully documents how James's mysticism inflects his theories of language. In a first draft of a paragraph meant to open the Gifford Lectures, James sets words against vitality. It begins by explaining the ineffability of mysticism, as James formulates it, the way that "something in life, as one feels its presence, . . . seems to defy all the possible resources of phraseology" (259). James continues, "Life defies our phrases, not only because it is infinitely continuous and subtle and shaded, whilst our verbal terms are discrete, rude, and few; but because of a deeper discrepancy still. Our words come together leaning on each other laterally for support, in chains and propositions, and there is never a proposition that does not require other propositions after it, to amplify it, restrict it, or in some way save it from the falsity by defect or excess which it contains. . . . Life, too, in one sense, stumbles over its own fact in a similar way; for its earlier moments plunge ceaselessly into later ones which reinterpret and correct them" (258). Here, James figures life itself with a tacit image of the abyss and the way the abyss foregrounds in that it both anticipates and contrasts with epiphanic mystical experiences. James goes on to discuss singular moments, moments that do not lean or plunge but refuse such support. Such a moment, James writes, "stands and contains and sums up all things; and all change is within it" (258). Words and concepts are therefore "spread-out" (259), while the most vital, most intensely lived moments, as James puts it, "melt in a kind of chemical fusion" (259). By opening *Attitudes toward History* with James's tendency to fuse perspectives, Burke extends the work he began in *Permanence and Change* on mysticism's body and on perspective by incongruity, emphatically maintaining mysticism's energetic vitality and ethical openness even as he moves into mysticism's role in his emerging theory of language.

In fact, in the next section of *Attitudes toward History*, Burke picks up on exactly this sort of Jamesian synthetic fusion in his extended consideration of the grotesque, the poetic category that, as Burke notes at the outset, "focuses in mysticism" (57). In this discussion he sounds notes similar to those heard in both his earlier letter to Tate and the later passage in *A Grammar of Motives* when he writes, "mysticism *as a collective movement* belongs to periods marked by great confusion of the cultural frame, requiring a radical shift in people's allegiance to symbols of authority" (57–58). Burke goes on to describe the grotesque as a "deadly earnest" move to feature contradictory impulses simultaneously, best described by Burke as "the cult of incongruity *without* the laughter" (58). In this discussion he returns to James, this time to James's treatment of Hegel. As Burke recounts it, "James felt that Hegel's key concept, the synthesis of contradictions, was essentially a mystic insight, and he preferred the insight of the logical frame by which Hegel strove to make it rationally negotiable" (59). Perhaps James's preference for a mystical reading of Hegel stems from his sudden nitrous oxide–induced Hegelian clarity. The approach that James and Burke both dub Hegelian very nearly approximates the approach that Gunn calls "imaginative dialectic" and attributes to Gurdjieff (38).

For Burke the poetic device of mysticism is the grotesque, inasmuch as it synthesizes through its simultaneous, melioristic rendering of opposites. The grotesque, in Burke's scheme, names a "symbolizing of parallels, 'correspondences,' whereby simple notions of identity become confused, as *one* thing is seen in terms of *something else*" (62; emphasis in original). Burke's literary examples include Joyce "charting modern life as a parody of the *Odyssey*," "Eliot expressing the mystic's sense of 'drought' by borrowings from the lore of primitive magic" (63), and Thomas Mann recasting biblical characters at various periods in history (63–64). And in another, now lesser-known example, the opening of Robert Cantwell's proletarian novel *The Land of Plenty* shows workers "seeing in the dark" by obtaining the deepest understanding when the factory lights go out. The mystical grotesque provides a symbolic counterpart to Gurdjieffian stop exercises, altering identity by thwarting automatic habits—in this case of seeing or reading—and thus enables identity to change before one's very eyes (60, 64). Jamesian in spirit, the grotesque works to loosen up otherwise restrictive perspectives. As Burke winds up the passage, he phrases its implications in this way: "If we are ever to recover from a world of nouns, going from a philosophy of *processes* to a philosophy of *categories* (perhaps to something like 'process-categories') without merely dismissing by snobbery and legislative fiat all the enlightenment that process-thinking has brought with it, such an analysis of associational clusters or constellations may have to be undertaken" (68). That paragraph's culminating example proposes a grotesque "*phenomenological* science of psychology" that, according to Burke, would resist the "tenuousness of the purely introspective or the impoverishment of the purely behavioristic" (68). By closing the paragraph in this way, Burke reveals the ability of the mystical grotesque to draw together phenomenology and psychology—body and mind—into one investigation. It would be, following James, a "wayward" investigation, conducted in a wide-ranging, curious, at times "tootle-voiced" and "disorbited" style. Such an incongruous method is exactly what Burke relished in James. In concluding these first three chapters of *Attitudes toward History*, he writes: "We have attempted, in the foregoing pages, to illustrate some of the major factors involved in the 'strategy' of writing and thinking. We have tried to reveal the subterfuges to which the poet or thinker must resort, as he organizes the complexity of life's relationships within the limitations imposed by his perspective" (106). And yet this conclusion does not tell the whole story. That is, for Burke the recurring method in the previous pages is a mystical one, and the mystical method works precisely by challenging and expanding the limitations of one's perspective, by invoking the as-yet-unseen, and thinking beyond the now by thinking the now in exaggerated, even grotesque terms.

As such, mysticism offers up an incongruous approach to all modes of knowledge making—literary, artistic, political, and the everyday. And the political emphasis must, for Burke, be kept in sight. To this end his review of Perry's book on James contains one important equivocation that does not appear in *Attitudes toward History* but that merits consideration here. After reflecting at length on the virtues of James's mysticism, Burke qualifies his celebration of James by noting "an almost total absence of historical and economic considerations" (124). In this way Burke strives to keep his political concerns—the concerns, recall, that he voiced to Tate in 1933—in play. While the review levels a cautionary critique, *Attitudes toward History* fills the space with Whitman, who provides the missing emphasis on "brotherhood, work, democracy, and . . . Lincoln" (18). In contrast to Whitman, "the mention of politics" in James, Burke writes in the Perry review, "is rare, and naïve" (124). Burke goes on to discuss further what is for him a troubling deficiency in James's work, namely the lack of "a critique of economic relations as such" (125). Indeed after careful searching through Perry's two-volume work, Burke locates only one instance "containing such an emphasis," in a letter from John Dewey recommending the work of a man who studies issues of class interests, technological conditions, and social organizations (125). With this Burke ends the review on a note of caution: "When such themes were not explicitly and exhaustively assigned their place, students could be exposed to Jamesian influence, could be graduated into a flowing, Jamesian world, and still contrive to forget the profoundly Jamesian lesson" (125). The lesson, of course, comes from James's mystic side—the refusal to settle for one perspective. It is a lesson that for Burke has profound political implications. In following James's lead, Burke expands his featured crew of mystics to three. Whitman thus holds the place for historical and economic concerns. Even as he functions as "the poetic replica of James" with his "disintegrated," ecstatic assertions (*ATH* 14), Whitman helps Burke augment James, as Burke himself culls what perhaps might be called a grotesque, or synthetic, political mysticism.

Early on in Yeats and in Gurdjieff, and later in Whitman and James, Burke saw the possibilities of a "mystic turned radical," to invoke the title of a 1913 essay written by the socialist writer, editor, and early haunter of Greenwich Village Randolph S. Bourne. Bourne observes that "the mystic must answer that most heinous of all charges,—of being unscientific. By tradition he is even hostile to science. For his main interest is in wonder, and science by explaining things attacks the very principle of his life" (207). "But the modern mystic," he continues, "must not only recognize the scientific aspect of the age—he must feel the social ideal that directs the spiritual energies of the time" (210). Science, Bourne held, must be made to reach beyond itself. Such impulses—of nonforeclosure and of reaching beyond—are distinctly mystical, as I hope is by now apparent. Indeed, as Gunn demonstrates, "many brands of occultism—from ECKANKAR to Gurdjieff—can be understood as confronting the 'rational' and scientific vocabulary of modernity" (47). And as such confrontation frequently entailed a Hegelian-style synthesis or a Blavatskian "Middle Way," rejecting science is of course out of the question. Which is why Burke's time working among scientists at John D. Rockefeller's Bureau of Social Hygiene, considered in the next two chapters, figures prominently both in his development of his mystical method as well as his interest in bodies. For Burke, that is, the mystical imperative to reach ever beyond, to see "around the corner" of things (*ATH* 222), applies to bodies, communities, domains of knowledge, and entire nations: as he puts it in his discussion of the grotesque, "the matter cannot be handled properly unless a collective enterprise is organized about the search" (*GM* 68).

Burke could not, in other words, let the abyss—that "awful internal chasm"—conclude his engagement with mysticism. Instead the abyss goads such an engagement and must be grotesquely fused with mundane everyday movements for a heightened sense that all directional movements—bodily, cultural, political, disciplinary—hang in the balance.

3

Burke on Drugs | *Efficiency and the Valuation of Habits*

In his review of Ouspensky's *New Model of the Universe*, published in 1931, Burke tries out some drug humor: "The author," he writes of Gurdjieff's follower, "has examined holy texts, in particular the religious lore of the East. His chapter on 'Experimental Mysticism' would lead us to suppose that he had made many tests with hasheesh, deriving from it that sense of impersonality, of the subjective merging into the objective, of 'unity,' which this drug seems to have induced even in people much less mystically inclined than he" ("In Quest of the Way" 104). And yet in this joke resides a sincere connection between mysticism and drugs: their twin abilities to alter perception radically. In the chapter under consideration Ouspensky reminds the reader that his previous book defines mysticism as "all cases of intensified feeling and abstract knowing" (274); his is a definition that as Burke's joke recognizes would easily include opium or marijuana use. Indeed Ouspensky's *Tertium Organum* gathers the "anaesthetic revelations" that James documents under the subhead "Unusual Mystical Experiences." Here Ouspensky writes sensuously about how "the deliciousness of some of these states seems to be beyond anything known in ordinary consciousness" (266). Drugs, as chemical intensifiers that enable the body to reach beyond its "normal" state, had long been used to stimulate mystical experience, as the last chapter's examples of Hart Crane, Benjamin Paul Blood, and William James attest. Burke himself figures the relation as one of close substitution, writing in *A Rhetoric of Motives* that "even if you believe in the validity of certain mystic revelations, you must agree that, besides mysticism and its 'fragments,' there are substitutes for mysticism, *Ersatzmystiken*, as with drugs, insanity, crime, and the many fantastic appetites by which men are goaded, as by demons" (331).

It happens that Burke knew something about these altered states as well.[1] As many Burke scholars know, he completed two stints with the John D. Rockefeller Foundation as a full-time researcher in the 1920s and 1930s, first on criminology, funded by the Laura Spelman Rockefeller Memorial Trust (June 1926–August 1927), and then at the Bureau of Social Hygiene (BSH) in New York (from 1928 until the mid-1930s) (Selzer 134; Jay 152; KB to MC, October 15, 1928, Penn State), where he was hired by Colonel Arthur Woods to research drugs and drug use. Until recently when Jordynn Jack and I began examining the evidence more carefully, not much was known about this period of Burke's experience; those who do mention it tend to figure the researching stints, as Selzer does, as a kind of transitory period, one among many strung-together jobs (134), or as work that proved useful later on when Burke wrote about Coleridge's opium habit (Jay 152).[2] In a 1983 interview with Roy Skodnick, Burke himself describes his drug-researcher days somewhat sketchily: "Ironically enough, all my notes on that stuff have disappeared. All that work I'd done just vanished. The stuff I used in *The Philosophy of Literary Form* was part of it. I wouldn't have any of it but for the parts included there. . . . Some of it turns up once in a while, but most of it's vanished. Maybe it's in the FBI files for all I know. That was such a crazy period" (8).

Yet, if examined closely, all of Burke's books following that period—not just *The Philosophy of Literary Form*, but also *Permanence and Change* and *Attitudes toward History*—yield trace evidence of Burke's work at the BSH, and together these traces suggest that Burke's drug-researching job did much more than keep him employed or acquaint him with the details of Coleridge's addiction. Burke's work with Colonel Woods at the BSH helped make him more receptive to mysticism and also helped him to formulate more pointedly his concepts of efficiency and piety, even as it offered him new and different vantage points on the body and communication. In other words, far from vanishing, Burke's work at the BSH stayed with him—arguably more closely than he realized. What follows will focus specifically on the ways the BSH seems to have broadened Burke's approach and helped solidify his method. Burke emerged from his years at the BSH, that is, with a more heavily theorized method of study, a firmer commitment to rhetoric, an affirmed yet altered take on the theories put forth in *Counter-Statement*, and a heightened interest in the body's role in rhetoric and identity production. His work as a researcher, together with his resistant relation to his ultraconservative boss, ultimately galvanized his interest in bodies in ways that might not have been possible had Burke relied exclusively on the realms of music or mysticism for his early theories of the body. Indeed, as his mystic, fusive method suggests, it is necessary to make the transdisciplinary push beyond artistic and religious realms of music and mysticism into the realm of science. What is more, the scientific discourse Burke studied at the BSH offered a rhetorically effective kind of cultural authority, as he indicated parenthetically to Cowley in October 1931: "I am interested primarily in making my argument tell, and less in claiming it for my very own, so if I can retreat behind authorities—you know my vast respect for them, after living among them at the Bureau of Social Hygiene, the whole cow-milking lot of them—behind authorities I shall retreat" (October 22, 1931, Penn State). This offhand comment in all its color best characterizes Burke's ambivalent relation to scientists and scientific knowledge. On one hand he held science in high regard, rhetorically well aware of the cultural authority enjoyed by scientific knowledge. And yet on the other hand, especially when it came to legislating morals in the name of "hygiene," Burke's relation to the BSH was frequently one of irreverence. But his was a productive irreverence, one that helped structure his critical method.

Efficiency Refigured

Burke's work as a drug researcher affected his theoretical writings and his critical scope by at once confirming hunches developed in *Counter-Statement* and expanding them for *Attitudes toward History*. A case in point is Burke's thinking about the concept of "efficiency," which undergoes subtle but revealing transformations during the years Burke worked for Colonel Woods.

Burke's initial consideration of efficiency in *Counter-Statement* appears in "Program," an essay on the purpose and future of art that he wrote in late 1927, just after the end of his first stint with Rockefeller's Spelman Trust and a year and a half before Colonel Woods hired him at the BSH.[3] In this essay, where Burke first ponders efficiency as a value, the stakes for him lie in the question of aesthetics. According to Burke "efficiency" functions as the dominant historical value at the time he is writing, and insofar as it is deemed by many as "practical" (111), it stands against the aesthetic. In Burke's version the value of efficiency aligns with science, prosperity, and "progress" (111) and is thus mechanistic, industrial, and self-proliferating (107, 119). As discussed in chapter 1, Burke responds by arguing that the artist must dialectically oppose these values—"the aesthetic must serve as anti-mechanization, the corrective of the practical" (111); or, as the book's title suggests, art must offer a "counter-statement" to those who valorize efficiency and what Burke somewhat cynically terms its "healthy club-offer" grouping of values—"prosperity, material acquisitions, increased consumption, 'new needs,' expansion." Such a counter-statement would instead offer, among other values, "inefficiency, indolence, dissipation, vacillation, mockery, distrust, 'hypochondria,' non-conformity, bad sportsmanship . . . experimentalism, curiosity, risk, dislike of propaganda, dislike of certainty" (111), and innovation.[4]

Yet this counter-statement is more than a dialectical assertion that counters by negation. Instead Burke develops a method of resisting efficiency in *Counter-Statement* that might be characterized as "refusal through rearticulation." That is, Burke suggests effecting a transformation of the system itself: "When inefficiency becomes a danger, we should so alter the system that inefficiency ceases to be a danger" (120). Such a rearticulation in this instance involves slyly swapping the terms *efficiency* and *inefficiency*, whereby what would be deemed "inefficient" in a Taylorized factory can be deemed, from the artist's perspective, efficient. By conjuring an artistic "counter-efficiency," Burke effectively names his own method: "An important aspect of the artist's 'efficiency' resides not in an accumulation of products, but in a ceaseless indwelling, a patient process of becoming expert in himself" (118). In other words, Burke's model of artistic efficiency involves protracted engagement with material in order to know it thoroughly, intimately. As such, the slow, painstakingly careful version of artistic practice becomes a resistant counterpractice in the realm of mechanistic, output-focused, high-speed efficiency.[5]

Such a method, Burke believes, will produce responsive, artistic "innovations," innovations that "must be, in some way, the humanistic or cultural counterpart of the external changes brought about by industrialism, or mechanization" (108). He clarifies: "By 'innovations,' incidentally, is not meant something new under the sun. By innovation is meant simply an emphasis to which the contemporary public is not accustomed" (110). The job of the artist, then, is to notice the habits and practices ushered in by an era and to respond by adding an unfamiliar perspective into the mix.

In "Program," then, Burke works through the problems with efficiency, and by doing so articulates what would become his signature method: such a "ceaseless indwelling," that is, an ever-complicated, multidirectional, extended, mystically open and thorough consideration of the subject at hand, which produces "innovations," unfamiliar, sometimes strange ways to formulate a situation. Such is the approach he takes when thinking and writing about language, life, and art on his own time, as much as it was when he was researching and writing about drugs on the BSH's time. Burke's time there, in fact, effectively expanded his critique of efficiency—taking him beyond the realm of art—even as it affirmed his conclusions in *Counter-Statement*. As the letter to Tate considered in the last chapter suggests, the "innovation" Burke himself turned up is a renewed focus on the body. The body, that is, becomes his cultural counterpart to the efficient, bureaucratic machine. Before detailing his innovation, however, I want to consider more carefully just how Burke's notion of efficiency changed during the time he worked for the BHS.

Efficiency reappears in newly expanded form most prominently in *Attitudes toward History*, the book Burke completed just after his work for the BSH ended. Here *efficiency* can be found in the "Dictionary of Pivotal Terms," with four and a half pages devoted to the entry. This time Burke figures efficiency as that which "throws strong light upon something, and in the process cast[s] other things into shadow" (248). While Burke's discussion of efficiency in *Counter-Statement* takes place, for the most part, in the realm of art and work, in *Attitudes toward History* he sees efficiency everywhere—from the emphasis on pleasing the palate in the production of breakfast foods to war's "efficient" mobilization of a nation's efforts, to caricaturists' tendency of "stressing certain considerations and omitting others" (249). The result, Burke complains, is overspecialization, overemphasis, and, inevitably, imbalance. In Burke's words *efficiency* becomes that which "endangers proper preservation of proportions" (248).[6]

Burke's primary example of efficiency, however, turns out to be journalism, which has "developed out of an organized method for assembling a literary product with maximum speed" (250). By figuring news as at once mass-produced and literary and expanding the literary and the artistic to broader meanings (as he does in *Permanence and Change*), Burke is able to fold in the views on efficiency put forth in *Counter-Statement*. Yet at the same time, the more general conception of art enables a broadened perspective and more elaborate critique of efficiency. Guided by "headline thinking," journalism, according to Burke, is the "bureaucratization" of what was, in ancient times, an inefficient "imaginative procedure"—the transmission of news through bards, who "shaped their statement . . . [by] *saying* only what could be *sung*" (250; emphasis in original). The entry then moves from the metaphor of song to the more contemporary metaphor of money: "'Efficiency,' to borrow a trope from the stock exchange, is excellent for those who approach social problems with the mentality of the 'in and out' trader. It is far less valuable for those interested in a 'long-pull investment.' Otherwise stated: It violates 'ecological balance,' stressing some one ingredient rather than maintaining all ingredients by the subtler requirements of 'symbiosis'" (250). Here Burke reiterates that the value of balance gets violated through efficiency; yet the trope of the stock market does more than advocate a diverse portfolio. By invoking the stock market—where he had actually invested the money from his 1929 *Dial* Award[7]—he brings in the question of investment and, at the same time, reintroduces the issue of commitment inherent in his programmatic *Counter-Statement* call for a "patient process of becoming expert." That is, Burke still favors—arguably with more resolve—a kind of "long-haul" mentality over and against the unreflective opportunism he sees at work in more efficient models driving the bureaucracies of journalism and advertising. The ancient bards who "inefficiently" "said only what could be sung" inhabit a special place for Burke, for theirs is a model of news distribution that emphasizes the sort of purposeful "indwelling" he champions in *Counter-Statement*. As he puts it later on in *Attitudes toward History*, "the future is really disclosed *by finding out what people can sing about*" (335; emphasis in original). Such singing necessarily entails immersion in a subject matter, a kind of inhabiting. That Burke privileged such committed work is evident when he mentions to Malcolm Cowley that he was not, at the moment, thrilled with John Dewey, who, as Burke puts it, "seems too external to his subject" (March 30, 1934, Penn State).

The model of resistant, inhabitive, artistic efficiency presented in *Counter-Statement* thus reemerges in *Attitudes toward History* as the commitment of the "long-pull investment." The dictionary entry ends with an illustrative "parable" that brings together the revised account with the earlier account, and does so with direct reference to his work at the Bureau of Social Hygiene. The parable features an artist who, painting the same scene as other artists, chooses to emphasize a flea "with startling singleness," thus revealing the scene anew. But the flea receives so much attention that a "Flea School of Art" develops, with other artists clamoring to depict fleas, because fleas are, in a sense, of the moment. Burke's problem lies not with the first flea artist, who identified strongly with the flea and whose incitement involved intimate, artistic commitment. The school of art, conversely, according to Burke, fetishizes the flea, overemphasizes and thus overdramatizes the flea, and, as Burke puts it, "picks up the *mannerism* without the *drive*" (252). At this point the "imaginative"—the moment of intimate connection with the flea—becomes, in Burke's words, "thoroughly bureaucratized" (252), devoid of poetic force. Efficiency, that is, averts commitment, intimacy, and drive, therefore precluding the sort of intense, reflective, protracted involvement with the subject Burke favors in *Counter-Statement*. Burke develops this critique with a lengthy footnote, wherein he wonders whether all journals, "even our better journals, have done anything other than to 'bureaucratize' . . . by bringing the communicative resources of the whole world to bear upon an isolated theme" (251n). Here Burke offers yet another justification for why he has broadened the scope of his work so significantly since *Counter-Statement*. He has decided, in short, that he must combine the artistic (counter)efficiency laid out so carefully in *Counter-Statement* with a counter-refusal of overspecialization. In other words, instead of worrying strictly about the category of the aesthetic, he will obsess intimately about countless categories. Burke accomplishes such a regrouping by rearticulating what counts as artistic, as evident when he admonishes readers to "distrust hypertrophy of art *on paper*. More of the artistic should be expressed in vital social relationships. Otherwise, it becomes 'efficient' in the compensatory, antithetical sense" (259). Here Burke sees problems with the "counter-statement" logic and offers that an approach to aesthetics must be retooled as well—what he wrote in *Counter-Statement*, in hindsight, was itself a bit too efficient with its narrow parameters. What is more, such a hypertrophic focus risks leading to gross exaggerations, a telltale mark of efficient methods. The explanatory footnote discussed above then goes on to invoke explicitly his boss and his work at the bureau in relation to the narrow, overly dramatic approach Burke disparages: "We refer among other things to the ideal of horror, whereby the author 'sells' his masterpiece in competition with his competitors, by contriving to make the issue even more calamitous than they do. We once did ghosting work on a drug book—and our employer soon taught us that the 'best' preparation for a proposal to control drugs was a picture of the world being destroyed by drugs. Find the threat of drugs everywhere—and you have established the 'crying need' for the proposed legislation" (251n).

Burke's expanded sense of efficiency is owed, then, at least in part, to Burke's boss at the BSH, Colonel Arthur Woods, who exemplified "hypertrophic" efficiency. To avoid such an imbalanced model of "efficiency," to explore "vital social relationships," and to keep subject matters open while engaging in patient, intimate study of diverse fields would become Burke's program, newly revised and expanded. A June 1932 letter from Burke to Cowley helpfully documents his conflicted memory of his work with Woods: "I could never respect myself while hired to keep morphinists from getting their morphine, or to treat crime as an absolute. (It would take me a lifetime to explain the damages and the rewards of my work with the Colonel. It was here that I first learned of the virtue racket)" (June 2, 1932, Penn State). *Dangerous Drugs*, the book Burke ghosted for Woods, shows Burke enacting subtle resistance to Woods and the BSH's mission—the "virtue racket"—as his patient, "inefficient" methods stand out as markedly distinct from Woods's hypertrophy. What results is a provocatively incongruous—even inefficient—book.[8]

The Colonel

While only six years older than Burke, with perhaps even better connections, Colonel Arthur Woods was, in so many ways, a counter-Burke. Harvard-educated, a Republican and Episcopalian, Woods, a member of the ruling class, was always in charge of something, from education (he was schoolmaster at a wealthy private school in Massachusetts at the turn of the twentieth century) to law enforcement (commissioner of the New York Police Department from 1914 until 1918) to the military (named colonel, Aviation Section, in 1918). From there Colonel Woods became a key behind-the-scenes political figure: in 1918 he was appointed associate director of the Committee on Public Information for Foreign Propaganda, and in 1919 he was named assistant secretary of war; in the 1920s Woods became chairman and trustee of the Spelman Fund of New York, a fund started in the memory of John D. Rockefeller's wife, Laura Spelman. Woods subsequently served as a trustee of the Rockefeller Foundation from 1928 until 1935 (Fosdick 310). Woods later became an adviser to the League of Nations on drugs and drug trafficking, and in 1930 he temporarily left his post at the BSH when summoned by President Hoover to lead the Emergency Committee for Employment. Burke himself somewhat humorously invokes Woods as helmsman when he refers to him in a letter to Allen Tate as "the Captain my Captain" (October 17, 1929).[9]

Woods also authored two books early on, *Crime Prevention* (1918), a manifesto for "law, protection, and order" (7), and *Police and Public* (1919), which is part guide to the profession of law enforcement, part public relations document bespeaking the valor and courage of police work, and part handbook for producing ideal police workers. Colonel Woods celebrates policemen in these books and looks askance at all others as potential criminals—with special attention, in

Crime Prevention, to "mental defectives" (56), ex-cons (90–94), "emotional types" (94–96), the unemployed (40–48), alcoholics and drug users (71–81), and young boys (101–4). By identifying these risk categories, Woods embodies his own ideal of the "preventive policeman," whom he refers to as "the policeman of the future" (*Police and Public* 123). The police activist author of these books is staunchly prohibitionist, antidrug, and promilitary and, above all, is a man whose mission it is to detail and valorize the policeman's job (*Crime Prevention* 123; *Police and Public* 13–15).

What is more, the ideal police officer, for Woods, was an efficient worker with an efficiently trained body. Woods argues variously for the use of military drill (*Police and Public* 158), equating the sturdiness of courage with sturdiness of body: "The courage of the men will be made more sturdy and instinctive if they have confidence in their own powers, in their marksmanship, their ability to use their hands and bodies, and if they keep themselves in sound physical condition, hard and supple" (159). Woods's desire to make courage more "instinctive" illustrates his militaristic need for an ultraefficient operation. He therefore scorns the public's view of policemen as "portly, slow moving, with their gait showing fallen arches," offering instead his own depiction: "alert, active, intelligent,— flat-fronted, instead of flat-footed. As the arches of his feet are up, so should his aspect be, his eyes, his mien, his aim" (163). Woods, however, lamenting that very little work is "done as well as it might be," in his quest for the most efficient law enforcement possible enlists the public as surveillants of police work and ultimately argues that "the public is entitled to be furnished with complete and accurate police records" (169). As his logic goes: "Inefficiency and negligence are hard to conceal if results have to be furnished" (172). Woods's first two books are thus saturated with the value of efficiency, with a heavy emphasis on the centrality of juridical matters.[10] An efficient police force, would, for Woods, produce a smooth-running, equally efficient society. This much is indicated in a line from *Crime Prevention,* which insists upon a direct correlation between law enforcement and society even as it forecasts the major premise of his later book, *Dangerous Drugs,* the book Burke helped Woods write: "The policeman has come to the conclusion that if the traffic in these deadly drugs could be stopped much crime would be stopped also" (74). The swift, causal connection between drug traffic and crime displays the logic that Burke complains about in *Attitudes toward History,* and strongly resists while working for Woods. Moreover, the moralizing rhetoric of Colonel Woods in *Dangerous Drugs* makes it fairly easy to locate Burke's contributions, and the passages that were most likely written by Burke reveal a developing preoccupation with how drug use produces dispositional changes. This general interest in bodily mannerisms and affect, I will argue, helped Burke shape his notion of "piety," a concept that effectively unpacks efficiency in *Permanence and Change.*

A Ghost of Incongruity

As the full title hints, *Dangerous Drugs: The World Fight against Illicit Traffic in Narcotics* bears a hard-line political agenda. Focusing mostly on opium, morphine, and heroin, the book details social ills caused by the trafficking of illegally manufactured drugs. The self-proclaimed purpose of *Dangerous Drugs* goes like this: "The writing of these chapters was undertaken for the purpose of clarifying and emphasizing certain measures which we believe must be enforced if this devastating narcotic drug traffic is to be controlled. There are medical, psychological, and educational aspects of the problem of combating drug addiction which we will not attempt to discuss thoroughly, for we are concerned with the subject from the standpoint of legal and police measures" (4). This passage perfectly illustrates the sort of efficiency that made Burke grumble—right down to the language with which it is written. The passage, that is, swiftly moves to the sole and narrow purpose of "clarifying and emphasizing certain measures," skipping over all the complicated ways that drugs link with bodies, minds, and education in favor of the more narrowly focused "standpoint of legal and police measures." It is clear from Woods's publication and work history that the "standpoint" of legal and police measures is undoubtedly his own.

Yet a noticeably different standpoint inhabits the book, one that is far less concerned with the police officer–as–hero or the derelict drug user, but a standpoint that is more concerned with—indeed, fascinated by—historical attitudes toward and physiological effects of drugs. Burke's nonjudgmental fascination is indicated early on in his novel *Towards a Better Life*: "For four purposes men have had recourse to drugs: for happiness, phantasy, intensity, and sleep. In the chemical subterfuge of morphine some have for a time found happiness" (79). Such a view of drugs does not jibe well with the "virtue racket" Burke encountered at the BSH, and yet its odd persistence in *Dangerous Drugs* makes it relatively easy to trace Burke's imprint. *Dangerous Drugs*, in fact, bears ample evidence of clashing efficiencies, as Woods's swift and sure proclamations stand starkly against Burke's broadly historical, intimate, protracted consideration of drug use.

These divergent standpoints—that of the policy-minded law enforcer (Woods) and the philosophically minded, physiologically focused researcher-for-hire (Burke)—make *Dangerous Drugs* a weirdly incongruous book. Colonel Woods has an explicit purpose ("to deal with the primary evil, the matter of Drug Supply itself" [4]), and the book, as noted earlier, was funded by the BSH, a Rockefeller-supported office whose professed mission was "the study, amelioration, and prevention of those social conditions, crimes, and diseases which adversely affect the well-being of society, with special reference to prostitution and the evils associated therewith."[11] The introduction frames the book Woods no doubt envisioned, repeating the word *evil* in sentences such as these: "But we purpose to deal with the primary evil, the matter of the Drug Supply itself" (4), and "We should set promptly and efficiently about the business of freeing ourselves from those evils which are less 'necessary'" (6). The introduction leaves no question about the book's primary aim: "The Drug Menace should be one of the first to go, for not only is this a degrading burden with which society need not be saddled, but there is a definite course of action by which it can be removed, as subsequent chapters will attempt to demonstrate" (6). In extending the mission laid out in his previous book *Crime Prevention*, Colonel Woods is also setting up the book's somewhat dramatic, bureaucratic approach to drugs by offering, as Burke put it in the passage quoted above, "a picture of the world being destroyed by drugs."

The second chapter, "The Alkaloids," departs radically, however, from the tone, scope, and mission laid out in the first chapter. This departure, I contend, bears strong indications that Burke was the chapter's ghostwriter. First, the chapter does anything but demonstrate "a definite course of action"; nor does it, as promised in the introduction, explain "as briefly as possible the nature of the drugs, the nature of the users, and the nature of the traffic" (4). As anyone who has read anything of Burke's knows, succinct description was not exactly his forte, and his "counter-efficient" method disavowed mere surface engagement. He is known, instead, for giving his subjects a wide-ranging breadth of consideration, an approach that reflects his by now trademark multidirectional ruminations. Burke himself recognized this style of thinking late in his career when he offered the term *counter-gridlock* as a description of how he would "go every which way," so that his thought process often resembled, to him at least, the reverse of a New York traffic jam (Skodnick 5).

In *Attitudes toward History*, where such an approach most closely approximates a methodology, Burke writes that the job of the social critic is "patient study of the 'Documents of Error.'" (258). He goes on to explain: "To avoid 'cultural vandalism' there must be constant exposure to the *total archives* accumulated by civilization (since nothing less can give us the admonitory evidence of the ways in which people's exaltations malfunction as liabilities)" (259). Here Burke describes the approach he seems to have taken while working on *Dangerous Drugs*. As a result the writing in the book's second chapter departs noticeably from the moralizing generalities found in the introduction, opting instead for a more scholarly, inquisitive tone that borders on fascination with drugs, their histories, and their physiological effects. In fact the entire chapter, when placed next to the overblown rhetoric of the first chapter, seems rather humorously mismatched, if not dreadfully out of place. It begins, for example, in the "archives" of civilization: "The history of man's acquaintanceship with opium leads us back among the vaguenesses of remote antiquity" (7). What follows is a seemingly exhaustive list of physicians who prescribed opium, took opium, and, for the most part—at least according to the writer—loved opium. The beginning of the chapter, that is, takes a leisurely stroll through the words of ancient medical texts stretching back to Galen, the second century C.E. Greek physician who enumerated all the medical benefits of opium, up to the sixteenth-century German Paracelsus, who referred to opium as "the stone of immortality." While Colonel Woods might have called opium the stone of "immorality," the writer of chapter 2, in contrast, seems far more fascinated with the drug's cultural history than perturbed by its popularity. The chapter goes on to cite Alpinus, another sixteenth-century physician, who notes energy loss and deteriorating functions in the bodies of opium users and then continues:

> Platerus of Pasle, and the Belgian van Helmont used it with prodigality, the latter to such an extent that he became known as Doctor Opiatus. In the seventeenth century, the Dutch physician, Sylvius Franciscus de le Boe, said that he could not practice without it, and Sydenham, one of the foremost English physicians, stated that "among the remedies which it has pleased Almighty God to give to man to relieve his sufferings, none is so universal and so efficacious as opium." Our tincture of opium of today was developed from Sydenham's laudanum. Haller, the greatest among medical minds of the eighteenth century, wrote of the drug and, according to Lombroso, was himself addicted to enormous doses. (9–10)

This passage hardly takes the morally outraged, "efficient" stance taken in the book's initial chapter. Rather, the passage—and the entire chapter, for that matter—reveals the intensive, protracted research that must have gone into the writing, "the constant exposure to the total archives accumulated by civilization." The chapter goes on to detail the invention of the hypodermic syringe and the effects of subcutaneous delivery, making a subtle but strong case that this invention led to more widespread use of opium and its alkaloid partners, morphine and heroin. Such an argument continues to undermine Woods's aim by suggesting that the problem might not be so easily or efficiently "removed" as the introduction would have readers believe. The passage ends with a snappy (and not terribly moralizing) sentence: "By the time the danger of heroin became generally recognized, the underworld, in America at least, had been sniffing it for years" (13).

From there the chapter departs even more noticeably from the book's aim, building a subtle case in favor of morphine by pointing out that it is the "perfect drug" for doctors to become addicted to, "through taking it at the end of a hard day's work when some new responsibility turns up which means that they must be alert for several more hours" (15). The drug is "perfect," the writer contends, because "it dulls the body's complaints of weariness without producing any of the distortions of behavior or causing the inaccuracy in work which might have resulted from alcohol taken as a bracer under similar circumstances" (15). Again, the writer of chapter 2 portrays upstanding members of society as addicts—but addicts who are apparently nonetheless productive, thanks in large part to their morphine.

"The Alkaloids" is thus a long, rambling chapter that departs noticeably in style, tone, and argument from the other chapters and from the purported scope of the book. Its tone is more that of investigative history than that of swift denouncement. Rather than chiming in with the overblown, moralizing rhetoric of the introduction, the chapter reveals instead the work of a patient, meticulous researcher subtly mounting a case against the book's very premises. What is more, the chapter that bears Burke's distinctive imprint also reveals an intense fascination with bodily processes, pointing to the BSH as a place where Burke's interest in the body was itself subject to his efficient method: surrounded by scientists and scientific resources, he could multiply, patiently, and thoroughly learn about bodies. And as this chapter, and the next two chapters show, that is exactly what he did.

An Intimate Knowledge of the Body

Burke certainly came to the Bureau of Social Hygiene with an already-percolating interest in the body, as evidenced in his writings on music and mysticism as well as in *Counter-Statement,* where he invokes the body as "a generator of belief" in the context of artistic value (105). In the section on "the appeal of forms" discussed in chapter 1, Burke articulates something approaching a bodily affinity for poetic form: "The appeal of form as exemplified in rhythm enjoys a special advantage in that rhythm is more closely allied with 'bodily' processes. Systole and diastole, alternation of the feet in walking, inhalation and exhalation, up and down, in and out, back and forth, such are the types of distinctly motor experiences 'tapped' by rhythm" (140).

While Kumiko Yoshioka (33) and Robert Wess (*Kenneth Burke* 66) treat these bodily moments in *Counter-Statement* as problematically essentialist, and while Burke himself in retrospect seems embarrassed by his "naturalistic" emphasis (*CS* xv), I offer that this passage is neither overly naturalistic nor essentialist at all. At first glance the passage seems to posit a kind of "natural" bodily rhythm, but the point is about how the body's movements—what Burke calls "motor experiences"—have the capacity to fall into a discernible rhythm, as discussed in chapter 1 in the context of music. Recall from that discussion how the regular rhythms of pulse, of breathing, of walking mark the body's movements as prone to rhythmic patterns, attuning the body to yet other kinds of rhythm, such as those produced in music or in poetic form, Burke's primary concern in *Counter-Statement.* The focus here, in other words, is on a meeting of rhythms, and the ways the rhythms of the body can fall in sync with rhythms of prose. As

Burke figures it, the body, as a generator of rhythm, is also attuned to rhythm in particular ways—as such, the body is figured as capable of a certain kind of belief in the "ideas" "imported" along with the rhythm.[12] He goes on: "The rhythm of a page, in setting up a corresponding rhythm in the body, creates marked degrees of expectancy, or acquiescence" (140).

Writing about the reader, Burke continues: "In becoming receptive to so much, he becomes receptive to still more." Once bodily movements have been hijacked by the poem, there is no turning back: "In all rhythmic experiences one's 'muscular imagination' is touched" (141). Burke's work on rhythm guided his attribution of rhetorical tendencies to the body and its affective capacity for taking on new habits, new beliefs. That "muscular imagination," Burke learned at the BSH, can be touched by more than musical and poetic tones, shaped by something other than the ancient mystical postures and ritualized dance movements; it can also be altered by synthetic chemicals.

Burke's curiosity about the body, like his thinking on efficiency, would be sustained and taken in new disciplinary directions during his time at the BSH. When viewed in terms of bodily rhythms and susceptibility, for example, drug users and readers of poetry bear striking similarities. Burke's description of the rhythmic reader—"in becoming receptive to so much, he becomes receptive to still more"—might as easily be applied to a trembling coke addict. In fact, as Burke's syncretic work suggests, both drugs and poetry can be figured as transformative substances, both induce affective change, and both tap into bodily rhythms, creating and increasing receptivity.

The body also figures strongly in the alkaloids chapter of *Dangerous Drugs*, as the ghostwriter Burke keeps an eye on bodily processes, specifically the "tendency of the morphinist to increase his dosage" (19). The gradual production of the habit through a steady increase of doses seems to captivate Burke's attention, as he describes how a user "finds himself taking several grains merely to establish the same physical and mental tone that formerly resulted from the fraction of a grain" (19). Burke also details physiological symptoms of withdrawal—muscular tremors, watery eyes, abdominal cramps—symptoms by which "the morphinist is usually revealed" (17). Then, in a telling moment, the writer turns from an exhaustive consideration of withdrawal's effects on the body to its effects on the mind: "Naturally, such acute physical exhaustion has a direct mental parallel. The addict becomes depressed, even to the point of delirium. . . . His plight is pitiable, all the more so since there is but one quick remedy for all the suffering: another dose. This fact makes it almost impossible for an addict to rid himself of the drug habit unassisted. All during the period of his suffering, he knows that if at any moment an injection of the drug is given him, his troubles are over. In a flash Mr. Hyde becomes Dr. Jekyll. His composure returns, the body falls back into its accustomed ways. He is restored to the addict's equivalent of normality" (17).

Here Burke describes a case in which bodily rhythms have been overtaken by drugs. If the body considered in his music criticism and in *Counter-Statement* is receptive and susceptible, the body in *Dangerous Drugs* is that and more, insofar as it comes to depend on its substance, and when the substance is present "the body falls back into its accustomed ways," its acquired set of habits and rhythms. Burke's work on drugs, then, drew his attention to the bodily dogma even more, showing him that habits and beliefs created in the body through sustained repetition are tenacious, relentless, and, most of all, impervious to reason. That is, while the dramatic paragraph above sets itself up to discuss the "mental parallel" of bodily dependence, it can never turn completely away from the body, because the habit so clearly exists on a physiological plane. Thus the description, like the drug habit, begins and ends with the body, but not without invoking what Burke calls in *Permanence and Change* "physical parallelisms of the mind" (see, for example, 158). His account of cocaine traverses between body and mind in a similar fashion: "A small dose makes responses quicker, muscular strength greater. Repeated doses tend to develop extreme excitability, with mental and physical stimulation, and the addict can talk without ceasing. . . . He is, in short, generally on edge, tingling with a false sense of vitality which may be either pleasant or disturbing, or even both simultaneously" (26–27). In these and other descriptions physiological and mental conditions are intractably combined, as Burke the writer-researcher figures the cocaine user as a bundle of sensations, intensified with each dose.

The chapter Burke most surely ghostwrote pays special attention to affective change—how a habit such as a drug habit dictates the body's "normality," how desire works on and through the body, and, moreover, how pain and addiction conjoin mind and body through sensation and movement.[13] In yet another way, then, the Alkaloids chapter exceeds the brief historical "sketch" promised in the introduction and instead raises questions about the mind-body relationship, with specific attention to the relationship between habit and affect. "The Alkaloids" argues about the intense, physiological staying power of drugs rather than their inherent evil (the introductory chapter's favorite assertion), and in doing so, it treats the "medical, psychological, and educational aspects of the problem of combating drug addiction" that the introduction places outside the book's purview. The focus, in short, is on the body rather than on the traffic of drugs. Moreover, both the rejection of Colonel Woods's moralizing tendencies discussed earlier and the focus on mind-body associations can be found in *Permanence and Change*, the book in which the body figures most forcibly for Burke and, not coincidentally, the book he was writing while he was working for Woods.[14]

Piety, the Body, and (a Drug) Habit

Both Woods and the drug user, as figures, come to inhabit *Permanence and Change* in relation to Burke's concept of piety. Woods, that is, seems to be a major force behind Burke's attempt to crack open piety and disentangle the word from its strictly religious associations whereby piety often comes with prepackaged notions of "good" and "evil." Instead Burke describes piety as an act of creating linkages—"the sense of what properly goes with what" (74)—and from these linkages different ethical models, different "altars," emerge. Piety, as Burke puts it, "extends through all the texture of our lives" (75), and in this way "we may expect to find great areas of piety, even at a ball game" (76). As illustrations Burke offers what he terms "pious" associations, such as an unhappy person's linking of distress with the sound of the doorbell (76) and the "pious" vulgarity shared by "gashouse gang" members—for example, the "correct way of commenting upon passing women, the etiquette of spitting" (77). Burke finds these instances of "what goes with what" compelling for their seeming "deviance" from more typical, "pure" associations with the word *piety*. He continues: "These considerations force us to reinterpret what jurists or social workers often look upon as decay, degeneracy, disintegration, and the like. If a man who is a criminal lets the criminal trait in him serve as the informing aspect of his character, piously taking unto him all other traits and habits that he feels should go with his criminality, the criminal deterioration which the moralist with another point of view might discover in him is the very opposite of deterioration as regards the tests of piety" (77). It is difficult not to read Woods in this passage, for the perspective criticized here is the perspective offered by Woods in *Crime Prevention, Police and Public,* and the introduction to *Dangerous Drugs.*

Burke's account of the formation of criminal character suggests that he himself occupies the position of "moralist with another point of view," one who sees the "criminal" as a conglomerate of focused habits bound together by the pious logic of criminality. This view, of course, contradicts that held by Woods, for whom criminality embodies decay and degeneracy. If the connection to Burke's work at the BSH is not already apparent, then Burke turns to the morphine addict as an exemplary figure: "Similarly with the 'drug fiend,' who can take his morphine in a hospital without the slightest disaster to his character, since it is called medicine there; but if he injects it at a party, where it has the stigma of dissipation upon it, he may gradually organize his character about this outstanding 'altar' of his experience—and since the altar in this case is generally accepted as unclean, he will be disciplined enough to approach it with appropriately unclean hands, until he is a derelict (77–78). The scare quotes around "drug fiend" demarcate the voice of someone such as Woods, whose pious linkages draw on the hypertrophic, "efficient" language Burke describes in *Attitudes toward History* and who, as a result, sees a derelict wherever he sees a drug addict. Burke's reformulation of piety can thus be read as a direct counterresponse to Woods's overly moralizing account of drug users. Burke not only draws his examples from his experiences at the BSH, but he also devotes his critical energies to dispelling the logic of the bureau itself. And just as Burke's resistance in *Dangerous Drugs* leads him to focus on physiology and habit, the broadening of the concept of piety enables him to consider the body's role in ritualized, habituated practices. In other words, practices lead to habits that lead to more associative practices; over time the accumulation of associations produces a radically transformed yet finely tuned piety. Thus the body is where something like beliefs and even morals are formed.

The moral foundations of the BSH and Woods thus stand for all Burke tries to counter with his reformulation of piety. As he did with the concept of efficiency, Burke produces a "refusal through rearticulation" whereby he counters the moral "ground" of religious-toned piety by rearticulating the concept more generally, in reference to associative practices that lead to something like deep conviction.[15] This rearticulation subsequently leads Burke to consider bodily practices and habits. His reformulation and new focus come together most notably when he develops the gashouse gang example, wherein he frames piety as both a visible bodily phenomenon and way of seeing—that is, interpreting the visible bodily aspects of others. He elaborates this notion by pointing out how humorously out of place someone of "high culture" and "refined" taste would seem when placed amid a group of spitting, catcalling men. He writes, "If we can bring ourselves to imagine Matthew Arnold loafing on the corner with the gashouse gang, we promptly realize how undiscriminating he would prove himself. Everything about him would be inappropriate: both what he said and the ways in which he said it" (77). In other words, a long string of associative, bodily, and discursive practices have gone into making Matthew Arnold utterly incapable of blending in with the working-class gashouse gang, and Arnold's carefully cultivated bodily demeanor would no doubt betray what Burke would label impiety in the gashouse context. Such formative practices, Burke explains, continue to press on and press out one's character. As he puts it, "There is, of course, a further factor involved here: the matter of *interaction*. Certain of one's choices become creative in themselves; they drive one into ruts, and these ruts in turn reinforce one's piety" (78). After a certain point, that is, Matthew Arnold may act no other way—unless, of course, he got hold of some heroin.

Recall that in *Dangerous Drugs* Burke pays particular attention to the Jekyll-Hyde phenomenon of the drug user, and he does so throughout the chapter with sentences such as these: "If the addict is denied his accustomed drug for as short as a time as twenty-four hours, his entire emotional and physical make-up may be altered" (16). It is worth noting here how, as with the gashouse example, the alteration happens at the level of affect. In *Dangerous Drugs* Burke spends a good deal of time detailing the difficult and time-consuming process of getting someone off drugs—the tenacity of habit takes its own hold on Burke the researcher.

In this regard Burke's research on opium and hypodermic syringes surfaces in his until recently unpublished tract "Auscultation, Creation, and Revision," written sometime between 1930 and 1934, while he was at work on *Permanence and Change*. In explicating Bertrand Russell's work on cravings and physiological desire, Burke draws on the historical research he did for *Dangerous Drugs* to dwell on the intensity and tenacity of a physiological craving:

> It was noted that opium-eaters developed, besides their need for the drug, a distinct opium hunger, a craving for the *taste* of opium. Accordingly, when the hypodermic needle was invented, earnest practitioners who had no need of metaphysics in their daily rounds decided that the craving of the palate could be eliminated were they to administer opiates by injection, since the patients would thus never learn the *taste* of opium. Great was their exaltation on finding this subterfuge for removing an important lure to relapse—and they were some time in discovering that the morphinist, instead of a craving for the taste of opium on his tongue, now suffered a greedy fascination at the thought of a hypodermic needle puncturing his veins. (79–80)

That the locus of the desire for opium could transfer from the taste buds to the subcutaneous regions of the limbs fascinated Burke, who counted drugs as one of many "pious linkages" one's body might establish and subsequently cling to.

Vascular craving appears more obliquely in *Permanence and Change*, where Burke likens a drug habit to a kind of poetics when he describes the intensely addicted user as "hypnotically entangled in the texture of his poem" (78). The word *poem* here is not metaphoric, but rather refers to Burke's tendency (especially in *Permanence and Change*) to figure poetry generally as a creative act—that is, something everyone is capable of in some way, as with piety: "Indeed, all life has been likened to the writing of a poem, though some people write their poems on paper, and others carve theirs out of jugular veins" (76). In what might be an oblique reference to drug use, Burke effectively truncates the more extended point made in "Auscultation, Creation, and Revision" this time demonstrating how the body can be "tapped" with poetic force. The drug addict's pious poem is composed, then, of the habitual body-drug relation to which the addict is utterly devoted, or in Burke's formulation, "by the ruts which his experience itself has worn" (79).

Burke therefore uses a drug addict as the ultimate example of a more encompassing piety, one that focuses on the formation of "ruts" rather than their inherent good or evil. His figuring of piety can be read as a direct counter to Woods, whose "piety" would be in line with religious, moral associations set forth by institutions such as the Episcopalian Church or the Bureau of Social Hygiene. Burke's newly formulated account of piety, then, is to a large extent underwritten by his work for the BSH and by Woods himself. And Burke's attention to what he calls "the range of piety" enables him to return to what was percolating in *Counter-Statement* and became even more evident in the case of the drug user:

the rhythmically receptive body overtaken by new chemically induced "rhythms," resulting in a new sense of "normality."

As the religious aspects of piety remind us, belief is more often than not accompanied by rituals—bodily practices such as kneeling and closing the eyes and material artifacts such as altars and cups. When in the context of piety Burke equates the "texture" of one's "poem" with the "ruts of experience," he effectively extends the discussion of "the body as generator of belief" begun in *Counter-Statement*. This time, however, Burke focuses on the body's capacity to be affected by so much more than poetic form or even music—but by observing rituals, by mimicking others, by "following" the ways of a criminal, gashouse gang member, or drug addict. At stake in these examples are questions of bodily learning and habit formation—in other words, the means of creating and solidifying "pious linkages." All these identity practices, that is, happen by association, and all become manifest on the bodily level and on the communicative level, as Burke maintains in an explanatory footnote on "style" toward the end of *Permanence and Change*: "Style is a constant meeting of obligations . . . a repeated doing of the 'right' thing. It molds our actions by contingencies, but these contingencies go to the farthest reaches of the communicative. For style (custom) is a complex schema of what-goes-with-what, carried through all the subtleties of manner and attitudes" (269n). Here, Burke opts for the term *style* to figure what he has thus far referred to as *piety*, the "sense of what properly goes with what." The footnote shows how style and piety come to settle in the very bodily rhythms Burke discusses in *Counter-Statement*. Note, for example, how a repetition of actions is conjoined with a "knowledge" of what is "right." Bodily repetition and knowledge of propriety are so reciprocal as to become almost identical. That is, action is molded by repetition, whereby the body falls in sync with the "contingencies"—whether a broad sense of "criminality," how spitting rightly accompanies catcalling, or how one must kneel in church when the priest makes the requisite hand motion. All these linkages bear on "the subtleties of manner and attitudes" in a way that, through repetition over time, equips a body with the "right" mannerism and actions for the situation.

Such habit formation is akin, for Burke, to the way a child who appears to have learned to walk, has really only learned "*a certain kind of walking* that is adapted to floors and streets, for instance, but poorly adapted to rough mountainsides," or in his other example whereby "the skilled sailor, having learned to walk by taking the roll of a ship into account, rolls when on firm ground" (*PC* 105; emphasis in original). The "ground" here thus approximates the contingencies of which Burke writes in the style passage above—a bodily sense of how something is done in a particular context. The "farthest reaches of the communicative" in the above passage thus demarcates Burke's place for the body. Here, "communicative" might be read as deliberately adjectival, in the sense of a communicative disease, thus marking the transport or contagion of habituated mannerisms and actions—the "schema of what-goes-with-what, *carried through all the subtleties of manner and attitudes.*" Bodies in this way become, to return to Burke's *Counter-Statement* verb, "tapped" by, and hooked on, certain styles/pieties.

Such full inhabitation of piety, however, can, like a drug habit or like Wood's juridical habit, become so engulfing as to become destructive, thus reintroducing the dangers of efficiency. In the rest of the lengthy footnote, Burke explains how style and piety, when taken to extremes in a social milieu, create a dangerous imbalance: "Style can have its own form of deterioration. For in societies greatly marked by class prerogatives, style itself tends to become a competitive implement, as a privileged group may cultivate style to advertise its privileges and perpetuate them. Style then ceases to be propitiatory. It becomes boastful. . . . As style assumes this invidious function, there is a corresponding social movement from inducement toward dominance. Its congregational qualities are lessened, its segregational qualities are stressed" (270n). The tenacity of bodily habits, and the way these habits and manners are looped into identity, can, if unchecked and picked up by others, lead to imbalance and overemphasis and most likely back to the moralistic associations of piety that Burke so strenuously resists. It is therefore incumbent on the social critic—much as it was for Burke's early conception of the artist—to attend to the hypertrophy of style or piety in order to "counter" the onset of ecological imbalance, or worse, divisiveness.

In this cyclical, recursive way, then, piety remains tethered to efficiency. In a retrospective interview conducted in 1980–81, the language of drug addiction can still be heard in Burke's discussion of habituated styles of thinking: "I believe, absolutely, you do get hooked to a vocabulary. If you really do live with your terms, they turn up tricks of their own. You can't get around them" (Skodnick 10). The interviewer, following Burke's metaphoric lead, poses the follow-up question—"What dynamic is at work and responsible for such a fix?"—to which Burke responds: "They do run you by vocabulary. . . . You're picking the terms and they always have an angle beyond which you use them and then *they* use *you*. There's no question about it. Sometimes a person writes a book and the book sells, and he writes another book . . . and it's wonderful. He's making money. Then it turns out that his way of writing gave him psychogenic cancer! That's a part of the anguish of your body when you were writing these books. Take someone like Sylvia Plath. Here's a woman who really lives with her work, means it, every damn thing she writes. She gets more and more efficient on suicidal themes. Then you're going in that groove" (Skodnick 10; emphasis in original). The "groove" here aligns with the "ruts of experience" considered so extensively in *Permanence and Change*. In this conversation Burke emphasizes the reciprocity of the "substance"—here language: just as with the cocaine addict and the addict's substance, a writer uses terms and the terms use the writer. The reciprocal movement produces a fusion of the substance and body, producing the "user" anew. The subsequent movement of Burke's answers from the language of addiction to the language of bodily transformation is therefore both easy and habitual for Burke. He figures styles of speaking and thinking as habits and language itself as a drug, thus suggesting just how deeply ingrained—habituated, even—his work as a drug researcher had become.

Burke's years as a drug researcher were therefore formative in at least two ways. First, by placing him in direct relation to an "efficient" boss, the time at the BSH helped him refine and reformulate the work he did in *Counter-Statement*. The result is a broader approach to social matters, yet one that nonetheless draws on and benefits from his early aesthetic criticism. Such an approach is altered through his developing method—the counter-efficient style of scholarship no doubt made more explicit to Burke through his oppositional relation to Colonel Woods. Perhaps more important, Burke's scope is also altered as he brings his patient methodology to bear on his assigned subject of study. The consideration of drugs and drug use in the context of "social hygiene," that is, opens for Burke all sorts of windows onto bodily learning and habit formation, even as it equips him with a remarkably broad perspective on the sociopolitical implications of how such habituated bodies get formed and formulated. Even though Burke claimed it would take him "a lifetime to explain the damages and rewards" of his work with Colonel Woods, it is clear that the rewards lay with his newly resolute commitments to secularizing piety and to the lessons of openness he first learned from mysticism. And another reward lay in the value of what is now referred to as science studies: in his research at the BSH Burke encountered various scientific discourses that would remain of deep interest to him as he continued his rhetorical project. Two such sciences—endocrinology and constitutional medicine—will be considered in the next two chapters.

4

From the Rhetoric of Science to the Science of Rhetoric | *The Case of Endocrinology*

When the name Kenneth Burke appears in studies on the rhetoric of science, it usually accompanies a Burkean term for analysis. Such terms include *identification, dramatism, metonymy, form, bureaucratization of the imaginative,* and *terministic screens.*[1] Burke's conceptual legacies, that is, help scholars to examine more carefully the rhetorical workings of scientific discourse. And yet these critical applications only tell part of the story of Burke's usefulness for the rhetoric of science. But for a few exceptions in which scholars discuss Burke's notion of metabiology (Crable, "Ideology as Metabiology"; Thames, "Nature's Physician"; Wolfe), his direct engagements with science have been largely overlooked. Burke's time at the Rockefeller Foundation, in addition to paying conceptual dividends in the notions of piety and efficiency discussed in the previous chapter, gave him a unique opportunity to work among scientists. His Rockefeller stints, as this chapter will demonstrate, equipped him to theorize not only the rhetorical dimensions of science—though he did that too—but also and importantly his time at the Bureau of Social Hygiene exposed him to the scientific dimensions of rhetoric, language, and meaning-making by taking him, quite literally, deeper into the body. In funding Burke as a researcher, Rockefeller also sponsored a curious instance of transdisciplinary work.

This chapter will focus on one particular—and particularly new—discipline that caught Burke's intellectual fancy during his days at the BSH: that of endocrinology, the study of the body's internal secretions. As Burke characterized his position from the vantage point of the 1980s: "The name Rockefeller opened all the doors for me. I could ask any question. Endocrinologists, they'd tell me anything" (Skodnick 8). What follows will offer a historical account of endocrinology in order to get at what endocrinologists might have, in fact, told Burke. As it turns out, the scientific knowledge he gleaned from endocrinologists helped him to formulate an account of meaning making based on a theory of body-mind mimetics that, among other things, offered a more satisfactory (for Burke at least) alternative to psychoanalysis.

Burke shared suspicions of psychoanalysis with his fictional character discussed in chapter 1, David Wassermann. Wassermann, remember, ranted that the edges of psychoanalysis were too dull, its vocabulary and hence its diagnoses too predictable. When writing fiction, of course, Burke could craft hilarious barstool screeds about the ills of psychoanalysis, but as a social critic he had to ensure that his account was tempered and well supported. It is important to note that for Burke psychoanalysis had a lot to offer. For one thing, as a technique psychoanalysis offered a solid instance of his favorite method of incongruous naming, of casting "out demons by a vocabulary of *conversion* . . . calling them *the very thing in all the world they are not*" (PC 133; emphasis in original). And yet Burke's biggest issue with psychoanalysis has to do with its consistent return to the repressed—its negative view of what, for Burke, is simply "*the nature of attention* in the first place" (PC 141; emphasis in original) as evident by his adaptation of terms such as *trained incapacity* and *occupational psychosis* from Veblen and Dewey, respectively. His own view leads Burke to propose that "the metaphor" of psychoanalysis "be tentatively shifted from a legalistic one suggesting repression to an optical one suggesting focus" (PC 141), which would lead the critic/therapist to examine the shiftiness of interest itself. Though only one of many "psychoses" Burke would draw upon to try to see things differently (another will be considered in chapter 6), endocrinology nonetheless provides an interesting case study for Burke's tweaks to psychoanalysis and, more to the point of this chapter, his contributions to the rhetoric of science through the science of rhetoric.

The previous chapters of this book have first discussed how bodies seem to have nudged Burke into rhetoric in the first place and then detailed how his critical mystical and efficient methods were developed alongside—even through—his thinking about bodies. This chapter, a case study of Burke's brief but strategic uses of endocrinology, shows those theories and methods in action as he responds to psychoanalysis as a dominant mode of interpretation and treatment. As such this chapter and the next two follow the tracks of bodies in the development of Burke's most important critical contributions.

Endocrinology functions rhetorically for Burke in a couple of ways. First, it offers him the rhetorical heft needed for his poetic approach in *Permanence and Change*: "After all, the devices of poetry are close to the spontaneous genius of man: in naming a corrective philosophy with poetic standards, we should have a point of reference which was in turn 'biologically' grounded. In this respect, poetry could enjoy an authority drawn from the scientific psychosis itself, a criterion based upon pragmatic demands and not offered as revelation. This is an important fact, since any new rationalization must necessarily frame its arguments as far as possible within the scheme of 'proprieties' enjoying prestige in the rationalization which it would displace" (66). This passage, one of the most explicit discussions in *Permanence and Change* of that book's aims, resonates with the claims Burke made to Tate about the "genius of the body" and its promise for providing mystical insight, and at the same time sets in motion Burke's rhetorical strategy of efficiency discussed in the previous chapter by altering the accepted terminology of science. And finally the passage promises to enact the mystical method of "placing together things formerly apart"—in this case the standards of science and poetics (writ large). Recall that Burke's efficient method requires a suspension of belief in the order of things, achieved by shifting perspectives, as he puts it later in *Permanence and Change:* "Where the accepted linkages have been of an imposing sort, one should establish perspective by looking through the reverse end of his glass, converting mastodons into microbes, or human beings into vermin upon the face of the earth" (120). Here, in detailing his mystical, efficient method, Burke offers the necessity of looking at everything differently. Indeed he almost seems to be proposing a shift in focus from the distinctively *human* aspects of humans—consciousness, rationality, dominion over the earth—to a focus on humans as collections of tiny, scurrying entities. In the 1920s and 1930s endocrinology—insofar as it figures human bodies as systems of glands interconnected by a matrix of fluid and "pulses of energy" (Cannon, *Wisdom* 19) supported by finely calibrated parts of water, salt, sugar, and fat—seemed to offer just what Burke was looking for. The science, named for its focus on that which is innermost (*endo* = within, inside, inner), effectively turns human bodies inside out, attributing all manners of bodily disposition, appearance, and behavior to internal chemical bodily processes.

As a point of focus or "psychosis" in Burkean terms, endocrinology not only lent Burke the rhetorical force of science, but its then-emerging conclusions about the human body edged Burke's body theories even closer to language by offering him new ways to figure how meaning making—humans' engagement with words as symbols—frequently happens deep inside the body, at the level of glands, chemicals, and organs. As it happens, endocrinologists made matters even easier for Burke, relying as they did on the language of communication in their early discussions of the body's internal secretions and, in one notable case, explicitly formulating psychiatry itself as above all a bodily matter.

Endocrinology as a Discipline

Endocrinology had only recently emerged during the 1910s and 1920s as a field in its own right following what contemporary endocrinologist Jean D. Wilson calls "the rapid, almost explosive growth of the new discipline" (389). As early as the end of the nineteenth century, physiological scientists had discerned a clear link between specific glandular organs and pathologies such as diabetes, acromegaly, and giantism (390). During the second decade of the twentieth century, various endocrine societies were formed and journals devoted to the discipline were published in the United States, Italy, France, and Germany (390).

Such novelty and promise drew the attention of the Rockefeller Foundation in the form of research grants, new alliances with the National Research Council, and the creation of the Bureau of Social Hygiene. As Rockefeller adviser and former research scientist Raymond B. Fosdick puts it, "so intricate and relatively obscure is the subject of endocrinology, and so intimately related to the growth and function of body and mind, that the Medical Sciences division . . . gave long-continued support to a few investigators who have possessed an unusual blend of chemical knowledge, tenacity of purpose, enthusiasm, and critical judgment" (126). In addition to the foundation's direct support of endocrinologists, the Rockefeller-funded Bureau of Social Hygiene, together with the National Research Council's Division of Medical Sciences, formed a Committee on Research in Problems of Sex in 1921. As historian Jennifer Terry shows, this placement of the committee within the NRC's Division of Medical Sciences seemed to ensure a focus on laboratory studies that would maintain scientific legitimacy (136–37). That two of the original twelve committee members—embryologist Frank R. Lillie and Harvard physiologist Walter B. Cannon—specialized in endocrinology ensured that a primary focus of the committee would be endocrinological studies. So before the Rockefeller reorganization in 1928, endocrinology was being supported by at least two wings of Rockefeller's expansive foundation—its own medical sciences division and its Bureau of Social Hygiene. Cannon's legacy for endocrinology includes the "emergency theory of response"—also known as the "adrenaline rush"—and his experiments figure prominently in Kenneth Burke's theories of bodily interpretation.

So, just as the Rockefeller Foundation was stepping up its support for studies in endocrinology, Burke was at work studying crime and drugs at the Bureau of Social Hygiene. It is easy to imagine how his work in both these areas intersected with that of endocrinologists. As an example, in 1928, the end of Burke's first round at the Bureau of Social Hygiene, a book titled *The New Criminology: A Consideration of the Chemical Causation of Abnormal Behavior* was published. Written by a neuropathologist and a science/mystery writer, *The New Criminology* dramatically locates the "source" of a criminal mind in the cells, nerve endings, and endocrine glands. The book's aim, quite simply, is to "show that criminal actions are in reality reactions caused by disturbed internal chemistry of the body" (Schlapp and Smith 29). At the time theories proliferated widely regarding hormonal imbalances and all sorts of social and visible "deviances"—from criminal behavior to schizophrenia to dwarfism and cretinism. Indeed, in the late 1920s and early 1930s a spate of books were published in the United States on how endocrine activity shaped bodies and behavior. The science was ascribed immense import, as evidenced by a selection of titles alone: Ivo Geikie Cobb's *The Glands of Destiny* appeared in 1927; Louis Berman's 1921 *The Glands Regulating Personality* was revised and reissued in 1928; Theodore Hubert Larson's

Why We Are What We Are: The Science and Art of Endocrine Physiology and Endocrine Therapy was published in 1929; and *The Physical Basis of Personality*, by Charles Stockard, who worked on the Experimental Morphology Farm at Cornell Medical College, appeared in 1931. And R. G. Hoskins's 1933 *The Tides of Life: The Endocrine Glands in Bodily Adjustment* encapsulates its own moment with much drama, crediting endocrine activity with practically all vital activity: "One of the fascinating new chapters in the book of science is the story of internal secretions. Their potency is almost unbelievable. Their influence is pervasive in all that we do and are. In the present they cooperate in determining the forms of our bodies and the workings of our minds" (23–24).

Aside from endocrinology's contributions to criminology and studies of personality in general, it also, as suggested earlier, linked to question of drugs and drug use, Burke's other research area at the Rockefeller Foundation. Cobb's *The Glands of Destiny* notes that drugs such as strychnine "produce their effect by stimulating the adrenal secretion" (63), and much early endocrinology involved developing the exact formula for substances such as adrenalin and insulin so that they might be manufactured synthetically (71) and injected into subjects experimentally. Harvard physiologist Hoskins observes of hormones: "considered as drugs they are astonishingly potent" (22). In fact, when the British physiologist E. H. Starling famously coined the term *hormone* in 1905, he placed hormones in "the same category as drugs of our Pharmacopoeia" (Croonian Lecture 340). H. H. Dale, secretary of the British National Research Council, would later proclaim hormones "the natural drugs of the body" (Harrower 55). So too Burke, writing in 1933, refers to the endocrine glands and neural channels as "the body's drug factories" (*PC* 150).

Perhaps because of its movement inward, as well as its related imbrication with psychiatry, endocrinology offered Burke a handy dialectical counterpart to psychoanalysis. Whereas psychoanalysis tended to start with behavior and speculated about what happened on the interior (in the psyche or mind), endocrinology began with internal chemical processes and moved to external behavioral manifestations. In the somewhat forceful words of endocrinologist Larson, writing in 1929, "We are all barometers and register in external manifestation our endocrine relativity and endocrine exchange, which makes us what we are. Learn to interpret the barometer" (348).

Endocrinology as Internal Communication

And yet the dominant metaphorics of endocrinology were not those of barometric pressure. From very early on the body's internal secretions were figured as a kind of bodily communication. In his initial formulation of hormones, Starling not only called attention to their "druglike" behavior, but, mixing the metaphor of drugs with one of communication, he also called hormones "chemical messagers" (340).[2]

In his brief history of endocrinology, physiologist John Henderson shares the story of Starling's consultation with the Pindar scholar W. T. Vesey when it became clear that he "needed a word for an agent released into the blood stream that stimulated activity in a different part of the body" (9). Vesey suggested the Greek word *hormaō*, meaning "to excite or arouse," and that apparently did the trick (Henderson 9). The base meaning of *hormaō* bears importantly here, for it indicates motion or movement. Only through movement can a hormone transmit its information. When Starling introduced the term in his now-famous Croonian Lecture, he underscores the importance of hormones as movers and carriers when he uses the metaphor of messengers: "speeding from cell to cell along the blood stream . . . coordinat[ing] the activities and growth of different parts of the body" (340). This double understanding of hormones as druglike and communicative substances took hold and can be found throughout endocrinology research in the late 1920s and 1930s. In fact Starling's epithet "chemical messenger" is used in virtually all discussions of endocrinology from the period.

The early formulation of hormones as "chemical messengers" encouraged extensions of the communication metaphor found in the work of neurophysiologists W. B. Cannon (who was part of the BSH-created Committee for Research in Problems of Sex) and his colleague R. G. Hoskins. Cannon and Hoskins, both Harvard physiologists working at the intersection of neurology and endocrinology, conceptualized the relationship between the endocrine and nervous systems as that of a giant communication network. Cannon, known by many as one of the "main pioneers" of neuroendocrinology, focused specifically on how emotional and affective responses were transmitted chemically to and from the nervous system.[3] Cannon's instructive *Bodily Changes in Fear, Hunger, and Rage*, diagrams the interrelationship between glandular and nervous activity and features the curious drawing below.

At first glance this body that is nothing *but* organs looks something like a telephone switchboard, but upon closer inspection it is even more intricate. Whereas a telephone switchboard funnels multiple signals into one location for targeted redistribution, the messages in this diagram are distributed to various locations in the central nervous system, represented by the spindly image on the left, and then redistributed even more broadly. The text itself shows Cannon using the analogy of a mass communication system to imagine how the endocrine and autonomic nervous systems interact. After observing that the brain and spinal cord's outlying neurons are "never innervated directly from the central nervous system" (23), he describes instead a process of translation and redistribution: "I have suggested that possibly these outlying neurons act as 'transformers,' modifying the impulses received from the central source (impulses suited to call forth the quick responses of *skeletal* muscle), and adapting these impulses to the peculiar, more slowly acting tissues, the secreting cells and visceral muscle, to which they are distributed" (23).

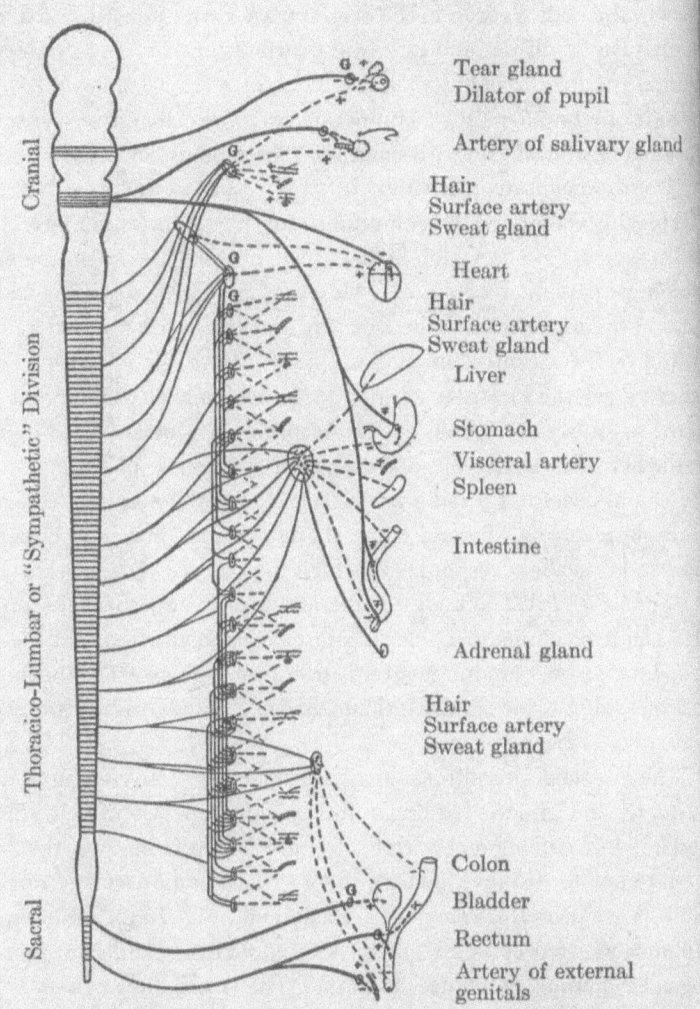

FIGURE 1.—Diagram of the more important distributions of the autonomic nervous system. The brain and spinal cord are represented at the left. The nerves to skeletal muscles are not represented. The preganglionic fibres of the autonomic system are in solid lines, the postganglionic in dash-lines. The nerves of the cranial and sacral divisions are distinguished from those of the thoracico-lumbar or "sympathetic" division by broader lines. A + mark indicates an augmenting effect on the activity of the organ; a − mark, a depressive or inhibitory effect. For further description see text.

Walter B. Cannon's representation of the autonomic nervous system, from *Bodily Changes in Pain, Hunger, Fear, and Rage* (1915). Reproduced by permission of Sarah Cannon Holden

For Cannon the adaptation and distribution of these impulses to various parts of the body, as seen in the diagram, are both extensive and diffuse. It is this mechanism of diffuse and extensive distribution that "is of prime importance in accounting for the bodily manifestations of affective states" (26). These states include the familiar list of autonomic responses: digestive disruption, the hair standing on end, shaking, perspiration, goose bumps, all visceral conditions resulting from momentary intensities.

Hoskins elaborates the communication metaphor even more explicitly in his 1933 *Tides of Life,* in which he likens the nervous system on the one hand "to a telephone system of a great city. Messages are constantly going from the various parts of the organism to a coordinating and distributing center and thence transmitted to the various send stations" (328). With the endocrine system, on the other hand, "the messages are not . . . individually distributed but are broadcast to the organism as a whole" (328). According to Hoskins, the proper analogy for traffic between the nervous and endocrine systems is not a telephone system with individual users but a radio broadcast, whereby the same message goes out to multiple receivers. "By and large," he continues, "hormone broadcasts are utilized to bring about responses in which the body as a whole or major portions of it respond" (328). The body, figured as an intricate web of neuron transformers and gland receptors, becomes a site of mass mediation, a critical instance of broad, affective, communicative distribution. The extension of the communicative metaphor likely led to Hoskins's use of the soon-to-be cybernetic term *feedback* to endocrine systems.[4]

The effects of this diffuse, highly dispersed internal communication bears importantly on Cannon's reading of human emotion—Cannon, it should be noted, had a highly visible break with his friend William James over this very matter. In an attempt to disprove James's theory that emotion comes directly from the body—that tears, for example, precede and produce the emotion of sadness—Cannon injected college students with adrenalin in order to mimic the physiological symptoms of intense emotions ("The James-Lange Theory" 113). The aim of the study, quite simply, was to prove that the emotions in question did not, in fact, arise from the physiological condition, but rather that the cognitive perception of emotions effectively comes first. Cannon's study, together with a similar study conducted by Spanish endocrinologist Gregorio Marañon, concluded that subjects injected felt "no specific emotion" and instead described their state in comparative terms. Cannon writes that of his student subjects, "a few who had been in athletic competitions testified to feeling 'on edge,' 'keyed up,' just as before a race." Similarly the "normal" subjects of Marañon's study made such remarks as "'I feel as if afraid,' 'as if awaiting a great joy,' 'as if moved,' 'as if I were going to weep without knowing why,' 'as if I had a great fright yet am calm' 'as if they are about to do something to me'" ("The James-Lange Theory" 113).

Marañon's more extensive study included "normal" and "abnormal" subjects, such as those with hypothyroidal condition or those subjects who were already in a "known" state of specific emotional distress—after talking about "sick children or dead parents," for example. Curiously in these cases, according to Cannon, a "real emotion" developed following the adrenaline injections (113–14). For Cannon the resulting behavior of both the "normal" and "abnormal" subjects suggested that emotion had to precede the physiological condition and thus went a long way toward refuting James's visceral theories of emotions.

For Burke, however, such conclusions about an internally communicative body provided a new way to think about how affect shapes interpretation. That the unaroused patients related their sensations to previous "knowable" affective moments, and that the aroused ones let their prevailing affect rise to new heights, was highly suggestive for a kind of bodily poetics, which is just what Burke tries to articulate in *Permanence and Change*. Endocrinology provided a window into the body's internal processes and thus helped Burke to formulate a multidirectional, somatic response to the science of psychoanalysis. Much as a drug habit, chemicals such as hormones help craft meaning—and meaningful commitments—on the level of the body, and the work of endocrinology helped Burke to make this point in response to psychoanalytic accounts of meaning making.

Glandular Translations

In the *Permanence and Change* chapter titled "Meaning and Regression" Burke begins his none-too-subtle critique of psychoanalysis with a meandering hypothetical example of an insomniac named "Mr. Squib," whom he describes as "a very mild and tolerant fellow, distinguished for a certain humorous charitableness, harboring no grudges, worried over the fate of mankind, and really doing much good for those with whom he comes into contact" (148). And yet Mr. Squib's acute insomnia begins to reshape the way meanings exist. Burke asks readers to suppose further that this insomnia-induced orientation persuades the otherwise mild-mannered Squib that "he stands beneath a Damoclean sword or that he bears a Bellerophontic letter, or that his hungers are being fed by the mocking mimetics of a Barmecide feast" (149). "If some primitive response arises under such a situation," Burke muses, "are we not really dealing with something so *intellectual* as a matter of interpretation, and is not the affective response (the primitivism of terrors, vengeances, or collapse) quite in keeping with the meaning of the situation as it presents itself to him?" (149). In other words, what might be dismissed as highly affective delusions are actually *conclusions* formed by Squib's insomnia-shaped intellect. Burke's "hypothetical" conundrum points to the difficulty of separating the affective from the rational.

Burke then further clarifies his stance, leveling a more pointed critique of psychoanalysis: "In noting that the rational is shaped by the affective, psychoanalysts did great service—but too often the discovery led them to underrate the fact that, once the rational has arisen and taken form, it brings forward demands of its own, and guides us as to what the affective response should be" (149). In other words, because psychoanalytic accounts of regression focus on the moment of origin, the diagnostic enterprise fails to follow through what an affective rationality might mean for questions of future affective responses, interpretation, and meaning making. The issue of rationality's affective contours thus leads Burke to intellectualize affect even as it edges him closer to the question of language. In a telling example he explains how it requires "highly intellectual equipment... to be terrified at a gun the first time in one's life a gun is pointed at one, and without ever having been shot" (149). This moment when the body so immediately and decisively translates "gun" into "run" is exactly what drew Burke to endocrinology and what scientists such as Cannon had begun to chart. Burke then goes on to delineate the concatenations of meaning that go into making the gun such a "pure" stimulus. "Thus," he continues, "even though one grant that the original formative factors of the rational are affective, one cannot jump to the conclusion that henceforth all rational manifestations must be considered as a mere phosphorescent glow arising above the affective. . . . Instead, our interpretations of the signs, be they true or false, can instigate the most intense affection" (149).

What Burke effectively offers here is a serialized process of meaning making whereby affect enters at every step, forming and reforming what is called rational. In the case of fear of a gun, the fear's moment of origin (presumably the question of psychoanalysis in Burke's schema) becomes less crucial than how a gun has come to signify something that ought be feared—that is, through the affective attachment of meaning to the very idea of gun, resulting in an overarching interpretation guided by associative fear of death and pain. The process of signification here is rendered concatenate, serialized, and, always at every turn, affective. In order to support his argument, Burke turns to the discourse of endocrinology. What results is a footnote as important for his arguments as it is long and convoluted. The first part of the footnote reads as follows:

> To be complete, this discussion of the relationship between meaning and affect should also consider at great length the mind-body parallelisms suggested by such sciences as endocrinology. Some research which I did in drug addiction leads me to suggest that the interaction between intellectual interpretations and the secretions of the "body's drug factories" (the endocrines and their neural channels) would be as follows: Such a response as fear arises from our interpretation of a situation as dangerous. This fear response also sets up in the body a glandular constellation which can make for extreme wakefulness (since alertness is biologically part of our defensive equipment, being precisely the sort of attitude that would best help us

protect ourselves against the thing or situation interpreted as a fear-sign). If such wakefulness is prolonged, the state of exhaustion adds new factors to be interpreted as danger-signs. (150–51)

This footnote, which presses the hypothetical instance of Squib the insomniac, spills over onto the next page in the first and subsequent editions of the work and offers a rare reference to Burke's drug research, and, much as does the 1983 interview with Roy Skodnick, explicitly links his thinking about endocrinology to his days at Rockefeller. Moreover, the footnote shows Burke using the discourse of endocrinology to interrogate not only body-mind parallelism, but also, more specifically, the body's role in shaping interpretation—the bodily, affective processes that shape rational, and ultimately rhetorical, associations. The "glandular constellation" accompanies a fearful interpretation so that the sign *gun* translates into the word *run* through the adrenaline-fueled emergency response. Of course fear can be aroused by something far less obvious than a gun—a doorbell or a ringing phone, in the right situation, could cause this sort of a glandular surge. Like Walter Cannon and Gregory Marañon with their experimental injections, then, Burke assigns the immanent interpretive act priority, regardless of its degree of rationality or its verifiability.

At the same time, or almost immediately after (Burke is unclear about which), the interpretation—in his example, the fear of the gun—"sets up in the body a glandular constellation which can make for extreme wakefulness." The resulting wakefulness, or fear response, turns out its own interpretations on subsequent events or situations, and the cycle spins on. In blocking out the rational "glow" of ideology, Burke is able to isolate a view of the body as an equal or even primary participant in interpretive critical acts. The footnote continues: "Now, if we reverse the process, beginning with the endocrine constellation (which may arise purely from some physical glandular infection), we find the organism in a state of alertness—and since extreme alertness is part of the danger-equipment, it may in turn lead the sufferer to interpret his situation as a danger-situation. In this way his endocrine disorder may lead him to discern fear-elements in events outside him which would not be so interpreted if the disorder were removed (as it can be temporarily, for instance, by a sedative)" (151). Here Burke uses endocrinology to suggest that internal processes can form interpretations: chemicals can shape or regulate meaning. He also shows how a system of reciprocal, associative feedback gets "set up" in the body, and the feedback itself is accomplished by what he formulates as "the insertion of shuttle-terms." The footnote presses on: "But we should also remember that in the devious ways of the mind the simple correlation between danger and fear can be greatly altered by the insertion of shuttle-terms. For *solace* belongs as much to the danger category as fear does. Hence wakefulness may also lead to an elaborate structure of solace, as in the case of scientific, religious, or poetic insomniacs who may convert the burden of sleeplessness into output" (151). Such conversion of "disorder" into productivity is in line with Burke's suggestion earlier in the chapter that "instead of calling the intense response a *disease*, we might consider it quite accurate" (148). In other words, by means of the shuttle-term *solace*—much like the injection of a synthetic hormone —insomnia might be rhetorically transformed from a disorder to artistic production.

It would seem this footnote takes Burke's readers a long way from his point, but as Burke's footnotes frequently do, it instead fills in the scientific discourses and rhetorical moves that lead to his claims in the first place. Indeed the footnote appears at the end of a paragraph on affect, a paragraph that begins: "Thus, though our orientation rises out of the affective, it in turn calls forth affective states" (150). Thus, in considering all the forces that produce affective states, Burke turns to endocrinology. And there he finds a system of translation and communication that both mimics and mingles with symbol systems. What results is an association of concepts through bodily impulses and flows of energy—a chemical sort of rhetoric.

Matter over Mind: Attitudes toward Insulin

By now it should be apparent that this relatively new study of the body's internal secretions helped galvanize Burke's critiques of psychoanalysis even as it helped refine his theories of orientation and interpretation. Not only did endocrinology offer him new ways to theorize processes previously considered solely the province of mind—processes such as emotion, meaning making, and thought itself— it did so in a way that featured the body more prominently from the beginning. In keeping with the incongruous, mystical methods laid out in the previous two chapters, the closer Burke comes to the mind, the more emphasis he places on matter. In other words, as the mind's mimetic, reciprocal counterpart, the body, for Burke, seemed to hold more promise as a starting point for "reorientation"— read "therapeutic treatment"—than the mind. What is more, a controversial psychiatric treatment derived from endocrinology helps Burke to reflect on mimetic mind-body relations.

A passage on "secular prayer" from the "Dictionary of Pivotal Terms" section of *Attitudes toward History* most pointedly illustrates how endocrinology informed Burke's mimetic mind-body theories. The opening of the entry moves quickly to a point about bodies and prayer: "Secular prayer would not, by our notion," Burke writes, "be confined to words. Any mimetic act is prayer. Even 'psychogenic illness' may be a prayer, since it is the 'substantiation of an attitude' in a bodily act" (322). The passage raises dance, music, and the graphic arts as forms of prayer, he writes, "in our technical sense of the term," simultaneously invoking points about piety and character engaged in the last chapter. From there, Burke continues, "Secular prayer is the *coaching of an attitude by the use of mimetic and verbal language*" (322; emphasis in original). The notion of mimetic language is obviously crucial for understanding how Burke's bodily theories meet language and will receive further consideration in chapter 7. For now, however, I want to focus on yet another sprawling footnote that spans the bottom third of the next four pages and spins out of the rather surprising suggestion that psychogenic illness—the name of which indicates its origins in the "psyche"—might be productively considered as "attitude" substantiated in a "bodily act" (321–22). The footnote begins by positing the sort of reciprocal mind-body feedback espoused by Cannon and Hoskins:

> The two-way relationship between the mental and the physical, in other words, can lead from the physical to the mental as well as from the mental to the physical. The mimetics of agitation may lead to a state of agitation, or a state of agitation may lead to the mimetics of agitation. Hence, such a state of mind as guilt or fear may induce its corresponding visceral expression (in glandular and nervous actions), or *v.v.* Applying such considerations to the matter of "psychogenic illness," we should say that the mental sufferer is an actor—and in the process of enacting his role as sufferer, he adopts the mimetic expression (including visceral, glandular responses) in keeping with his attitude. (322)

As it is, the footnote may as well stop there. Burke has thus far underscored, by way of a double chiasmus in the first two sentences and chiasmatic shorthand ("v.v") in the third, the reciprocity between mind and body, and he has elaborated his hunch that the reciprocal relation functions mimetically—and in doing so mind and body remain in close touch, as "body-mind." In offering the "mental sufferer" as "an actor," Burke is not attributing agency so much as he ascribing character of that kind that has been "built up" through one's—and one's body's—pious commitments, much as with the heroin user. But the footnote persists, posing tentative and rather bizarre questions about what a mimetic theory might mean for treatment of mental illness: "Might we speculate on a paradoxical attempt to arrest *mental* disorders by deliberate infection with the corresponding *physical* disorder?" (323n).[5] As an example Burke follows up on a point earlier in the footnote that asthma, in psychoanalytic theory, is marked as a particularly regressive ailment (322n) by suggesting that a psychopathologist might stem the "ravages of mental regression" by "finding the material means of *giving his patient asthma*" (324n; emphasis in original). "In other words," Burke writes, "might a little of the *physical* disease be introduced as homeopathic inoculation against the full ravages of the *mental* disease?" (324n; emphasis in original). The assumption here is that the physical manifestations of an illness would be more manageable for a mental patient, a point he makes quite clearly later in the footnote when he calls "material equivalents" of "mental terrors" "psychologically *more negotiable*" (325n; emphasis in original).

At this point, rhetorically, Burke cannot afford to end his speculative footnote with the odd suggestion that psychiatrists trying to arrest regression might as well produce legions of asthmatics, and so he goes on to cite an even more startling instance of the latest therapeutic method in which psychiatrists, by means of insulin-filled syringes, were taking legions of patients diagnosed with schizophrenia in and out of hypoglycemic comas and seizures—for days, sometimes weeks at a time. Burke quite plainly invokes this controversial practice, known as insulin shock therapy, to illustrate his hunch that body-mind mimesis can extend to treatment: "Something of this sort seems to be going on, in the experiments with the arresting of dementia praecox by injections of insulin. Is it not possible that the *physically* engendered fear imparted to the patient by the injection serves as immunization against the ravages of his subtler and vaguer *mental* fears?" (324n; emphasis in original). That Burke refers to such a contemporaneous method of treating dementia praecox (schizophrenia) is itself remarkable and suggests that he either came across the practice in the course of his drug research at the BSH or later when in the final throes of writing *Attitudes toward History*.

The first reports on the use of insulin shock to treat schizophrenia came out of Austria in 1934–35, during which time Burke was working at the Bureau of Social Hygiene, where psychiatry, along with other medical sciences such as endocrinology, received ample funding. Since the early 1910s the Rockefeller Foundation had partnered with—and supported—the National Committee for Mental Hygiene, and according to Fosdick, "it was in the broad field of psychiatry that the Division of Medical Sciences placed its major concentration as the century rounded into its third decade" (127). By 1933, when Burke began his second stint with the foundation, Rockefeller had made psychiatry its primary emphasis in an attempt to redress the breach between psychiatry and other forms of medical knowledge, such as anatomy, neurology, and endocrinology. According to Fosdick, until that point "little attention was paid by either the professional psychiatrist or the practitioner in other branches of medicine to the interplay of body and mind in every illness" (129). Indeed, according to Fosdick, bolstering psychiatry with "scientific methods," thereby bringing together body and mind, was named as an explicit mission for the foundation at an April 1933 trustees meeting (129, 320n6). The foundation's objective was to "infuse medicine with psychiatry," thereby following through on the promise of psychiatry and offering a more integrative approach: "With all its wisdom," Fosdick, himself a former trustee, writes, "if medicine neglects what integrates and harmonizes the functions and organs, its picture will be out of focus and its comprehension incomplete" (129). This sort of transdisciplinary work was exactly what the sprawling

Rockefeller Foundation was equipped to encourage. In so doing it would follow the leads of—and take up research begun by—experimental psychiatrists working overseas, such as Manfred Sakel, the Austrian psychiatrist who developed insulin shock therapy.

Sakel accidentally hit upon the idea in his research on morphine users whom he was treating with insulin. He noticed "remarkable mental and characterological changes which followed severe hypoglycemic shock" (*Pharmacological* 1) and speculated that the treatment might be useful for schizophrenia. Given the lengthy focus on morphine in his writing for Woods, Burke, who would have been quite comfortable reading articles published in German, may well have hit on the practice before Sakel's work was made available in English between 1934 and 1935, two years before the practice actually caught on in the United States. Nevertheless, in December 1936 Sakel visited New York to lecture on, demonstrate, and teach his technique, prompting more than twenty New York hospitals to begin administering insulin to patients diagnosed with schizophrenia.[6] By 1937, the year *Attitudes toward History* was published, New York had become a hotbed of insulin shock treatment. No fewer than twenty-eight scientific articles appeared in the 1938 volume of *Psychiatric Quarterly* sharing clinical results from this trial period.[7] In 1938 the Nervous and Mental Disease Publishing Company in New York printed an English translation of *The Pharmacological Shock Treatment of Schizophrenia*, Sakel's own description of his methods and results.

Sakel's volume is worth considering in some detail here for its explicit theorizing of what he calls the "somatic orientation" of his method over and against psychoanalysis. If Sakel and other practitioners of insulin therapy were not at the time quite certain about how exactly the treatment method worked, they nonetheless grounded the method in pointed theories of the body's importance for psychiatry, theories about mind-body reciprocity that Burke quite explicitly favored. In his introduction to the English edition of *The Pharmacological Shock Treatment of Schizophrenia* Sakel claims on no uncertain terms that his book—and by extension his new treatment method—"is meant to show . . . that there is an indivisible unity between the purely physical manifestations and the psychotic and psychic phenomena which are consequences of physiological phenomena, and thus the products of the living being" (xvii–xviii). In short Sakel offers what he calls a "pathophysiological basis for psychotic processes" (xviii): the success rates of insulin shock therapy, which by most accounts at the time hovered around 70 percent, buttressed his claims that the body, in fact, should be given equal consideration with, if not priority over, the workings of the mind in matters of mental illness. The author of the book's preface, neurologist Foster Kennedy, explicitly hails psychoanalysis, impatiently proclaiming, "Surely the time has come to put away the notion that psychiatry deals just with mind-disease" (ix), and comparing the psychoanalyst to Polyphemus, Homer's one-eyed

Cyclops (xi). Such metaphorics of limited vision are in line with the same discourse used to spur Rockefeller's funding of work across the medical sciences and psychiatry and would of course appeal to Burke. Still, in *Attitudes toward History*, in the same footnote where he accepts the psychoanalytic theory that asthma is a "regressive" disorder, he objects to therapy as a method of psychological treatment: "Our objection," he writes, "to most psychotherapy, as now conducted, is that it is accomplished, insofar as it is accomplished at all, by the systematization of triviality. Its dissociative modes of treatment, in being nonmoral, are immoral; its lack of social co-ordinates makes it function anti-socially. There is a need to broaden its individualistic, isolated co-ordinates to embody attitudes that fit into a larger social texture. In short, there must be a remoralization of therapeusis" (325n). While the irony of offering insulin shock therapy as a potential counter to the "immoral" practice of psychotherapy was not yet evident, the point remains that Burke leans more toward an approach that takes seriously the concatenate, chiasmatic process of meaning making (body-affect-language-affect-body). In other words, if affect operates through impulses—neural, glandular, vascular, and otherwise—trafficking through the body, then a method of treatment that remains solely on the level of the psyche would simply not do.

And yet in the scheme of Burke's entry, the entire title of which is "Secular Prayer—or, Extended: Character-building by Secular Prayer," a "lump" that according to the book's conclusion names "the complex intermingling of these three levels (the mimetic, the intimate, and the abstract)" (341), the critique of psychoanalytic treatment is secondary to the larger point about the mimetic level, or "mimetic sphere," which most closely aligns with physicality for Burke and which is most easily theorized through "mimetics of agitation." In other words a psychogenic condition such as dementia praecox, much as a person with insomnia or a drug habit, exposes most noticeably mind-body mimetics and its role in concatenate and diffuse processes of interpretation. As he points out in a parenthetical explanation of his epithet for the human body, "the original economic plant," glandular secretions frequently play a role in the mimetic positions the body might take: "Thus the body," he writes parenthetically, "as an 'economic enterprise,' may on occasion prepare itself by the increased secretion of adrenalin, which induces an increase in muscular tension, and may in turn be correlated, in the 'superstructure' of emotions, as fear or rage" (339).[8] Rage, in turn, can be made manifest on the body, the point at which Burke ends his earlier engagement with endocrinology in *Permanence and Change* when concluding his short chapter on meaning: "Since passing anger can be externalized in a curl of the lip, why cannot the exaltation of any prolonged 'insight' be found finally in the shaping of the organs, if we but know how to read the characters there? . . . The connectives would be remote, like the relationship between emotionality and glandular change. But they would be there nonetheless, in the physical parallelisms of the mind" (158). So endocrinology models the distributed, concatenate connectivity about which Burke is writing, and as such helps him to get beyond the limits of psychoanalysis in his theory of orientation and his meditation on the body's role in meaning making. *Attitudes toward History* thus pursues the somatic line of inquiry begun in *Permanence and Change*, moving more deeply into the glandular body, refining his position on psychoanalysis and, ultimately, the science of rhetoric: such correlative biological processes, are, for Burke, often and everywhere folded into interpretive, critical, and ultimately rhetorical acts.

What Burke arrives at, then, via his rather circuitous route through endocrinology is that the questions of orientation and motive (the questions that concern him as much as they do any psychoanalyst) might be best explored not just in a tracing backward in an individual's history, but by tracing inward and outward, noting bodily responses to situations and momentary "translational" shifts. Such a bodily hermeneutics considers the body and affect at every turn, thus resisting the severe compulsion always to explain with one vocabulary. In considering moments of "agitation"—indeed, in preferring the term *agitation*—Burke also resists the compulsion to pathologize, a tendency that will be central in the next chapter on body morphology, a form of scientific knowledge that takes Burke from the body's interior communicative processes to its external features.

5

Seeing "Deviance" as Inclination | *Kretschmerian Constitutions and Bodily Occupations*

Chapter 5 of the third part of *Permanence and Change*, titled "The Search for Motives: Magical and Scientific Interpretation," broaches the book's central question; indeed it is the question that Burke returned to time and again: what makes humans act? The question of course seeks a common denominator that drives human action, a fundamental motive, and it is itself transdisciplinary in that it cuts across disciplinary concerns of sociologists, rhetorical theorists, psychologists, political scientists, anthropologists, philosophers, and historians.

In considering the question of human motives Burke's chapter effectively decides that such a question, like all questions, is unanswerable without a place from which to answer it. In doing so the chapter anticipates much feminist standpoint theory of the 1980s, as well as the situated knowledges of postmodern feminism, providing one occasion to align Burke with feminist interventions into Western philosophy.[1] The same chapter, as it happens, provides at least two more links to contemporary feminist theory. First, Burke's stress on biology aligns with recent attempts to draw together feminist studies and science studies productively in a way that refuses the too-easy claim that biology, as a reductionist science, is strongly antithetical to feminism's goals. Elizabeth Wilson's *Psychosomatic: Feminism and the Neurological Body* both calls for and successfully performs a suspension of disbelief in biological reductionism. At stake in such an effort is a second, broader question of the body, a question broached variously by theorists such as Elizabeth Grosz, Judith Butler, and Susan Bordo in the 1990s. Wilson's argument that "the question of the body has yet to be posed as comprehensively as it could be" (5) both engages and moves beyond earlier feminist interventions with its insistence on taking scientific knowledge seriously for what it might tell us about bodies and bodily difference.

All of these connections to feminism remind us of the ever-present philosophical and methodological issues that must be confronted when working with and talking about bodies, and Burke patiently works through many of these in the chapter on motives. For him the selection of a perspective such as religion, Marxism, or psychoanalysis necessarily presses one's answers into an frame of causality—of a greater being, of economic forces, of repressed experience—and such singular causality, in Burke's scheme, often tilts toward the sort of efficiency he blasted early on. Yet these sorts of perspectives count as *preference* or purpose, and according to Burke, "man lives by purpose—and purpose is basically *preference*" (235); "every system of exhortation hinges about some definite act of faith, a deliberate selection of alternatives" (235). Burke then reveals his own preferences for action or participation, cooperation and communication, ultimately equating the entire cluster of preferred terms with life: "Life, activity, cooperation, communication—they are identical" (236). His emphasis on life as activity and not just passive existence helps to situate his strong preference for keeping biology in the mix, and his preference for posing the related questions of bodies and motives as comprehensively as possible. Doing so calls for a hard look at the principle of variation in so many scientific discourses; and as contemporary feminist theory teaches, it is difference itself that vexes such a universalizing question as "What makes humans act?" In order to pursue the question of motives in tandem with the question of bodies, one must take seriously bodily difference. Such a question takes us, then, much as endocrinology does, into the realm of the individual body.

The next chapter of *Permanence and Change*, "Occupation and Preoccupation," takes up the question of bodily difference, but it does so by raising a series of questions about that most socioeconomic part of life—occupation: "What are our occupations? Is their number confined to the trades and professions listed in a business? Are people solely occupied as plumbers, bakers, bank clerks, doctors, writers, and the like?" (237). These questions have less to do with issues of labor than with reevaluating the notion of vocation, stretching it beyond what someone does for a "living" in the economic sense to how one's life—and hence one's "perspective"—is shaped by one's commitments, occupations, and preoccupations. Burke does so by counting things such as obsessions and hobbies as occupations, but also bodies: "Is it not also an occupation," Burke asks somewhat provocatively, "to be a hunchback?" (237).

With this question Burke makes good on his book's subtitle (*Anatomy of Purpose*), offering the body itself as one important way to extend prevailing notions of occupation. Such an extension resists the tendency, in an era dominated by what Burke called "brain work," to forget the body altogether. As he laments earlier in the book, "a modern state requires a whole army of brainworkers whose activities hardly engage their physical genius at all" (185). The notion of "physical genius" thus inhabits a special place within the chapter on occupation, the bulk of which describes the role of inclinations or capacities in shaping one's perspective. Such inclinations can take the form of a "gift," as in musical acumen; a practiced art, such as boxing; or a disease or deformity, as with his hypothetical hunchback (241).[2] Such inclinations, that is, frequently begin with bodies.

As this chapter will show, Burke's treatment of the body as a set of inclinations grows out of an engagement with German psychiatrist Ernst Kretschmer, whose work, as described by Burke, "is concerned with the description and measurement of bodily types, and of the mental patterns correlated with these" (*PC* 243–44) or, in the title of Kretschmer's book that most interested Burke, the relationship between *Physique and Character*. In this enormously influential 1925 treatise, Kretschmer develops a typology of three bodily shapes: pyknic, which he also called "circular" (short and roundish), athletic (muscular), and asthenic (long and thin). These types formed the basis of what he called a "psycho-physical correlation"—that is, the three body types corresponded to particular personality types, psychological disorders, and intellectual leanings (*Physique* 38). So while Kretschmer's types would later be taken up by such famous anthropologists as Margaret Mead and adapted by other constitutionalists into the now more commonly known body types—ectomorph, endomorph, and mesomorph—they more immediately informed a new approach to psychology.[3] As is by now clear from his fictional rants against psychoanalysis and his ongoing transdisciplinary quest for alternative views, Burke resisted the too-narrow standpoint of psychoanalysis, and in doing so joined a whole host of thinkers keen on finding new perspectives.[4] The synthetic morpho-psychological approach, which begins with the surface, size, and shape of the body rather than the recesses of the psyche (as psychoanalysis did), appealed to Burke, who shared Kretschmer's interest in avoiding an easy pathologizing stance on motive. Kretschmer's typology instead operates as an index of inclinations, and as such helped shape Burke's early preoccupations with psychosis, genius, and also with vision.

Still, how did Burke become preoccupied with the synthetic, scientific questions that drove Kretschmer? Was it his days as a researcher associated with the Rockefeller Foundation, where such transdisciplinary, synthetic practices formed both the spirit and the mission of its programs in the medical sciences?[5] Or was it, more simply, Burke's "occupation"—at 5′ 4″ with a big, round head—as a pyknic type?

Translating Constitutions: Ludwig's Literary Biology

Burke's Rockefeller-based work in psychosomatic fields of drug research and criminology as well as his own body type kept him preoccupied with Kretschmerian questions of constitution, but the occupation that most likely first introduced him to the matter was a job he got as a translator. Sometime in 1926 or 1927 Burke translated from German a book by the biographer Emil Ludwig titled *Genie und Charakter (Genius and Character)*. By this point Ludwig, a Polish-born Swiss citizen, was gaining international popularity as a biographer of famous figures, past and present. His subjects ranged widely and included Goethe, Bismarck, Cleopatra, and Jesus. His biography of Napoleon, made available in

English in 1926, drew much attention in the United States, reaching number two on the nonfiction bestseller list in 1927.[6] Ludwig's book appears to have factored importantly in Burke's thinking about the body's relationship to character formation, but most important it stands as an early link to Kretschmer's more overtly scientific project.

In the preface to *Genius and Character* Ludwig characterizes his own work as a portraitist and compares himself to the ancient biographer Plutarch, who, much as Ludwig would, wrote about the lives of figures from years past. In comparing himself to Plutarch, however, Ludwig makes one important distinction: whereas Plutarch's domain was demarcated clearly as history, Ludwig stakes a cross-disciplinary claim on psychology and biology. "The renewed interest in memoirs," he writes matter-of-factly in his introduction to the work Burke translated, "is biological: and perhaps the portraitist of today, who is first of all a psychologist, is much nearer to the biologist than to the historian" (*Genius and Character* 4). Biology, then, was central for Ludwig, yet he, like his translator, worked in many different disciplinary modes, and his methods fall somewhere between second-wave phrenology (by-then outdated) and constitutional analysis.[7] Writing of his own occupation in the third person, Ludwig claims that as a portraitist he "can exploit the dramatic form, or the short essay, the detailed, exhaustive life history, or the editorial" and with all available discourses: "With a kind of naïve cynicism, he appropriates the scientist's laboriously collated facts for purposes of his own: an artist who ransacks the flower beds and leaves a pillaged garden behind for a grumbling caretaker, while he himself goes off with a superb bouquet gleaming in his arms" (7).

On Ludwig's list of "floral pillages" are the methods of constitutional analysis. He thus attends carefully to photographs and paintings of his subjects, attempting to decipher what Burke translates as "silent betrayals"—subtle yet legible features of the body and face that give indications of the bearer's values, interests, and temperament (6). For Ludwig the revelatory sloping noses, giant foreheads, and physiques large and small broadcast the subjects' innermost character: "So that pictures," he writes, "provide the biographer with material as valuable as letters, memoirs, speeches, conversations—when the scientific investigator has found them authentic—or as handwriting. For this reason, the biographer cannot obtain adequate results unless he has a picture of his subject to work from" (6).

Ludwig's mix of the nonscientific, the scientific, and the quasi-scientific also provides a useful opportunity to distinguish constitutional analysis from physiognomy and phrenology. With his focus on facial morphology he hearkens back to the derided phrenology of the previous two centuries, especially in his assumption that external appearance is a gauge of internal worth, which inscribes what Lucy Hartley calls a "moral order" (7) with a special emphasis on what the form of the head can reveal about the mind itself. As Laura Doyle puts it, "phrenology rendered the mental and the emotional—in a word, metaphysical—capacities not only observable but measurable" (60). In such an economy the body is thought to make the mind more legible, to reveal one's place in a hierarchy of minds and morals.

If physiognomy and phrenology theorize the body as merely reflective of, or bearing the signs of, one's innermost character, then constitutional analysis views the body's size and shape as setting up particular propensities and therefore ascribes to bodies a more active role in one's talents, actions, or inclinations. Those propensities can, in turn, be found through a scopic analysis of the body, and so the system depends on copious and fine-grained measurements. According to physical anthropologist Edward E. Hunt Jr., another crucial difference between phrenology and constitutionality is that "phrenology and physiognomy can be regarded as holdovers from an earlier age . . . based on ill-defined single cases rather than statistical correlations in samples of people" ("Old Physical Anthropology" 342). In fact, by most accounts the related inquiries of phrenology and physiognomy count as pseudosciences, whereas Kretschmer's constitutional studies fall under the class of science (Tucker and Lessa 436–37). Constitutional analysis therefore relied on broad swathes of data, though the question of its validity nevertheless remains an open one.

In Ludwig's work constitutionality ekes out the body-as-window approach of phrenology in his discussion of certain figures, such as German leader Otto von Bismarck, whose body sets him up for success, as Ludwig exclaims in his characteristic celebratory style: "How much was Bismarck indebted to his physique, although he hardly ever came to actual tests of fist and muscle! His body and his accomplishments were identical: the will of a giant vibrant with the electric charge of magnetic nerves" (*Genius and Character* 41). Ludwig also describes Vladimir Lenin as an "undersized man with the freckled somewhat fawnlike face." "This physique," he continues, "which gave him his energy and his endurance, and his care-free laughter—this is the second key to his nature, and to his success" (*Genius and Character* 131). Ludwig's zeugmatic style reveals his belief in the link between body and character—it is a link that reaches beyond the body-as-sign to body-as-shaper. His physical descriptions, that is, do much more than establish a visual image for the reader. The bodily descriptions in *Genius and Character* indicate anything from temperament to values to styles of interacting with the world. For Ludwig, in short, bodies constituted biographies.[8] In part, then, Ludwig's "biological" approach approximates that of constitutional medicine, which, according to medical historian Michael Hau, sought to decipher "the psychological constitution of individuals, their character and mental abilities . . . from their physical appearance" (151). Physical constitution was an index of correlations between body and mind, and crucially the approach taken by Kretschmer did not posit a hierarchy among various body shapes (Hau 165).

Ludwig's anecdote-as-evidence approach, in contrast, assumes moral superiority. And yet despite his belief in the moral superiority of his subjects, Ludwig's fame as a constitutional biographer nevertheless both drew on and contributed to the popularity of Kretschmerian analysis.[9]

Kretschmer's Constitutional Types

For a more scientific "rationalization" of Ludwig's approach, and in order to develop "a point of reference" that was "'biologically' grounded" (PC 66), Burke would consult Kretschmer's work directly. Before considering his use of Kretschmer, however, I want to discuss the methodological and conceptual characteristics of Kretschmer's work with particular attention to those that came to matter for Burke—namely its synthetic, multidisciplinary approach to body and mind; its conceptual rearticulations of psychosis and genius; and its emphasis on ways of seeing.

Importantly Kretschmer himself hints that his own work might have been negatively spurred by the likes of Emil Ludwig, or at least the physiognomical and phrenological traditions from which he also drew: "Investigation into the build of the body," Kretschmer contends, "must be made an exact branch of medical science. . . . Belle-lettristic *aperçus* of a physiognomical nature do not help us much forward" (*Physique and Character* 5). He therefore put forth a more exacting set of transdisciplinary methods than Ludwig's merry skip through posies. Like Ludwig, however, Kretschmer sees his methods as necessarily cutting across disciplines, and he contends that his work on the body has immense implications for almost all realms of knowledge: "If we are successful in the application of . . . biological modes of thought to provinces of the psychic life which were hitherto foreign to it, and if on the other hand it is possible for clinicists and biologists to get a broad view over the problems of psychology from a well-grounded point of vantage, so that they can see problems which must hitherto have appeared too subjective, vague, and misty, then along these lines we shall have helped advance toward the firm synthetic articulation of the entire field of modern thought" (262). Here, in the last paragraph of *Physique and Character,* Kretschmer reveals what he imagines to be the end result of his project: a synthetic, transdisciplinary "point of vantage" that would, as he notes earlier in the same paragraph, prove useful for "medical and anthropological purposes, but in particular for general psychology, and for the answering of certain aesthetic, literary, and historical questions" (262). Even if he wanted his work to inform art, literature, and history, he nonetheless adhered to strict scientific methods of constitutional analysis. That is, if the "problem," as Kretschmer puts it, "presses on indefinitely into the depths of biology and psychological science," then the solutions, he believed, lay very much on the surface of the body, and his science thus became a matter of learning to see. Early in *Physique and Character* he details his particular method: "We must plod along the bitter, wearisome road of systematic verbal description and inventory of the whole of the outer body from head to foot; wherever possible, measuring it with calipers and tape-measures, photographing, and drawing. And not only must we do this in a few interesting cases, but we must take hundreds of observations, using every patient we can get hold of, and for each must we make out the same complete scheme. Above all, we must learn again to use our eyes, to see at a glance, and to observe without a microscope or laboratory" (5). Kretschmer, in short, was interested in making all kinds of bodies legible to psychologists.

Such a broad view is evidenced in his insistence that the careful observation and note taking must be applied not just "in a few interesting cases" but on all kinds of bodies, "using every patient we can get hold of." As a result, while Kretschmer's mind-body correlations focus on the extreme or "abnormal"—schizophrenic and manic-depressive "psychic disturbances"—similar correlations were equally apparent in "healthy" individuals in the form of temperaments, all of which, Kretschmer concluded, still exhibited schizophrenic or manic-depressive tendencies, depending on the body type. He sought to bolster his argument about tendencies by finding the correlating tendencies, however latent, in every physical type.

In other words, because Kretschmer found his correlations across such a broad spectrum, his efforts effectively served to normalize clinical psychosis. In *Psychology of Men of Genius* he observes, "Among sound, normal people, the differences of bodily type, express themselves above all in differences of temperament; that is to say, in differences of emotional constitution and mental sensitiveness" (53). Such a focus on "normal" bodies follows from an observation frequently attributed to him, that "whosoever knows neuroses knows his fellow men" (see, for example, Eliasberg 207).

Building on the success of *Physique and Character*, Kretschmer's new broad scheme of physical and mental correlations thus effectively turned psychosis on its head, offering a scientific basis for stripping "deviance" of its negative connotation—or even subtly refuting deviance altogether. In other words, if all people with similar body types had the same tendencies, then there is no deviance per se, just different degrees of manifestation. Kretschmer, it should be noted, disavowed any connection between his constitutional investigations and race. Unlike the physiognomists and phrenologists before him, his aim was not to prove the superiority of any set of people, but instead to elucidate "human differences within populations or cultures" (Hunt "Human" 69). There were politically good reasons to disarticulate constitutional studies from racial considerations, and Kretschmer's desire to avoid racializing his typologies ultimately drove him to resign from his post as president of Germany's General Medical Society when Hitler came to power in 1933.[10]

Bodily Genius

Put most simply, *Physique and Character* replaces questions of deviance and inferiority with notions of body-as-inclination. This scheme carries over into Kretschmer's later book, *Psychology of Men of Genius* (translated into English in 1931). Here Kretschmer brings the constitutional approach detailed in *Physique and Character* to bear on the notion of genius. Unlike Ludwig, Kretschmer offers a quite lucid definition of genius, one that likely appealed to Burke for numerous reasons. In the introduction to *Psychology of Men of Genius,* Kretschmer calls geniuses "those men who are able to arouse permanently, and in the highest degree, that positive, scientifically-grounded feeling of worth and value, in a wide group of human beings" (xviii). According to Kretschmer, then, geniuses must be in touch with the moment—rhetorically.

In this sense Kretschmer explicitly follows Wilhelm Lange-Eichbaum's "sociological conception of genius as a 'bringer of value'" (xiii), and later in the introduction he figures the genius more specifically as "the producer of new and original things" (xix). Kretschmer's is thus a genius that emphasizes rhetorical, social connectivity as well as novelty and creativity. His genius also, importantly, attends to the importance of perspective:

> Scientific research, in so far as it is the work of genius, is to be explained largely according to the psychiatric formula of "overvaluation," or, as one used to say, of the "fixed idea." Men of strong reasoning powers, who are nevertheless possessed of a fixed idea, are characterized so far as they are abnormal, by the term paranoiac. The paranoiac thinker is usually a man of tenacious and deep emotionality who, through some acute experience, is forced into a definite line of thought. He then pursues the line of thought relentlessly and with the greatest consistency, so that his spiritual life becomes more and more tyrannically and one-sidedly controlled by it. With the fixation of such an overvalued idea in the emotional life of the individual there generally enters a systematized delusion, i.e. an increased power of combining impressions, extending to the smallest and most negligible matters of daily life, into a support for the original belief. Ultimately the controlling system of thought develops a whole array of tributary ideas, whilst everything that is of no use to it is shut out of consciousness and overlooked with complete, *passionate blindness*. (138; emphasis added)

"Passionate blindness" more accurately captures the full-on devotion of mind and body that Burke is after with his rearticulation of occupation as inclination. The notion of "passionate blindness" also names a sort of obsessive overfocusing, what Kretschmer calls "autohypnosis, a strained staring at a single point," an intense, protracted *anschauung* (140).

This emphasis on seeing, looking, gazing, known in German as *anschauung* (Hau 151), no doubt held appeal for Burke during the time he was writing *Permanence and Change*. Burke's book, after all, features *anschauung* as the root of *weltanschauung*, worldview or outlook, used interchangeably with the book's central term, *orientation*.[11] Kretschmer's synthetic, visual methods combined with an emphasis on bodily inclination as a way of seeing—or, in the case of "passionate blindness," of not seeing—to produce a dual emphasis on vision. Burke in turn folded Kretschmer's emphases together in order to formulate a new question: how does the morphology of one's body shape what one sees?

Built in to this question of Burke's is a crucial part of Kretschmer's scientific mission: to rearticulate the notion of "abnormal" and by extension to normalize psychosis, another of the key terms in *Permanence and Change*. Indeed, by using Kretschmer's typology to make psychosis into an issue of bodily difference, Burke both evenly distributes psychosis and figures the body as a set of inclinations. This in turn enables him to flatten "genius," a concept that he first encountered with his work on Ludwig and that, perhaps unsurprisingly, finds its way into his discussion of psychosis and the body.

In fact, while Burke rightly attributes his use of the term *psychosis* to Dewey, noting parenthetically in the "Occupational Psychosis" chapter that "it might be well to recall that Professor Dewey does not use the word 'psychosis' in the psychiatric sense; it applies simply to a *pronounced character* of the mind" (PC 40; emphasis in original), Kretschmer also provides a certain kind of psychiatric license to consider psychosis in this more general way, as a matter of emphasis or what Burke elsewhere and more famously calls "a certain way of thinking that went with a certain way of living" (PC 240). What is more, Kretschmer validates Burke's effort to consider the body as a material condition in which and through which such ways of thinking and living are encouraged and enabled, what Burke in the chapter "Style" terms "the eternal correlations between mental attitude and bodily posture" (PC 52).[12] Kretschmer therefore scientifically validates Burke's Dewey-inspired efforts to extract psychosis from the realm of the "abnormal" and reformulate it much more broadly.

In the "Occupation and Preoccupation" chapter of *Permanence and Change*, Burke offers Kretschmer as a kind of holistic (as in more encompassing) counterstatement to psychoanalysis. He begins by describing how Freud and the social anthropologist Bronislaw Malinowski approach the question of social patterns and values in patriarchal versus matriarchal societies. According to Burke, while Freud and Malinowski approach psychoses by beginning with the concept of the family and then moving to the individual, Kretschmer approaches from another direction—the individual body itself. In doing so he is following what Hunt, writing at midcentury, calls "a modern shift in anthropological awareness from the group toward the individual" ("Human" 55). Burke thus summarizes Kretschmer's work as a viable and crucial alternative to psychoanalytic views: "Another direction is revealed in the researches of men like Ernst Kretschmer . . . [who] would note different classifications of mind-body structure. Such differences of structure would amount in the end to differences in occupation, as each man tended toward forms of thought and action in keeping with his type or class" (*PC* 243–44).

After offering Kretschmer's constitutional approach as an alternative voice to psychoanalysis, a voice he believes must be considered, Burke follows the same rhetorical move in the next paragraph, invoking the work of William H. R. Rivers, a biological psychologist who performed experiments on soldiers during World War I. Here Burke cites an observation from Rivers's study of combat veterans that certain disorders correspond with certain ranks—for example, private soldiers experience hysteria more often, while officers experience repression (244). According to Burke, Rivers "ascribes this difference to distinctions in training, as the emphasis upon obedience enhanced the hysteric factor of *suggestibility* in the private soldier whereas the stressing of initiative and authoritativeness in the officers led them to intensify the *repression* of their fears" (244; emphasis in original). Again Kretschmer offers an intriguing—and for Burke a more satisfactory—perspective: "But with Kretschmer," Burke writes, "the *economic correspondences* between status and thought are of a more fundamental sort, as they vary, say, between the 'occupation of being a short and stocky man' and the 'occupation of being a tall, thin one'" (244). The distinction, for Burke, names a more basic one, one that explicitly offers the body as an alternative "ground" or starting point from which to theorize psychosis.

And yet psychosis and disease need not be deemed wholly negative. Bodily occupations, as Kretschmer teaches Burke, function as productive inclinations—what he terms elsewhere in *Permanence and Change* "the productive organic forces of the mind-and-body itself" (63). And if Kretschmer's early book *Physique and Character* offers Burke a theory of the body-as-inclination, his subsequent book, *Psychology of Men of Genius*, helps Burke to focus more specifically on another key concept, often seen as a partner term to psychosis: genius.

If Burke was curious about the category of genius before he began translating Emil Ludwig's *Genius and Character*, he likely found the book frustrating for its refusal to define the term. In spite of the book's lengthy discussions of genius, the concept itself is left in a realm of self-evidence, of the tautological and ineffable "we know it when we see it" variety. Or better, genius is something that might best be discerned by geniuses, as Ludwig suggests when he writes of his own art as a biographer: "When writing of genius one must draw upon resources in himself which are akin to its dominant characteristics" (*Genius and Character* 7). Indeed, the process of elucidating genius, for Ludwig, takes on a mysterious, magical quality: "Whereas he [the biographer] studies character without regard for genius, when he is finished genius has automatically resulted." The biographer thus works "with the intuition of the poet," with which he "penetrates his heroes' motives, tracking down the sources of their passions and their acts" (8). If Ludwig does not offer a definition of genius, he does offer a clear focus on motives and "sources" of "passions," a preoccupation that came to inhabit Burke.

In this way Ludwig's occupation as a close reader of the bodies and lives of so-called geniuses no doubt stayed with Burke, who observes in *Permanence and Change*, "In the case of geniuses, we readily note the preoccupational factor, as a man's exceptional aptitude in one category of action places him permanently in a different situation from that of ordinary men (or, otherwise stated: His special gift provides him with special motives)" (240). At least two points in this passage should be emphasized. First, when Burke applies what he calls in the preceding paragraph "the technique of perspective" to the category of genius, then "genius" becomes a kind of occupation, a situation equipped with different kinds of motives. What is important for Burke, contra Ludwig, is not genius's rarity, but the way its gift becomes motives. By emphasizing the motive side of genius, Burke makes room for a version of genius not rarified or magical at all, but simply differently inclined. Kretschmer effectively helps him to blur the distinction between deviance and genius, and in doing so to redistribute and redefine the two categories as propensities.

Burke's example of genius follows a paragraph packed with examples of how a focus on occupation helps account for motives and incapacities: a doctor steeped in the study of medicine is incapable of seeing life any other way; the current obsession with machinery (the obsession that perhaps confounds Burke the most) renders a nonmechanistic view untenable. And his third example is confined to a bodily condition: "Upon accidentally burning oneself," Burke writes, "one will be for the time occupied with this situation alone. One may even adopt measures of expression so exclusively attuned to this single situation that he will greatly outrage persons who, though present, are living in a totally different situation" (240). This sort of trauma—instantaneous or formed through more sustained physical experiences—becomes a special concern of Burke's, a way to bring occupation back to the body, trauma, and the intensive, relentless, zoomed-in focus that can result from certain conditions. Indeed occupation becomes yet another way to consider what in earlier and later books Burke calls efficiency. Yet the emphasis here is on the myriad—sometimes pedestrian, sometimes accidental, and often relentlessly physical—ways such preoccupations take hold.

The concluding example in Burke's discussion of genius/motive/preoccupation hits all these points quite nicely, moving as he does to what would become one of his favorite illustrations: "An encounter with a dog may leave a lasting impression upon one mind, while it contributes only a minor meaning to another; which is to say that one man was more gifted for being affected by the dog and the other was more gifted for not being affected" (240). Burke here translates a most mundane daily encounter—meeting a pooch on the sidewalk—as an action that simultaneously draws on and reinforces one's particular "gifts" or inclinations. Burke is not talking about a virtuoso sonata or a paradigm-shattering theorem—the stuff of genius in Ludwig's sense—but in a paragraph that begins with the topic of genius, through a series of moves that keep in place only the language of capacity, he is soon considering genius next to a sniffing canine. Another interesting feature of this example is how an encounter with a dog frequently occurs in the domain of affect—whether one fears or welcomes such an encounter, an encounter with a dog is more often than not extrarational and dominated by a frequently uncontrollable bodily response, a response that emerges out of a bodily meaning-making process.[13] Here we see Burke emphasizing the role of bodies and affect in shaping perspective, which turns out to be one of his major preoccupations, a preoccupation animated by his work on scientists such as Kretschmer.

Rhetorical Genius and "Hypochondriasis"

Kretschmer's *Psychology of Men of Genius* provides the validation Burke needs to assemble the examples discussed above under the heading of occupation and "gifts," always, especially, with an eye to the body. In this way Kretschmer's book offers another, more general, sense of genius, one formulated by Thomas Carlyle but attributed by Kretschmer to a nameless "famous writer": "'Genius,'" Kretschmer quotes, "'is the capacity for taking pains'" (136). Turning to the question of "the part which 'disease' sometimes plays in shaping occupational or preoccupational patterns," Burke writes: "In his *Psychology of Men of Genius* Kretschmer notes important correlations between the nature of a man's disorders and the nature of his attainments. Reversing the emphasis of Max Nordau's famous blast on *Degeneracy*, in which Nordau discredited the products of geniuses by showing their relationship to disease, Kretschmer tends rather to show the ways in which geniuses converted their liabilities into assets" (244). Here Burke considers an oft-repeated claim that genius of the rarified kind stems from illness, thereby assisting his efforts to bring deviance and genius closer together by focusing on capacities and inclinations. What is more, he uses the discussion to move into questions of art and society, the questions Kretschmer hoped his work could yield and moreover, the ones that got Burke interested in the body in the first place.[14]

In his discussion of Kretschmer Burke also reintroduces the term *hypochondriasis* as something of a synonym for *occupation*. That substituting move happens between the following two sentences: "Particularly in eras of great uncertainty, we might expect disease to appear significantly as an occupation—for though one be in doubt about all else, he finds an unquestioned authority in the reality of his own discomfitures. We might say that hypochondriasis is merely the restricted manifestation of the tragic mechanism, the man's physical and mental burden being in itself the monastery walls that hold him to his vow" (244–45).

Burke borrows *hypochondriasis* from the psychologist W. H. R. Rivers, who was made famous by his book *Instinct and Unconscious* and his application of psychoanalytic treatment to World War I soldiers. Earlier in *Permanence and Change* Burke uses the term as a term of "adjustment" to one's conditions, as he notes how "patients may reconcile themselves to their disease by becoming engrossed in its symptoms" (144). Such engrossments fall in step with Burke's mystical method as well as his devotion to inefficiency.

Hypochondriasis, it should be noted, is driven by symptoms, and as an example Burke describes Mann's recognition of the "hypochondriac incentive in his art" as a sort of forming form, with "the symptoms . . . providing him, by the very nature of the case, with an authoritative form into which the fluids of experience are poured" (245). Still, while the figure of the hypochondriac has generally come to signify something like self absorption, for Burke such absorption is by no means confined to one's individual symptoms, but rather such "symptoms" are necessarily translated into something larger than the individual per se: "Such an incentive," Burke continues," will transcend its beginnings in that the thinker attempts to socialize his position, and in doing so must include areas of symbolization not at all local to himself" (245). Hypochondriasis of the body therefore models the kind of intensive interest one might cultivate in response to particularly perplexing social and/or political situations.[15]

Burke later elaborates the productive aspect of rhetorical constraints, drawing once again, if tacitly, on Kretschmer's social notion of genius: "Whatever the source of a writer's preoccupations, he can communicate only by manipulating the symbols common to his group; hence there is much justice underlying the new schools of 'health,' at any rate if we mean by individual health a conformity with the psychosis of one's group" (245). Here Burke seems to suggest the impossibility of radical novelty, given that novelty must be presented in a recognizable form—in other words, novelty must be legible before all else. This rhetorical/social point does not, however, for Burke, only come after individual creativity. In fact he seems to settle on a kind of feedback loop—so that the preoccupation is formed by social conditions. In the hypochondriasis passage discussed above, Burke calls a disease an "occupation" and notes the "authority" one finds "in the reality of his own discomfitures" (244). So the disease—and the focus on and through the disease—has its etiology in larger social forces. Yet, drawing on Kretschmer and pursuing his own notion of hypochondriasis, Burke continues, "illness is both painful and creative" (245), and toward the end of the chapter he concludes that "the particular value of disease in insight, however, may arise precisely from the fact that the diseased man's burden sharpens him to some corresponding issue involving society at large" (245). Here Burke reaches for an even broader synthesis than Kretschmer's body-mind focus allows at first glance. Yet Kretschmer too offers a rhetorical notion of genius, one that acknowledges how inclinations and capacities, while inarguably productive on their own terms in his scheme, must connect in some way to larger values. As Kretschmer himself puts it in a succinct paragraph toward the end of *Psychology of Men of Genius*, "there are successful and unsuccessful inventors. The unsuccessful ones are called paranoiacs" (245). Similarly the insomniac, the schizophrenic, the drug fiend, and other figures of "abnormality" that populate *Permanence and Change*, instead of being "unfit," may instead be, as Burke puts it in his introductory chapter, "unfitt*ed* by being fit in an unfit fitness" (10; emphasis added). In other words, these figures do not fit because of unacceptably rigid ("unfit") standards of fitness. This clever play on words best illustrates Burke's attempt to swap meanings: prevailing notions of fitness are often themselves unfit.

So in Kretschmer Burke finds an intellectual model, one who offers an important countervoice to psychoanalysis by effectively "normalizing" abnormality and who, above all, makes the body his foremost preoccupation. In one or two extra steps Burke is able to extract from Kretschmer productive twin notions of genius and illness, and as such he refuses a reductive reading of the body as inhibitor to thought or carrier of disease—or as a site of visible deviance— and figures the body instead as productive capacity, a set of inclinations, thus generating the phrase "the genius of the body" (229). Burke also learns, through studying and following Kretschmer, how such bodily genius can—and must—be seen.

6

Body Language | *Paget and Gesture-Speech Theory*

So far, this book has considered when and why Burke first turned to bodies, how he culled a critical method from somatic mysticisms, and how his research into drugs, endocrinology, and constitutional morphology helped him to theorize further habits, communication, and meaning making—what humans see and say. By now it should be clear that Burke's transdisciplinary quest to theorize language and rhetoric consistently led him to bodily matters and back again, to language's edges. This account has so far focused mostly on Burke's work in the 1920s and 1930s, the decades of his first three books (*Counter-Statement, Permanence and Change,* and *Attitudes toward History*). Thanks in large part to the work of Jack Selzer and Ann George, those decades—and those books—are receiving due attention after a long stretch in favor of the 1940s and 1950s, during which time Burke published *Philosophy of Literary Form* and the now-canonical Motives books (1945 and 1950), which introduced the widely known concepts of identification, the pentad, dramatism, and symbolic action. It is tempting, then, simply to end my account here, thereby tacitly arguing for a new group of core texts. And yet to do so might suggest that Burke somehow got past his body hang-ups; that a concern for bodies was for him a means to an end, with the end being his most language-oriented concepts.

As this chapter and the next will show, though, such an account would be flat wrong: bodies figure quite centrally in the development of the later, better-known Burkean concepts, dramatism and symbolic action in particular. Burke did not "get over" bodies, but it was not for lack of trying. Try as he might, he could never shake the point that language always involves the body: writing and reading are physical acts, and most compellingly for Burke, the spoken word both depends on and channels physical effort and energy. This most apparent connection between bodies and language—that words need physical movements for their utterance—is probed most provocatively by evolutionary theorists, particularly one persistent theory that language itself began as physical gesture, the communicative efforts of the limbs, torsos, hands, and head.[1]

Unlike the theories offered by the "new sciences" of endocrinology and constitutional medicine, the gesture theory of language's origins dates back to the

Epicurean poet Lucretius, whose belief that gestures helped give early human sounds something like meaning (Kennedy 36) has had wavelike periods of resurgence thanks to proponents such as the eighteenth-century philosopher Etienne Condillac. Its best-known advocate is Charles Darwin.[2]

Burke's attention was grabbed by a less famous—though perhaps more thorough—advocate of the view that speech originated as bodily gesture: Sir Richard Paget, a full-time physicist and part-time philologist and fellow of both the Physical Society of London and the Institute of Physics. Paget later became known in speech and speech pathology circles for his role in developing the Paget-Gorman system of signed English, but in the 1930s it appeared that his signature contribution to the field would be his unique formulation of gesture-speech theory. He set out to prove gesture-speech theory with a clever mix of physical science and evolutionary theory. His 1930 book, *Human Speech*, not only asserts that language was formed by gesture; it also details a variety of methods drawn from his training in physics, phonetics, philology, linguistics, and acoustics (A. T. W. 364), as well as his study of Darwin, to assert why and, more intriguingly, how.

The book includes photos and long descriptions of his simulated vocal cavities complete with a larynx, tongue, and lips fashioned out of plasticine, paraffin, and a rubber band. These simulated cavities were meant to display the variety of "postures" performed during speech.[3] Such postures, formed through minute and articulated movements—gestures—of the human mouth and its connected parts, Paget surmised, are pantomimic outgrowths of bodily postures and gestures originally performed solely by the limbs, torso, and hands.

Human Speech sits on the shelf in the core of Burke's home office between Marx's *Capital* and the Modern Library's *Philosophy of Nietzsche*.[4] Burke folded Paget's theories into his own rhetorical theories at such an early point that they are both formative and forgotten, even, in one notable instance, snipped out between editions. Examined closely, Burke's use of Paget reveals an emphasis on the body's role in communicative practices heretofore missing from the discussion: spoken language as a physical act. The body, that is, both models and performs the physical movements to produce speech, and in doing so almost literally breathes life into words. Somatic theories such as Paget's, then, tend to yield rhetorical theories that focus on energy, vitality, and liveliness as rhetorical elements that cannot be fully accounted for by theories grounded primarily in cognition, reason, or epistemics.[5]

Given that Burke repeatedly uses Paget's gesture-speech theory as a suggestive, protracted thought experiment, overlooking this important historical connection leaves in most critics' hands rather deflated, decidedly *un*lively notions of Burke's most important conceptual legacies. The pentad (act, scene, agent, agency, purpose), Burke's dramatistic tool par excellence, so frequently tends to produce two-dimensional, flat analyses when it could, if historically reconnected with Burke's use of Paget's bodily theories, become much more lively.[6] In order to reconnect the twin Burkean legacies of dramatism and symbolic action with Paget and therefore with the body, I propose to examine in succession the moments when Burke engages Paget in his writings. Doing so chronologically, in the order that Burke wrote and revised (though not necessarily published), and filling in details from Paget's theories, will help give a full account of Paget's varied role in Burke's rhetorical theories and offer an alternative, somatic genealogy of Burkean dramatism, symbolic action, identification, and attitude. With Burke's help, then, I hope to offer a new and jarringly different way to think about bodies and rhetoric together, along with a historian's cautionary tale about how bodily theories of rhetoric, when used in strict service of reason, persuasion, and argument, can all too easily become bodiless.

This somatic genealogy pinpoints the first edition of *A Grammar of Motives* as the Burkean text that, in a departure from Paget's theories, produces an overemphasis on language and the mind that Burke later tried to amend. And because *A Grammar of Motives* remains the most consulted Burkean text, particularly in regard to dramatism, scholars such as Daniel O'Keefe are led to conceive of dramatism as a "distinctly non-physicalist framework" (8), and Dana Anderson and Sarah E. Mahen-Hays and Roger C. Aden locate Burkean attitude wholly in the mind or on the level of consciousness. In focusing solely on Burke's *Grammar of Motives*, these scholars therefore reproduce notions of dramatistic action that are too easily separable from the body.[7]

Attention to Burke's Pagetian side will show instead that attitude both stems from and manifests in generative, connective, bodily movement. Attitude forms one of Burke's most pointed amendments to *A Grammar of Motives* and to the dramatistic pentad. I consider this attitudinal revision in more detail toward the end of this chapter, to show how Burke's addition of attitude brings with it the crucial mind-body correspondences that his theories honored all along. Through this somatic genealogy of dramatism's core terms, I argue more broadly for the importance of keeping rhetoric, rhetorical theory, and rhetorical pedagogy more closely tied to bodies that generate, induce, and respond to rhetoric.[8] Before moving into Burke's writings, however, it is important to situate Paget's theory and its own allegiances more carefully.

Tongue-Tied: A Darwinian Origin of Speeches

Glossogenetic theories, or theories about language's origins, matter less to rhetorical studies for their loyalty to origins than for the assumptions they present about language's functions and rhetorical processes. Here Jacques Derrida's point about the "purely additive, mythical" force of origin theories is well taken (167), and so my purpose in examining Paget's glossogenetic theory and Burke's subsequent use of it is to identify their respective beliefs about language and rhetoric, and in particular to consider the implications of their account for figuring language as simultaneously a communicative and sensuous act. Glossogenetic theories, that is, mythical as they are, help to sort through the entanglements of biological, rhetorical, and linguistic apparatuses.[9]

In a recent treatment of glossogenetics, historian of rhetoric George Kennedy attributes humans' unique capacity for language to their ability to produce a variety of sounds "by manipulation of the lips, teeth, and tongue, and much greater control of the vocal cords" (29)—that is, to their facial and laryngeal morphology more than any "great chain" notion of "higher reason." Such a view, which unfolds as thoroughly Darwinian, leads Kennedy into a theoretical discussion of rhetorical situations and a highly speculative account of humanoid rhetoric (39–41). It also leads him, a committed Aristotelian, to a surprisingly naturalist view of rhetoric, and yet one that also centers on emotion and energy (3–4).[10] Paget, equipped with his training as both a physicist and philologist, takes his account far further than Kennedy, and yet both Kennedy and Paget stand in sharp contradiction to more widely accepted neo-Cartesian theories of language that assume its beginnings lie in humans' unique ability to think and reason.[11]

Because it begins with the body rather than the mind, with emotive force rather than reasoning ability, and with animals rather than humans, Paget's theory of gesture-speech also offers a way to trouble structural linguistics from a direction other than the poststructuralist critique of social structures, offering instead material, mutable, bodily structures. Whereas Saussure argues that the signifier—a word—arbitrarily invokes a signified, an image of meaning, Paget holds that the word is frequently not arbitrary at all but gestural, and it in turn evokes a gestural signified—that is, an image or sense of the gesture (rather than a concept or idea). Burke, building on Paget, offers neither a thoroughly structural nor even poststructural theory of language as most scholars have heretofore contended, but an accretive theory of language whereby the gestural force decreases by degrees as abstractions are built up. In the Burkean scheme, the building up of abstractions happens in reciprocal relation with biological processes and development, thereby producing a theory of symbolic action inseparable from—and indeed dependent on—the body's capacity for mimetic variation and migration, which results in what Burke formulates as bodies' "emergence into articulacy" (*Language as Symbolic Action* 67).[12]

Significantly Paget attributes his first flash of insight on mimetic articulation to his reading of Charles Darwin's observation in *Expression of the Emotion in Man and Animals* "that persons cutting with a pair of scissors often moved their jaws sympathetically, and that children learning to write often twisted their tongues as their fingers moved" ("Origin of Human Speech"; *Human Speech* 133; see also Darwin, *Expression* 40). Darwin raises these instances in his discussion of what he calls serviceable associated habits, whereby certain modes of expression such as lip biting or head scratching began as accompaniments to other more central actions or states of mind (nervousness, thoughtfulness) and are considered by Darwin to be vestiges of habit. And yet the mouth-focused instances cited by Paget—the "scissoring" of the mouth or the "writing" of the tongue—inhabit a murky area for Darwin, who introduces these examples with his own qualified verbal head scratching: "There are other actions which are commonly performed under certain circumstances, independently of habit, and which seem to be due to imitation or some sort of sympathy" (40). Darwin even broadens the mimetic, responsive sympathy to more collective scenarios, such as when audience members begin to clear their own throats when the singer they are observing sounds hoarse (40) or when his American physician friend while assisting childbirth "finds himself imitating the muscular efforts of the patient" (41n). While Darwin calls these associated habits "complex actions," the principle is itself rather simple: "When our minds are much affected, so are the movements of our bodies" (37).

Whether the body responds to actions going on elsewhere in the same body, as is the case with the tongue-twisting writing child, or in someone else's body, as with the grimacing doctor, the point here is that these sympathetic, mimetic movements operate on a logic of contagion, that physical actions have the capacity to affect other parts of the body, as well as others' body parts. It is this dual capacity for movement that Paget believes enables language's development: the migration of movements from one part of the body to the other, combined with his mechanical models that more or less reproduce laryngeal postures, helped him imagine gesture being converted into laryngeal and tongue movements, and the ability for those movements to "catch on" across bodies helped him account for the spread and resulting "staying power" of language, what Saussure calls its stability (72). Put still more simply, speech gestures are communicative because they are both communicable and communal.[13]

The result of the mouth's unconscious tendencies to mimic the emotional, postural state of the rest of the body, as well as its gesticulations, Paget concludes, is human speech. As he puts it in *Human Speech*, "human speech arose out of a generalized unconscious pantomimic gesture language—made by the limbs and features as a whole (including the tongue and the lips)—which became specialized in gestures of the organs of articulation, owing to the human hands (and eyes) becoming continuously occupied with the use of tools" (174). "The gestures of the organs of articulation," he adds, "were recognized by the hearer because the hearer unconsciously reproduced in his mind the actual gesture which had produced the sound" (174). Paget even uses a curious dramatic analogy when in *Human Speech* he casts the tongue, lips, and jaw as "understudies" of the hands: "The consequence was that when, owing to pressure of other business, the principal actors (the hands) retired from the stage—as much as principal actors ever do—their understudies—the tongue, lips and jaw—were already proficient in the pantomimic art" (133). Enter a new set of stage stars.

Paget's theory is itself remarkable for a variety of reasons, not the least of which is that it sets up a physical sort of philology, whereby words result from the mouth's physically performing their originary gestures and in doing so, according to Paget, preserve the vestigial gesture as meaning. Words, for example, that contain the consonant blend *sp*, "commonly mean something that comes to a fine point or edge or jet—as in *sper, spire, spout, spit, spue*" (*This English* 2), and those that begin with *str* "mean something that extends longitudinally—as in *stream, string, strap, stretch, strain, stroke, street*" (2).[14] The explanation, that is, is not about a root "meaning," as in traditional philology, but rather about a root motion—in order to form *sp* the lips form a *sp*ewing motion, and the formation of *str* entails a kind of elongation of the mouth. Paget's physio-philological theory, in short, figures speech as a bodily, mimetic, even affective art, thereby imagining bodily feeling, gesture, and posture as unconsciously contagious and iterable movements, spreading from body part to body part, almost literally from hand to mouth.

In the 1930s and 1940s Paget's theory was considered by some to be the new replacement for origin theories already in circulation. In a 1943 issue of *Science* animal intelligence specialist E. L. Thorndike surveyed the various by then "dishonored" glossogenetic theories. First there was the "ding-dong" theory, wherein certain things mysteriously elicited certain arbitrary human noises that thus came to serve as names. The second theory is the well-known "bow-wow" theory, wherein "men formed the habits of using the sounds made by animals" (1), and then there was the even more opprobriously named "pooh pooh theory," which posits a set of instinctual interjections. Thorndike then comes to Paget's theory, which he calls "ingenious" and christens, appropriately and, I might add, eloquently, the "'tongue-tied' theory, meaning that the tongue is yoked with the body by subtle bonds of mimetic kinship" (3).

Before moving to Burke, I want finally to tie together Paget and Darwin, because there is a discernible Darwinian logic driving Paget's research premise and his methods. While Darwin did not himself detail a theory of language's origins in *Expressions*, an inkling of such a theory can be found in *Descent of Man*, where he writes, "I cannot doubt that language owes its origin to the imitation and modification of various natural sounds, the voices of other animals, and man's own instinctive cries, aided by signs and gestures" (87). Not foreclosing the possibility of gesture-speech theory, Darwin also articulates some of Paget's key premises in *Expression* when he speculates that "laughter, as a sign of pleasure or enjoyment, was practised by our progenitors long before they deserved to be called human; for very many kinds of monkeys, when pleased, utter a reiterated sound, clearly analogous to our laughter" (356).[15] Such bodily sonic reiterations also, importantly, mark a creature's vitality. A mere three pages later, when discussing the physiology of rage, disgust, and blushing, Darwin explicitly states that such expressive movements "give vividness and energy to our spoken words" (359), an assertion that Paget—and by extension, Burke—would take very seriously. The Darwinian origins of Paget's theories and methods help account for three crucial features of Paget's—and Burke's—theories of language: (1) the strong emphasis on language's rendering of bodily attitude, its energy and vitality; (2) the dual emphasis on the communicable (that is, contagious) and communal features of bodily language; and (3) the menagerie of animals both Paget and Burke use to argue their points.

Paget's Fox Terrier: Animal Attitudes

Darwin's imprint is perhaps most evident in the way Paget and Burke deploy examples from the animal world to support their arguments about language and gesture. Paget locates in animal communication instances of gesture as symbolic action, and he develops what will become key Burkean notions of *purpose* and *attitude* by extensive reference to the world of animals.[16] The section of *Human Speech* concerning glossogenetics begins with a section on animal gestures.[17] Here Paget leaves unstated his phylogenetic assumption that places species life on a developmental continuum. Instead, he simply begins, "We need not be surprised at this idea, for it is clear, when the evidence is studied, that gesture is a common method, in use throughout the animal world, for inducing action on the part of another individual" (126). Paget then goes on to cite his conversations with animal biologist and evolutionary theorist Julian Huxley, which yielded "some interesting examples of animal gestures" (126). What follows in Paget's chapter is a brief catalog of gestures ranging from courting Empis flies (126) to dancing bees (127).

In his discussion of insects, Paget is quick to set aside issues of intentionality even as he preserves a symbolic reading of these gestures: "In these cases," he writes, "it need not be assumed that the gestures are intentionally symbolic, or indeed that they are intentional at all" (127). He then goes on to recount an instance of an African gray parrot belonging to Lord and Lady Grey of Fallodon who had "evolved a gesture which meant 'I want to be let out'" (127–28). Apparently when it wanted out, the parrot "held on to the bars of its cage with its beak and left foot, and pawed the air repeatedly, at about 100 beats per minute, with its other foot" (128). In Paget's view the parrot's movements fall in the category of "truly symbolic gestures" (127). Such willful gestures show the animal body exhibiting what Paget calls purpose, much like the purpose he observes in his own dog, Joseph, a fox terrier who "was especially devoted" to Paget's cook, Mrs. Wright. He continues: "When Joseph wanted to be taken out for a walk, or thought it was time to be taken up to bed, he pulled Mrs. Wright by her skirt in the direction required" (128). Paget even includes a photomontage that illustrates a Joseph-guided trek to the stable yard. Such activity, he believes, is symbolic and purposive and, even more important for his theory, shows the dog's mouth joining in with bodily cues—Joseph's urging body is accompanied by (or in Darwinian terms, associated with) a gripping, tugging mouth.

Because dogs provide a host of bodily cues along with vocal movements, they allow Paget to theorize further the relationship between gesture and sound: "The bark or yap or growl signifies the emotional state, but purpose is expressed by action and expression" (128). This division of expressive or communicative labor whereby sounds convey feeling but the body performs purpose lays the groundwork for Paget's theory, in which the laryngeal area becomes the place on the human body where both functions converge—that is, through the bodily action or gesture of the lips and mouth and the emotive intonations of the voice. The resulting movements—words—combine and recapitulate the body's emotive energy and purposive action. Paget goes on to theorize that the art of gestures must have had a "sister art," which he believes is "based on the use of the larynx." He continues, "The power of expressing the emotions by laryngeal tones is (as we have noted) almost universal among the higher animals, and it may be imagined that, in early stages of human development, mankind roared and grunted and sung [sic], on the one hand, to express his emotions, and gesticulated and grimaced on the other to explain his ideas. In some cases he may have used both methods together, as when a dog makes the threatening gesture of showing his teeth and energizes or phonates this gesture by the addition of the laryngeal growl" (132). Paget's laryngeal theories are thoroughly documented at the book's outset and thereby form the bases for his theory of gesture-speech. His plasticine resonators—model larynxes—were carefully crafted to produce particular vowel sounds physically and repeatedly. The variation in size and shape alone suggests that different sounds depend on different positions, and Paget also re-created various chest resonances, which together with the laryngeal formation produce tone and volume. These resonating organs are all assisted by the tongue, which Paget describes as "a muscular organ, constant in volume, but highly and very rapidly variable in form. It can take a great variety of different positions inside the mouth, so as either to alter the shape of the cavity as a whole or close it altogether in different positions" (36). Paget's models are crucial for visualizing the astonishing variety of laryngeal movements, postures, and gestures that form the basis of his gesture-speech theory.

Paget's mechanical experiments with resonance, along with his observations of animal gestures, allow him to account for energy and emotion in language, and it is this lively account of communication as energy, as movement, and as bodily attitude that first attracted Burke to Paget. Paget's mechanical and animal models helped Burke to think about mimetics and to confirm his suspicion that attitude and purpose—two features that would form important components of the pentad—are crucial components of communication.

Auscultating Paget

The earliest appearance of Paget in Burke's writings occurs shortly after the publication of *Human Speech* in Burke's long-unpublished "Auscultation, Creation, and Revision."[18] According to Burke's "introductory note" to "Auscultation," the piece details his interest in "local literary processes as they may be related to broader biologic or historic processes" (61). His rather cumbersomely subtitled section "The Present State of Language and Ideology (the Chief Productive Force of Writers) as It Affects the Problems Peculiar to Writers" documents a twofold concern about the "present state" of language on an evolutionary continuum: (1) the move to a "terminology"-based language, which Burke calls "a very obvious process of conceptual naming" and which derives from a shift to a specialized, individualized, conceptual, even abstract way of thinking (126); and (2) a concomitant move away from language's attitudinal and collective forces. As a reminder of language's more attitude-based and collective beginnings, Burke offers Paget: "According to the mimetic theory of Sir Richard Paget (a theory which he offers in place of the old 'bow wow' school, which held that speech arose out of onomatopoetic naming), language arose as 'gesture speech,' not a way of naming, but a way of expressing attitudes. At first these attitudes were probably expressed by the set of the entire body, as a terrier's back bristles when he expresses the attitude of rage, or his tail wags and his body relaxes to express an attitude which we, without tails, convey by saying 'I like you'" (124). With this introduction of Paget, and with an oblique but altered reference perhaps to Paget's terrier Joseph,[19] Burke hits on what most interests him about Paget's theory: it takes seriously the body's role in communication. Of course there is a problem with this particular passage in that it makes tailless, wordy humans sound somewhat robotic by comparison to the animated, tail-wagging terrier. Burke redresses this problem at once: "even now we do not wholly convey our meanings in this way. If a man said 'I like you' in thunderous accents, frowning and clenching his fists, we should have the most uneasy doubts as to his real attitude. A good actor still expresses his attitudes by the set of the entire body; a fairly expressive person uses facial gestures to a large extent; and those who would draw one card when they have four aces can conceal their glee only by the rigid donning of a mask, the 'poker face,' that says nothing because it changes not" (124). Here, by moving from a hypothetical example to the scenes of drama itself and then to poker, Burke meditates on the body's purposive communicative action. The repetition, from the terrier passage above, of the phrase "the set of the entire body" indicates the analogical function of animals and also places disposition foremost on

Burke's list of the body's signifying capacities. The use—or restriction, in the case of poker—of "facial gesture" also betrays, according to Burke à la Paget, meaning, or better, sense. The body can reveal or conceal attitude. Here is Burke's summary of Paget: "Sir Paget suggests that by greater and greater economy, this gesture speech which generally began with the whole body was localized in the facial muscles, and thence even many of the facial gestures could be dropped as the conveying of attitudes became generally confined to the throat and the sounds issuing from it (the 'tone of voice' probably conveying different meanings, before this in turn was made more precise by sounds being schematized into words)" (124–25). This last parenthetical reference to "tone of voice" condenses Paget's theory of laryngeal sound, in which the division of communicative labor gets made more completely. Paget, again working with canine gestures, observes that "the bark or yap or growl signifies the emotional state, but purpose is expressed by action and expression." In Paget's and Burke's schemes, words as human analogs of barks or yaps become reinfused with emotive force, while bodily disposition and movement exhibit purpose. And yet if gestures and sounds come together in the larynx, as Paget contends, then human speech is doubly infused with emotion and purpose, and together these movements form a palimpsest with the broader "scene" of bodily movements. Bodily movements, that is, do not recede into the background but work in tandem with wordy movements. Recall that in Burke's first mention of Paget he renders the energy and emotion Paget locates in a dog's body and in the human larynx with a single word, *attitude*.

Attitudes I: Gagging on Cs

Burke's focus on Paget and attitude in "Auscultation, Creation, and Revision" carries over into the first edition of *Attitudes toward History* (1937), which contains a hefty thirty-page exploration of what Paget's theories might mean for a critical theory of language. This discussion can be found in Burke's "Dictionary of Pivotal Terms" under the heading "Cues," where, it should be noted, Burke pushes Paget to wild extremes. At stake in this lengthy entry, which may be read as a microcosm of the book as a whole, is the material basis of attitudes that form and inform what Burke would later call "symbolic action." For Burke "pivotal verbalizations," or words and phrases favored by particular writers, may offer material—indeed, physical—cues to a writer's "emotional overtones" (84). Recall that for Paget the dog's growl emotes, and in his evolutionary scheme the emotive function combines with bodily purpose when transferred into the dual shape and sound of words. According to Burke, treating "words as postures" (*ATH* 1e 92)—what he variously calls "tonal opportunism" (1e 92) and "the mimetic function" (1e 92)—should even "be traceable more often in the verbal saliencies of poetry" (1e 92). And yet the Pagetian implications should not, according to Burke, stop with verse: "But we are suggesting that the 'key' words of even a conceptual writer, the words *singled out* for extra duty because of a writer's unanalyzable preferences, could legitimately be examined with mimetic criteria in mind. For the repetition of a concept, its constant recurrence, does function in emphasis like a poet's alliterations, and hence would bear examination for its role as 'choreography'" (1e 92; emphasis in original). Burke of course is one such conceptual choreographer, so he tries out the method on himself, setting out to find some "cue" "as to why, with a whole world of sounds to choose from, we selected 'comic frame'" (1e 83). What he "came upon" in this analysis, which focuses on *Counter-Statement*'s Mann and Gide essay, is a peculiar bodily response induced by speech gestures: "And as we finished the essay, in the period of nausea that usually follows the completion we complained that the essay had 'gagged' us. And we cited its key terms: 'correspondence,' 'conformity,' cult of conflict,' 'conscientiousness,' and *c*orruption'" (1e 83).

While at the time, Burke contends, he "thought no more about it" (83), he nevertheless began to notice, through this Paget-inspired analysis of his own work, that the gagging "episode" suggested "emotional overtones that might be lurking behind our preference for the word 'comic'" (84). He continues, "And we were surprised to note how many words we have since selected as our coordinates similarly begin with the sound of a hard 'c.' To list at random some of them from the present work and 'Permanence and Change': coordinates, key concepts, cooperation, conversion, Catholicism, Calvinism, capitalism, conversion, cues, clusters, and criticism" (84). Burke goes on to identify three psycho-physical associations with the letter *c*. First, apparently a teacher of Burke's in Pittsburgh urged her students to pronounce the hard *c* "as though you had a fishbone caught in the throat and were trying to cough it up," a physical formation that Burke calls "a variant of 'gagging'" (84). His analysis radiates into his adolescent throat ailment, which led to an "obsessive fear that we might choke" (84) as well as a "decidedly 'formative' attack of whooping cough, strong in the experience of choking" (84–85).

Second, Burke notes Paget's discussion of "words as physical acts," and in particular his treatment of the hard *c* sound. He quotes Paget: "The grip of the back of the tongue against the soft palate which produces a *k*, *g*, or *ng* is either associated with such action as swallowing, or it refers to a grip at the back" (85). Significantly this observation leads Burke to write, for the first time, about an identification: "During adolescence, our closest friend and sparring partner was Malcolm Cowley. We were, in the wise popular usage, 'identified' with him. Also, our own given name begins with the sound of a hard 'c'" (1e 86). That Burke's engagements with Paget's work produce a somatic notion of identification becomes even clearer when he begins "tying it all together":

> A man writes his name, he says his number. Your correspondent's name and number begins with "c." In trying to appropriate the forensic material, he

continues to pronounce his name. He says "you" and "it," but he is secretly saying "I." He can do no other. He "identifies" himself with as much of the corporate, public material (in the contemporary, in history, in philosophy) as he can encompass. Yet, if we are correct in feeling that illnesses and our fears are also lurking, along with personal identities, behind the "quality" of this consonant for us, might not such a sense of choking or gagging (inherent in the mimetic act of pronouncing these "key" words in hard "c") contain therefore as overtones a preoccupation with death? (1e 85–86)

Here what Burke liked to call the "correspondences" between mind and body become apparent, and a focus on the physical gestures of language forms a crucial early component of Burkean identification. Identification, so frequently figured by scholars as a sheerly social formation, first presented itself to Burke as an alliance formed between sounds made through similar laryngeal postures, or through physical mimesis.[20] At least in its early formation, Burkean identification is as much postural and somatic as it is social and psychological. By the end of the "Cues" entry, Burke has settled on language with strong Pagetian overtones: "Words are rich in 'linguistic action' only insofar as there is a 'dance' implicit in their 'naming.'" (110). This "linguistic dance," reminiscent of Paget's dancing bee, helps Burke render the way that "words, used with engrossment, are 'attitude'" and, importantly, how such attitude is conveyed through rhythms and movements that are thoroughly physical.

It is important to note here that this "linguistic dance," especially in Paget's scheme, is not just a metaphor, but as he makes clear in *This English*, it serves to explain the connection between bodily and linguistic rhythm, a connection Burke had been working on since at least *Counter-Statement*.[21] Paget explains the dance in this way: "When language is realized as a system of descriptive mouth gesture, we shall be better able to understand the relationship between the purpose of rhyme and rhythm in poetry, and that of gesture and rhythm, or harmony and rhythm, in the sister arts of dancing and music. When we make a rhyme, we have momentarily brought our organs of articulation into the same posture as before; when we so time these repetitions of posture that they occur rhythmically, so that our gestures of articulation (as a whole) form a pattern in Time, we have performed a dance with our tongue and lips" (101–2). Such an explanation helps situate Paget's notion of verbal choreography, again marking a kind of literalness: speech is not like a rhythmic dance but performs one.

The Pagetian-inflected theory of linguistic dance developed in the "Cues" entry carries over into the conclusion of *Attitudes toward History* and leads Burke to figure verbalizations, or naming, as acts themselves.[22] "Such acts," he writes, "on the rudimentary biological or mimetic level, occur when the poet feeling, let us say, agitation gives us agitated sound and rhythm; or feeling calmness, he slips into liquid tonalities" (249). Here Burke returns to the idea of "verbal choreography," which he claims forms "the material basis of linguistic action" (1e 249–50): words and bodies exist and act in reciprocal relation. Again, to illustrate Burke draws from Paget in a long parenthetical comment, part of which reads as follows: "The body . . . may require *acts* of grasping—and these acts have their counterparts in *attitudes* of grasping when, in expressing some attitude of contact, he alliterates with the letter 'm'—or he may 'dance rejection' in another situation by the selection of words featuring the letter 'p,' etc." (250). And yet, through a process of what Burke calls "accretion," the physical mimetic level of linguistic action is "buried beneath many kinds of social accretion" (250), including the will to abstraction, the dull "transcendence" of overschematized concepts that Burke laments earlier as being on par with a "filing system" rather than a "linguistic dance" (1e 110). R. R. Marett formulates this accretive transformation as "the perpetual re-imitation of imitations, which alters and embroiders as when gossips repeat a tale" (60). What Burke's meditations on verbal choreography produce, then, is an extension of Paget by which the linguistic dance develops in reciprocal, mimetic relation between and among biological, psychological, and linguistic processes as suggested in his use of identification above.

And for Burke in 1936–37, the guiding force of this complicated tangle of relations is attitude: "Perhaps the most important thing is not our formulae, or any other formulae, as it is the *attitude* to which *any* formulae give substance" (256). Such attitudes are choreographed in part through bodily responses to situations, and the ways those responses in turn set up rhythmic expectations and corollary movements, such as gagging or choking or, in an example Burke develops in his next meditation on Paget, by spitting.

Toward a Bodily Poetics—or, On Spitting Symbolically

Burke's 1941 essay "The Philosophy of Literary Form" begins where he left off in the "Dictionary of Pivotal Terms" in *Attitudes toward History*, with the opening section called "Situations and Strategies," which emphasizes the cluster of attitudes, tonalities, and stylizations supplied by the body's energetic and emotive forces. He poses this mundane scenario: "Let us suppose that I ask you: 'What did the man say?' And that you answer: 'He said 'yes''" (1). Such an account, when appearing on the page as direct discourse, contains none of the important expressive bodily, facial, or tonal movements Burke discusses in "Auscultation, Creation, and Revision." With such atonality meaning is at best fuzzy; as he puts it after posing the scenario, "You still do not know what the man said" (1). At stake for Burke is the attitude of "critical and imaginative works," which he figures as "answers to questions posed by the situation in which they arose. They are not merely answers, they are *strategic* answers, *stylized* answers" (1). He continues, "These strategies size up situations, name their structure and outstanding ingredients, and name them in a way that contains an attitude towards them"

(1). The point is so important for Burke (and for this particular essay) that he more or less repeats it two pages later: "And in all work, as in proverbs, the naming is done 'strategically' or 'stylistically,' in modes that embody attitudes, of resignation, solace, vengeance, expectancy, etc." (3).

Then, in a section called "Symbolic Action,"[23] he sutures one of the earliest instances of this crucial phrase to attitude via the dance: "The symbolic act," he writes, "is the *dancing of an attitude*" (9; emphasis in original), and in elaborating this point he meditates on "the correlation between mind and body" by suggesting that "the whole body may finally become involved" in "this attitudinizing of the poem" (9). To illustrate, Burke turns to William Hazlitt's discussion of Coleridge's and Wordsworth's habits of walking. Drawing from Hazlitt, Burke contrasts Coleridge's movement across uneven terrain, his manner "more full, animated, and varied," with that of Wordsworth, who walked "up and down a straight gravel-walk, his manner 'more equable, sustained, and internal'" (9–10). The link between the poets' respective ambulatory habits and their poetic "manner" allows Burke—à la Hazlitt—to read their poetry as symbolic enactment such that "the whole body is involved in an enactment" (11).

The discussion of symbolic action as poetic enactment leads Burke to a kind of mobile, bodily poetics, even as it leads him back to Paget. This bodily poetics forms the basis of Burke's only Paget-directed critique, that "he offers his theory as a *philosophical* one, whereas it should be offered as a contribution to *poetics*" (13). This point builds nicely on the work Burke did in *Attitudes toward History* to theorize the social accretions that cover over evidence for Paget's theory. As Burke puts it in "The Philosophy of Literary Form," "Philology, because of its involvement in historicism, really deals with *the ways in which, if Paget's theory were 100 per cent correct, such linguistic mimesis as he is discussing would become obscured by historical accretions*" (13; emphasis in original).

The passage preceding this important distinction between philology and poetics helps seal the point, and since it is the most lucid of Burke's accounts of Paget available, I quote it in its entirety:

> Sir Richard Paget's theory of gesture speech gives us inklings of the way in which such enactment might involve even the selection of words themselves on a basis of tonality. According to Paget's theory, language arose in this wise: If a man is firmly gripping something, the muscles of his tongue and throat adopt a position in conformity with the muscles with which he performs the acts of gripping. He does not merely grip with his hands; he "grips all over." Thus in conformity with the act of gripping, he would simultaneously grip with his mouth, by closing his lips firmly. If, now, he uttered a sound with his lips in this position, the only sound he could utter would be *m*. *M* therefore is the sound you get when you "give voice" to the

> posture of gripping. Hence, *m* would be the proper tonality corresponding to the act of gripping, as in contact words like "maul," "mix," "mammae," and "slam." The relation between sound and sense here would not be an onomatopoetic one, as with a word like "sizzle," but it would rather be like that between the visual designs on a sound track and the auditory vibrations that arise when the instrument has "given voice" to these designs (except that, in the case of human speech, the designs would be those of the tongue and throat, plastic rather than graphic). (12–13)

The gripping Burke describes is the same gripping posture that is enacted by Paget's terrier Joseph, and that in humans migrates to the mouth through a Darwinian process first of association and then of migration—re-imitations of imitations. This theory of mimetic traveling has strong poetic overtones for Burke, in the sense that the gestures begin to travel materially through words themselves: that is, expressive rhythms arise through physical rhythms of movement and work (PLF 16–17). At the heart of this poetics is the utterance's enactment or performance, so that the letter *m*, in Burke's example above, performs what Paget calls the "closing, containing, or gripping actions" (*Human* 154). When the lip closure of the *m* is released, however, as in the letter *p*, the action is reversed, resulting in "bursting, expelling, releasing" (*Human* 154). The placement of an *s* sound before the *p* exacerbates such expelling or releasing, and that same movement, extended, forms an *f*, as Burke discusses in "The Philosophy of Literary Form":

> Let us suppose, for instance, that *f* is an excellent linguistic gesture for the *p* sound prolonged, and the lips take the posture of *p* in the act of *sp*itting—hence, the *p* is preserved in the word itself, in "spittle" and "puke," and in the words of re*p*ulsion and re*p*ugnance. The close phonetic relation between *p* and *f* is observed in the German exclamation of repugnance, "*pfui.*" Mencken, in *The American Language*, cites two synthetic words by Winchell that perfectly exemplify this faugh-*f*: "phfft" and "foofff." These are "nonsense syllables" Winchell has invented to convey, by tonality alone, the idea that is denoted in our word "*p*est." Here, since the inventor has complete freedom, there are no historical accidents of language to complicate his mimesis, so he can symbolically spit long and hard. (13)

For Burke, Walter Winchell's words, because they are made up and are therefore unencumbered by the "social" or historical, reasoned accretions that form on the surface of gesture speech, present an instance of pure symbolic action—a performance, through sound, of repugnance. Because Paget allows Burke to present an instance of words-as-postures, he is able to translate the bodily poetics into a hermeneutic that can begin to account for performed "meanings," what he also terms "tonal values" (*ATH* 2e 238) or attitudinal force.

Paget, placed at the beginning of Burke's crucially formative piece, reverberates throughout the long essay and returns as it builds to its crescendo with the section "Ritual Drama as 'Hub.'" Here Burke hits on drama as the most useful term for organizing his emergent principles of criticism: "The general perspective that is interwoven with our methodology of analysis might be summarily characterized as a *theory of drama.*" Such a perspective, he proposes, would treat "ritual drama as the Ur-form, the 'hub,' with all other aspects of *human* action treated as spokes radiating from this hub" (103; emphasis in original). Viewing all sorts of spoken and written utterances as drama would reveal the points of overemphasis: "An essayistic treatise of scientific cast, for instance, would be viewed as a kind of Hamletic soliloquy, its rhythm slowed down to a snail's pace, or perhaps to an irregular jog, and the dramatic situation of which it is a part usually being left unmentioned" (103). Here the focus of pace and rhythm, of speed and slowness as dramatic features, ties in with the energetic movements and signifying postures Burke gleans from Paget. Indeed the footnote Burke appends to the Hamletic sentence indicates as much: "The Paget theory of 'gesture speech' obviously makes a perfect fit with this perspective by correlating the origins of linguistic action with bodily action and posture" (103n23).

The last of ten principles Burke offers in "The Philosophy of Literary Form" as the "broad outlines of our position," or what he would soon call dramatism, makes a curious analogy between his burgeoning method and biology. Arriving at his tenth principle, he writes: "Being, like biology, in an indeterminate realm between vital assertions and lifeless properties, the realm of the dramatic (hence dramatic criticism) is neither physicalist nor anti-physicalist, but physicalist-plus" (116). When read through the Paget-inflected genealogy given here, this observation foregrounds a twofold role for the biological body. The first is analogical: each combines, as Paget did with his kinetic terrier and his plasticine resonators, things "vital and lifeless"; the second is reciprocal: the constant interaction between the biological body and dramatism exceeds the limits of life and matter. The term *physicalist-plus* thus exceeds the analogy itself, for what Burke is describing here is a vital method of always attending to bodily matters. The physicalist-plus axiom perhaps best characterizes what Burke renders, à la Paget, as attitude.

Attitudes II: Dramatistic Language

When in the mid-1950s[24] Burke faced the challenge of revising his two-volume *Attitudes toward History* for a one-volume edition with Hermes, he would also return to Paget, this time with a gagging, choking, cut. He excised a full twenty-one pages about Paget, including all the material discussed in the "*Attitudes* I" section above, and replaced them with a short, carefully qualified, and revealing explanation: "We have . . . omitted . . . speculations based on Sir Richard Paget's book, *Human Speech,* attributing the origin of speech sounds to 'gestures' of the tongue, throat, and mouth. However, the omissions should not be taken to imply any loss of faith in his theory, which still seems wholly convincing, particularly since it seems the perfect physiological counterpart to a 'Dramatistic' theory of language. But our discussion here lacked the distinction between *philology* and *poetics* which we consider essential for our purposes (as explained in *Philosophy of Literary Form,* 12–17)" (ATH 2e 238).[25]

In addition to reaffirming his allegiance to Paget, Burke reaffirms the philology-poetics distinction he hit on in *The Philosophy of Literary Form,* a distinction that rendered his work on Paget in the first edition of *Attitudes toward History* not necessarily moot but somehow, at least in the process of trimming, expendable. The point about poetics turns out to be utterly crucial to Burke's theories of language as symbolic action and to the pentad, and it is also his unique formulation of Paget's theories.[26] If the purpose of this chapter is to provide a somatic genealogy of dramatism, then the most crucial line from the above passage is the one in which Burke claims that Paget's gesture-speech theory offers "the perfect physiological counterpart to a 'Dramatistic' theory of language." This line, written more than a decade after Burke's dramatistic tome *A Grammar of Motives,* suggests that together Paget and Burke offer a complete account of language, or at the very least that the two theories enjoy a complementary relation.

And so even though Burke's *Grammar of Motives* does not contain a single mention of Paget, it still nevertheless wrestles with issues of the "body in motion," which Burke figures as the "basic unit" of dramatistic action (14). *A Grammar of Motives* also keeps alive the notion of "linguistic dance," bodily poetics, and attitude. Burke's counterpart line, however, can most usefully be read through his later tinkerings with both *A Grammar of Motives* and dramatism and is particularly revealing in relation to his shifting attitude toward attitude.

Burke's Attitude toward Attitude: A Representative Anecdote

The word *attitude* has historically made a shift from body to mind, which makes it both a tricky concept as well as a useful one for considering the conceptual difficulties Burke and Burkean theories encounter with regard to theorizing the body. According to the *OED* the earliest instances of the word occur in the design arts context as a substitute for *aptitude,* and to refer specifically to bodily posture or disposition, as in a statuary or painting. The bodily meaning persisted alone until the nineteenth century, when the cognitive overtones of the word moved in. Both bodily and cognitive uses persisted in both realms, with the dispositional associations moving into dance by the twentieth century, even as cognitive researchers officially took on attitude measurement as an area of study. While my somatic genealogy favors Paget's use of *attitude* in the bodily sense, it is safe to say that in Burke there is considerable migration, suggesting a reciprocal mind-body relation. Early on in both editions of *A Grammar of Motives*, Burke, in attempting to determine where attitude would "fall within our pattern," settles on its "character as a state of *mind*" and therefore wants to locate it pentadically near the "agent" node (20). Such a notion of attitude rubs against the Pagetian or Darwinian attitude, which forms and manifests physiologically, as their favored example of the bristling dog suggests.

Read in the context of this early *Grammar* line, a Pagetian genealogy of attitude suggests that Burke's location of attitude is ambiguous at best.[27] And yet of course he accounts for ambiguity in his pentad-driven method, when he emphatically states: "Accordingly, what we want is *not terms that avoid ambiguity, but terms that clearly reveal the strategic spots at which ambiguities necessarily arise*" (xviii; emphasis in original). A good example of this sort of ambiguity occurs later in Burke's discussion of agency and purpose with regard to motion: "Two men, performing the same *motions* side by side, might be said to be performing different *acts*, in proportion as they differed in their attitudes toward their work (276). When considered alongside Burke's "Strategies and Situations" discussion at the opening of *The Philosophy of Literary Form*, this example could easily lead to a consideration of how such differing attitudes are *danced* or performed on and through the bodies that differently enliven the labor and the motions with which one approaches labor. This reciprocal relation between motion and action and body and mind, a relation that Burke would later formulate as the nonsymbolic motion / symbolic action pair, is actually crucial for the ambiguous, shifting, situation-bound relations between and among the pentad's terms. When moving between the pentadic terms, attitude hangs in the balance, as Burke indicates retrospectively in an "Addendum for the Present Edition": "With regard to the Dramatistic pentad (act, scene, agent, agency, purpose), I have found one modification useful for certain kinds of analysis. In accordance with my discussion of 'attitudes' (in the section on '"Incipient" and "Delayed" Action,' pp. 235–247), I have sometimes added the term 'attitude' to the above list of five major terms. Thus, one could also speak of a 'scene-attitude ratio,' or of an 'agent-attitude ratio,' etc. 'Agency' would more strictly designate the 'means' (*quibus auxiliis*) employed in the act. And 'attitude' would designate the manner (*quo modo*)" (GM 443).

Quo modo—the Latin phrase for "in what manner"—designates not just manner, but insofar as it contains a form of the Latin *modus*, mode, also entails measure, quantity, or physical limits, and in its specialized poetic meanings encompasses issues of rhythm and harmony. The manner at issue here cannot be separated from the bodies that perform manner or move in a particular manner. Burke's example illustrates this bodily force of attitude: "To build something with a hammer would involve an instrument or 'agency'; to build with diligence would involve an 'attitude,' a 'how'" (443).[28] Diligence here involves just the kind of energetic force Burke ascribed early on, through Paget, to the body in terms of both attitude and purpose. The second edition's addendum therefore shows him emphatically adding attitudes back into dramatism. These attitudes are bodily ones, as indicted by a *Quarterly Journal of Speech* article he published in 1952, where he writes, "Dramatistically, we watch always for ways in which bodily attitudes can affect the development of linguistic expression" ("Dramatistic View" [part 1] 254n2).[29] He then adds parenthetically, "(We like Paget's theory of 'gesture speech' for this reason)" (254n2). This line, with its modest parentheses, buried in the middle of a near-column-long footnote, still shows Burke thinking about Paget, especially along the lines of the bodily poetics—the ways the body energetically and attitudinally forms language. Burke's interest in Paget's Darwinian theory of verbal choreography and its status as poetics persists, if intermittently and stealthily, for the next twenty years. It is detectable, for instance, in his constant return to the language of dance,[30] in his enduring respect for and insistence on rhetoric's energetic force, and in his wrestling with the reciprocally related Burkean pair nonsymbolic motion / symbolic action," a pair he contends informed his dramatistic method from the start.[31]

As its physiological counterpart and genealogical forebear, Paget's gesture-speech theory can never be fully separated from Burkean dramatism. And yet Burke's *Grammar of Motives,* by suspending his earlier concerns of the body, cleaves mind and body most thoroughly—albeit temporarily. The net effect of an overreliance on *A Grammar of Motives* is a disembodied pentad, which in turn can yield somewhat lifeless analyses. As rhetorical critics we would all do well to remember the lesson Burke learned from Paget: communication is difficult to separate from language's materiality, which is never far from communing, communicative bodies. The pentad, at long last, would have attitude.

7

Welcome to the Beauty Clinic

> But of all this daily drama of the body there is no record. People write always of the doings of the mind; the thoughts that come to it; its noble plans; how the mind has civilized the universe. They show it ignoring the body in the philosopher's turret; or kicking the body, like an old leather football, across leagues of snow and desert in the pursuit of conquest or discovery. Those great wars which the body wages with the mind a slave to it, in the solitude of the bedroom against the assault of fever or the oncome of melancholia, are neglected. Nor is the reason far to seek. To look these things squarely in the face would need the courage of a lion tamer; a robust philosophy; a reason rooted in the bowels of the earth.
>
> Virginia Woolf, On Being Ill

In the 1950s Kenneth Burke turned his attention to shit. For starters, as a critic he began to pursue intensely—and for some inexplicably—a critical mode begun in *A Grammar of Motives*, which would draw "upon the ambiguities of the cloacal, where there are united, in a 'demonic trinity,' the three principles of the erotic, urinary, and excremental" (301–2). That is, as part of the poetics section of his "Symbolic of Motives" project, Burke began to focus even more on the images of symbolic purgation in literature, most especially regurgitation, ejaculation, micturition, and defecation. This cloacal criticism is most forceful in his essay "The Thinking of the Body," where a children's tale functions as a "circuitous description" of potty training; a German opera dramatizes the tension between fecal and sexual motives; a French story equates the body with corruption (34); the fire and water of a Greek drama become sex and urine; and Burke's own novel, according to this analysis, sidles up to Freud, "trying to solve the Riddle of the Sphincter" (61).

Burke's cloacal criticism uses almost as many approaches as it does texts, at times following a Paget-inflected sound association whereby, for example, *faces* morphs easily into *faeces*, and the word *towards* found in so many titles (including Burke's own) becomes *turds* (62). At other times the analyses are of the more predictable symbolic variety: for example, a rain shower occurring in a short story would amount to a giant, breathtaking piss. Still other associations are etymological; the word *ammonia* in Flaubert's "Temptation of St. Anthony" is read in connection with its chemical creation, as Burke writes: "Ammonia is said to be so named because it was obtained by the burning of camel's dung" (34). Greek words for flow and loosening are ascribed their more scatological usages. As a whole, "The Thinking of the Body" is an extended enactment of reading incongruously—what might be called, following the mystical strain in *Attitudes toward History*, a "grotesquing": feeling around for a "locus of irrationality" by seeking "poetic pathos" in "bodily bathos" (46).

Until recently scholars of Burke have opted to pass over his bathetic writings in stony silence.[1] It is difficult, after all, to type while holding one's nose. Richard Thames, writing about the first time he read "The Thinking of the Body," Burke's essay most concerned with the expressive work of excretion,[2] recalls being "embarrassed, even disgusted" ("The Gordian Not").[3] William Rueckert has been the most outspoken of the essay's critics, calling Burke's writing "some of the most tortured and absurd analyses he ever wrote" (*Essays* xiii). He resentfully blames "body-thinking" for Burke's never completing the ever-longed-for "Symbolic of Motives," the book that would have rounded out the Motives trilogy. According to Rueckert, Burke's "work on the poetics. . . was bogged down in his attempt to work out the physiological counterparts of his theory of catharsis—the central concept in his poetics" (xiii). In an earlier account of the time line of the "Symbolic," Rueckert is more direct: "We can assume that he began ["Symbolic of Motives"] as soon as he finished *A Rhetoric of Motives* and then encountered problems in the 'Thinking of the Body' section where it ends and put it aside until he could rethink that section and what he really wanted to do" ("Kenneth Burke's 'Symbolic of Motives'" 99). As Rueckert observes, decidedly not liking it, "Like it or not, this mind-body thinking theory is an essential part of Burke's dramatistic poetics" (111). This disapproving head shake follows a brief section where he argues that Burke's "thinking of the body" signaled "the persistence of adolescent motives in Burke" that "made him turd-brained and pee-headed while he was working this theory out in the fifties" (110).

While Rueckert chooses "the thinking of the body theory" as "a good place to leave—to bid farewell to—Burke's dramatistic poetics" (111), and blames it for Burke's inability to complete the "Symbolic," Robert Wess reads the body right out of "The Thinking of the Body," intimating that Burke made what amounts to an error in nomenclature. "The phrase 'the thinking of the body,'" Wess concludes, "turns out to be something of a misnomer: If the body is not 'causative' but simply the source of imagery of bodily catharsis that the poet should use 'to be thorough,' the 'thinking' is really the poet's not the body's" ("Looking for the Figure").[4] Wess's dissociation of poet from body refuses Burke's concept of body-thinking more swiftly and resolutely than Rueckert's grumbling.

This collective effort to remove bodies from Burke's midcentury theorizing is enabled in part by a category of disembodied genius. Rueckert and Thames believe that Burke never finished his "Symbolic" because he was "a victim of his own genius" (Thames, "The Gordian Not"; Rueckert, *Essays* xv), and yet the stalling of Burke's project seems to owe at least as much to the "genius" of his symptoms. Throughout the decade he cataloged these symptoms in his letters with Cowley right alongside—and sometimes as—ideas. Rueckert and others, however, have for decades favored the latter, a starkly disembodied version of genius.[5]

Editors, too, however unwittingly, participate in this effort. Paul Jay's edition of Burke's correspondence with Malcolm Cowley frequently excises those discussions of health and illness that encase the discussions of ideas. The only exceptions are when Burke seems to offer a direct tie between illness and his work, as in the nosological reading discussed below. No doubt the long passages he devotes to his ailments add the bulk of the seemingly mundane.[6] When added back in to the correspondence, the body passages suggest that Burke becomes a "victim" of his "genius" only if we read genius in the sense of capacity—physical and intellectual—rather than gleaming, finished, disembodied brilliance.

That glowing, idea-based notion of genius falls into step with the effort to skim ideas from the cloacal scum of Burke's work in the decade, leaving aside not just important concepts but entire articles.[7] Adding irony to injury, these accounts of Burke fulfill his own prediction at the beginning of "The Thinking of the Body" that "persons who insist on keeping the subject of the poetic imagination *salonfähig* (or as the dictionary might put it, 'suitable for discussion in the drawing room') will resent such analysis" (25). In separating ideas from matter, a dramatistic theory of poetics from thinking bodies, Burke scholars produce a more polished and better-smelling, if slightly less prolific, decade.

If the previous chapter established the indebtedness of Burkean dramatism to gesture-speech theory, a theory that depends on an evolutionary account of bodies and communication, thereby resisting the urge to reify a disembodied concept in order to render it eminently usable, then this chapter will continue the re-embodying effort by suspending Burkean concepts themselves to examine Burke's painstaking process of concept making. As historians of science Steven Shapin and Christopher Lawrence suggest, intellectual work tends to insist on ideas, knowledge, and concepts as disembodied. When scholars in rhetorical studies extract dramatism from its material beginnings, they betray a subtle belief in concepts' attaining value only when they have "shuffled off their mortal coils" (1). "Accordingly," write Shapin and Lawrence, "intellectuals have enshrined their products, and the objects of their interpretations, in the transcendental and disembodied domain that knowledge itself was understood to inhabit" (2). An excellent case in point would be the recent efforts to purify Burke's "Symbolic of Motives," washing away the refuse. More often than not those offscourings are a series of disconnected texts commenting on pain, language, suspension, and breakdown. *Breakdown,* like the vomit and excrement that captured Burke's attention during this period, is something of a dirty word for us academics; our writings are expected to comprise smooth narrative arcs, obscuring our jagged, halting scholarly processes: we reify the "Beauty Clinic" on a number of levels. Virginia Woolf's exasperated observation that "people write always of the doings of the mind" contains the stark suggestion that people write always as if the body has nothing to do with anything that matters.

The muck and grime—and the bodies that expel or roll in them—are crucial parts of Burkean theory that cannot be so easily disposed. Moreover, dumping them risks dumping a host of theories that might find relevance today, most notably a rereading of Aristotelian catharsis that keeps bodies tightly yoked to language and revives Burke's commitments to ecology. The 1950s writings serve as a nuanced guide to Burke's nonsymbolic motion / symbolic action pair, the pair that eventually becomes his preferred shorthand for body-language relations. Indeed the idea of a "Symbolic of Motives" isolated from bodies and rhetoric contains its own death sentence: without warm and breathing bodies, words and ideas—the realm of symbolic—become lifeless.

Crucially the effort to expunge bodies from Burke's criticism also elides the role of a body—of Burke's body—which, apart from scattered glossings of his insomnia and the commonplace asides about his abiding love for the bottle, has also been purged from scholarly discussions. The absence is still odder given the distinct biographical tone of so much scholarship on Burke, and it becomes rather astonishing when considered alongside his letters from the 1950s, filled as they are with description after vivid description of his ailments and his "alky." Individually these snippets have tended to provide charming anecdotes with which scholars pepper their footnotes, but taken together they document a body undeniably involved with idea making as a physical, even painful process. Moreover, that involvement—of live, moving bodies with the generation of ideas and words—becomes most salient in moments of breakdown.

This chapter will therefore offer a somatic rendering of Burke in the 1950s. Such a rendering will inevitably offer a sort of physical biography.[8] I offer body biography as a possible way out of the intention trap that biographical criticism often risks. Body biography, that is, can set up a less-than-conscious index of writerly engrossments. Where Burke is concerned, the evidence that physical breakdown both preoccupied, directed, and stalled his work stands against the widespread yearning for the healthy completion of the Motives trilogy. The intrusive, interruptive work of bodies—sick, ailing, addicted—may well block and at times divert otherwise straightforward intentions.

Two broad aims, then, guide this chapter's organization and argument. First this chapter as a whole will offer an alternative view of Burke in the 1950s, one that emphatically resists the celebratory, teleological urge to save him from his genius by bringing the "Symbolic" to fruition and instead lingers on the productive work of breakdown. My second broad aim then is to examine how two bodies—the body in theory and Burke's own ailing body—both sculpted and stultified his writing during this period. Such a picture is at times not pretty, but then again this is not a "Beauty Clinic," the term Burke used to describe efforts to neaten up ideas and make them "presentable."[9] And so in reconnecting bodies with ideas, this chapter will perform and theorize the stakes of body biography for rhetorical criticism. In doing so it joins Davis W. Houck and Amos Kiewe, whose book on Franklin Delano Roosevelt has already initiated such a movement without naming it. It also joins a broader set of feminist writers and philosophers, such as Janet Browne, Heather Benbow, Richard A. Ingram, and Denise Gigantes (139–59), who have contributed body biographies, which is to say they examine how one's bodily life figures into philosophical, scientific, and literary invention. Taken together, these body biographies—of Darwin, Kant, Nietzsche, and Keats, respectively—offer a strong refutation of science and philosophy as disembodied efforts. Such work refuses to oppose the material and the authentically intellectual, the act of theory building and theory itself. Burke too refuses these oppositions. He had little choice in the matter.

"Ailments, Ailments, Ailments"

In the 1950s Burke's own body was falling apart.[10] While his life to this point had already seemed quite full of physical ailments, his 1950s correspondence in particular chronicles his chasing of pain—with procedures, with diagnoses, with sherry.[11] His letters—especially those he wrote to Malcolm Cowley—offer accounts of "progress" on the "Symbolic," page numbers and all, and this progress is ever wound around the "meanwhiles" of physical breakdown. Burke's letters serve as much more than a coherent index to what he was thinking about and planning for the "Symbolic"; they also document a heightening awareness of his body's role in his writing, speaking, breathing, and thinking. That role might best be described with the incongruous phrase "disruptive guide."

In a November 1950 letter to Cowley, Burke invokes nosology, the classification of disease, to discuss each book in his incomplete trilogy:

> Nosologically, as regards my great Migratory Symptom, the project seems to have developed thus: For the *Grammar,* high blood pressure; for the Devices portions of *Rhetoric* (still unpublished) a stinging, ringing burning left ear; for the aspects of the *Rhetoric* that lead toward 'pure persuasion,' a laggard heart, and when I got to the middle paragraph on 'suspended animation,' p. 294, I just about melted away; and now, for the Symbolic (or at least, the Poetics section of the Symbolic), a really sustained battle with the gaspo-gaggo-gulpo symptom, which I have had on and off, but which now

seems to want to move in permanently, for a spell at least. (November 16, 1950; Jay 302)

This equation of illness with occupations is of course not new in Burke's oeuvre; in *The Philosophy of Literary Form* he discusses such "occupational illnesses" as a high occurrence of stomach ulcers among taxi drivers (11). Here he reads the ulcers as "a bodily response to the intensely arrhythmic quality of the work itself, the irritation in the continual jagginess of traffic, all puzzle and no pace." His consideration of taxi drivers' ailments focuses on space and pace, movements and rhythms. "In such ways," he contends, "the whole body is involved in an enactment" (11). Recall too the equation between occupation more generally and what Burke, following Rivers, calls "hypochondriasis," the process by which people come to terms with illness by becoming engrossed in their symptoms.[12] In the 1950s Burke became simultaneously engrossed in his symptoms *and* his work, to the point where the line between the two became almost indistinguishable. The connection between ideas and bodies is one that Burke would not let go—or perhaps better phrased, it is a connection that would not let go of Burke. Indeed these ideas in particular for Burke were so palpably physical that they seemed to have him in a choke hold.

Recall Burke's longstanding interest in the gagging or choking sensation mimed by guttural words. As he describes it, words that begin with a hard *c* feel a lot like getting a fish bone stuck in one's throat. Burke believed that the "gaspo-gaggo-gulpo"—or alternately the "gulpo-gaggo-gaspo"—the names themselves a trio of gutturals, resided in his throat area rather than his heart. Earlier in that same November 16 letter, Burke confesses to Cowley that he is "still avoiding doctors" and is starting to think that his "fantastic gulpo-gaggo-gaspo session of recent weeks may be not heart at all, but asthmatic" (November 16, 1950; Jay 301–2). And the source of the blockage seems to Burke to be not fish bones but words: "The difference between throwing words out and letting them mull around inside (between lecturing and writing) seems to be becoming an abrupt change of quality with me; and almost within a few moments after I go to work on the internal kind, I find myself just about stifled. I fight for breath like a man sinking in a mud hole. Also, I find that, at such times, I have been holding my breath. Oh, this living and dying by the Word. A certain kind of interference with breathing is natural when speaking, so maybe I can fool the jinx by that subterfuge" (November 16, 1950; Jay 302). Noteworthy in this passage is the use of the phrase "throwing words out" in contrast to "letting them mull around inside." As opposing phrases, "throwing words out" and "letting them mull" posit an inside and an outside corresponding to lecturing and writing, as indicated by his parenthetical, "(between lecturing and writing)." That the physical act of breathing becomes caught up in these processes makes speaking or "throwing words out" all the more vital for Burke, while the act of writing—too "internal" for him—leaves him fighting for air.

Burke was not the only one detailing his symptoms, however. Cowley's letters in this period are dominated by tales of suffering as well, including lists of ailments such as "arthritis, heart stuff, and also indigestion (oh, and gall bladder issues)" (November 10, 1952), as well as multiple operations on his ear (August 28, 1954); both Cowley and Burke had teeth pulled (MC to KB, February 13, 1953) and were hospitalized at various points.[13] The two in fact traded symptoms for more than half the decade until Cowley, in response to Burke's playful taunt that he could "match" Cowley "symptom for symptom, any time" (September 17, 1956; Jay 329) and upon learning of Burke's bilateral inguinal hernia, finally pleads "No more matching symptoms. You win" (October 5, 1956; Jay 329). A year later, at Stanford, Burke sealed his "victory" with a frightening bout of Bell's palsy, which gave him "one big moon-sized eye that wouldn't close, and paralysis of some facial muscles" (December 29, 1957).

But amid all the epistolary symptom-trading, the one constant was Burke's irregular breathing. As he struggled with his "Symbolic" throughout the 1950s, his "gulpo-gaggo-gaspo" symptoms persisted,[14] as did his perception that the gulping, gagging, and gasping owed to his occupation as a "word man." In the nosological letter of November 16, 1950, Burke updates Cowley on the still-percolating "Symbolic." Two paragraphs in particular, excised from Jay's edition, are worth considering for the way ideas and intellectual plans get tucked into physical symptoms:

> Why all this? Well, such considerations belong at one point or another in the Symbpolic [sic], if I can contrive to find the strategic (diplomatic) way of presenting them. I may as well admit: No matter how much I modify or qualify, the Symbolic is in essence an "ego" realm, dealing with "identities" in their uniqueness. And that's why the study of Symbol-using as Somnambulism finally brings us back to the clinical use of the self, as test case. Mainly, I have notes on White Oxen and Turds a Beddy Love, which I think of using, for at least one long chapter. Thus: first section, on Poetics proper; second section, Symbolic, on the "dream" in general, on man's life as first rough draft of a poem; and then, why not, for rounding-out, to put the two together, a long chapter detailing the major points as regards our discoveries about our own sentences, by a critic who is <u>revenant</u> to himself as fictioneer?
>
> All this has been written, while I squirm and gasp, nearly below the surface of the mud, at one moment my legs heavy; at another, pains in my left arm; again and again and again, my lungs only half as ample as they should be—and then, lo! Ecstatically, a full breath incipit vita nova. O, on the edge of the abyss. O, by the seashore at night, the waves ripping. (I think of me,

in the south, like a sin, when I should be in the north, in winter.) O, jukebox tunes, made cosmic, by being heard thus, at the jumping-off place. (emphasis in original)

In addition to including one of countless schematic descriptions of the ever-morphing "Symbolic," the first of these two paragraphs also justifies his use of his own writing as a case study for cloacal criticism ("Turds a Beddy Love" being the cloacal handle for his novel, *Towards a Better Life*). Even more important, for the purposes of this chapter, though, is the swift move between the first and second paragraphs, between ideas and physical conditions. Burke's respiratory irregularity persists during his writing, and he uses the language of mysticism to narrate the teetering "gaspo" part of the sequence: "O, on the edge of the abyss." Burke's "gulpo-gaggo-gaspo" stresses the terrifying but life-affirming quality of his ailments, as evidenced with the ecstasy brought by a "full breath," which begins new life, *incipit vita nova*. The stopped breathing, that is, functions to underscore breath itself when it resumes. Ideas themselves follow the pattern of his halting breathing, forming in fits and starts. Toward the letter's close Burke mentions his exercise regimen, again quickly flipping from body to ideas: "I do my daily dozen every night, and I can feel the blood being pumped into the right places—and whether it is or not, I can feel it, and those ideas feel right." Ideas therefore flow along with breath and blood, fused with the stuff of life. And that "stuff" is not always smooth or neutral but is at times unpleasant, sputtering "nearly below the surface of the mud."[15]

As Burke wades through mud, his stubborn "gulpo-gaggo-gaspo" persists, and so does his theorizing about its relation to his work. At times he believes he is choking on political issues, as he writes to Cowley on February 22, 1952: "Nor do we ever for a moment overlook the breath-taking nature of the current political gagging." But political issues are not fish bones, though the McCarthy-era gagging of which he speaks was very much real. And yet his effort to pinpoint an immediate and local material cause is suggestive, as when he establishes a sensorial link between contemporary politics and the gagging stench of newsprint: "Though I am fascinated by the crookedness of our journalistic rhetoric-hacks, in press and radio, I listen with a horrified sense of being gagged (To think that our children's destiny is in the hands of so dingy a priesthood!) There is a pungent odor of newsprint, 'emotionally' neutral, though I suppose an old newspaperman to whom it meant home could come to love it; when I was taking notes from my chapter on the newspaper, sometimes this smell was strong enough even to become stifling. I have a hunch that my troubles are spreading from sources such as these" (KB to MC, January 6, 1951). The overpowering smell of print mingles with and becomes the overpowering "crookedness" of the world, thereby arresting the otherwise smooth, unconsidered process of breathing and—by (quick) extension—of ideas and beliefs.

At other times, however, Burke finds the source of the gagging in ideas themselves—unscented, nonchemical ideas. In 1952 he wrote again to Cowley of his vague, doctor-diagnosed "coronary spasms," "what amounts to a psychosomatic explanation" (February 22, 1952; Jay 303): the symptoms, that is, spring from his inventional processes. He continues:

> Meanwhile, all sorts of ideas, even apparently innocuous ones, will of a sudden produce in me a kind of stoppage so that, literally, I forget to breathe. The engrossment that goes with the pursuit of an idea, at such times, seems to produce a "state of arrest." . . . And since so much of my work is done by prolonging the area of suspense (carrying a lot of things in an unresolved state, in the hopes that they will eventually fall into a pattern), I'm pretty much up against the old Biblical saying, "Who lives by the qwertyuiop dies by the asdfghjkl, or, if he can contrive a delay, by the zxcvbnm." (Jay 303)

This paragraph neatly parallels Burke's meditation on the stench of newsprint, especially in the way he renders the material arrangement of typewriter keys in his adaptation of the passage from Matthew. Even more intriguingly Burke describes his critical method as one of suspension—of "carrying a lot of things in an unresolved state." His addition to the biblical passage—"if he can contrive a delay"—links his suspension method with the deferral of death. The arresting of breath and work leads to a reaffirmation of life and, eventually, writing: breakdown gets folded into invention.

Cowley's response muses, "Funny, the doc's report on your condition tends to confirm my hypothesis (yours too, I note) that your health is in some measure an effect of your work—when you're taking things easy your health is good, and when you're trying to invent new theories, when you're riding your demon until your demon takes to riding you, then heart and mind start acting up" (February 28, 1952). As usual Cowley has it about right when he casts theories as demons, miniature mobile entities simultaneously regulating Burke's invention and respiration.

Demon, asthma, or something else altogether, the "gaspo-gaggo-gulpo" becomes a regular topos in Burke's letters to Cowley, and his numerous mentions of the conditions suggest that arrhythmia, of the kind discussed in the first chapter, has become the norm. In the spring of 1951 Burke "awoke at 5:30 in the morning, feeling about to die." After recounting a day of suffering with "aches and pains" and a fever, he writes that he "didn't get back to work until yesterday—and today am all gaspo, gulpo, gaggo" (March 2, 1951). In response to a letter full of Cowley's ailments, Burke urges him to "be glad, at least, that you don't have to stop every now and then, and remind yourself to breathe." He then adds parenthetically, "(Extra. Extra. Motives Expert Purposively Motivates

Breathing.)" (March 25, 1952). Later in 1952 Burke begins to sound a little like Fred Sanford of the 1970s sitcom *Sanford and Son,* attesting that he has "been gasping-gagging-gulping most fantastically, and about two or three times a week I start saying goodbye (literally)" (November 10, 1952). And then in 1954 he writes uncomfortably about a mellow period: "Often my fantastic ailments ease up for two or three days at a time (much to my bepuzzlement, since I had come to take gasping and gagging as a normal aspect of my occupational psychosis)" (August 15, 1954). He even jokingly converts his pentad to "gasping, gagging, bulping, burping, yawning" (August 22, 1954). By this point the halting, interruptive rhythms, "fantastic" as they are, seem to have replaced his normal respiratory rhythms. They have altered his work habits so that he writes—as he breathes—in irregular bursts.

In mid-decade Burke revisits what happens, returning to the writing/speaking distinction:

> Anyhow, I race in a sluice of this sort: Certain situations (foods, happenings, ideas?) increase my insomnia; then, after a certain stretch of the insomnia, this fantastic respiratory symptom settles on me—and I suspect that, in struggling to fill my lungs, I unintentionally so tighten things all around my chest that I interfere with the proper circulation of my blood. In any case, after I have been beset thus for a while, the muscles around my solar plexus are as stiff as stone. At other times, similar symptoms come from engrossment in reading or writing, but talking is a relief. Quite a muddle. (KB to MC, March 16, 1955)

Burke's relationship to his ailing body, as evidenced in his painstaking account of his symptoms' correlation—indeed, response—to the flow of ideas, approximates a belief that persists in the writings of both Virginia Woolf and Friedrich Nietzsche: a belief in the transformative power of illness. Illness, in this view, can be as creative as it can be stifling; ailments can open up new perspectives and expand the intellect (Ingram 25–26).[16] Such a view on illness is in keeping with the insights Burke gained from his interludes with the constitutional perspectives of Ludwig and then Kretschmer. Pain and illness often inspire through stultification and swerves, and perhaps it is no coincidence that the "Symbolic," the Motives project that Burke associated with reading-induced respiratory arrest, was also the project that sputtered and finally stalled.

Neither is it a coincidence that the same scholars who seek to banish bodies from Burke's work do so in their respective attempts to reconstruct, in a past though too-imperfect tense, what Burke would have published under that heading. To focus on the end results—in Burke's case the theories sputtering out of arrest—is to miss the crucial role that pain, illness, and suffering play in their formulation, and it is also to miss Burke's own fascination with the relationship between his body and his ideas, as well as his homeopathic antidote: two parts alcohol, one part Aristotle.

Burke's letters contain ample evidence—in the form of typographic slurs as well as explicit discussion of drinking—that he wrote them with a side of liquor. For instance, in the November 16, 1950, letter excerpted above, a letter Burke closes by noting that he has "done a hell of a lot of 'admitting' in this letter," he writes, "I admit it, as this letter continued, so early in the morning, yes, I dwank. I poured myself one dwink, and then anudder (again on the sumjick o' them oxen), and then anudder. And now all is relaxty waxty. And maybe I'm just a new wrinkle in alcoholics. Wouldn't that be a wonderful soloosh? So long as the liver and kidneys hold out."

After another particularly slurry letter to which Cowley responds with some concern, Burke reassures him, "Agree with you, that I must watch Friend Alky. He helps me unbend, which is all to the good. But he unbends me to the point where I'm twisted the other way. The final economics of the matter may be this: Use alky to relax after writing. But don't start drinking while writing (as I sometimes do, the last hour or so before lunch" (March 4, 1952). It becomes clear in the mid-1950s that drinking provides some relief to Burke's ailments. In January 1955 he writes of a "damfool ladybug" falling in his drink while he is working, and later in that same letter he notes that he had gotten up the previous night at 3 A.M. for a nip of sherry, "to ease the cardiac antics" (January 22, 1955). In an interview three decades later Burke theorizes drug and alcohol use as attempts "to be all body." He elaborates: "The rule I'm most proud of is this one: The only cure for digging in the dirt is an idea. The cure for any idea is more ideas. The cure for all ideas is digging in the dirt. That's the whole damn thing. Body back to body. That's your relation between ideas . . . that's the body talking for you" (Skodnick 12). At no point is this "body back to body" move more palpable than in the 1950s, when his attachment to alcohol tightens, even as he began to theorize catharsis—the processing and purging of pain, suffering, and toxins. Burke's fondness for "digging in the dirt" correlates with his ecological commitments, commitments that get revived in this decade as well.

It makes a certain quirky sense, then, that Aristotle—the philosopher of temperance whose fleeting comments on catharsis have befuddled critics for centuries—became another of Burke's occupations. In early January 1951 he announces to Cowley, "At present, am writing a long essay built around my comments on 'Aristotle's Poetics, 'Dramatistically' Considered.' It's a me-and-Aristotle sort of thing" (January 5, 1951). As Burke's respiratory condition persists, he takes Aristotle as something of a conceptual pacemaker: "Meanwhile, Gaspo-Gaggo-Gulpo, while me and Aristotle have got to typewritten p. 40 of our cooperative venture. (He's a nice man to work with. Despite his great fame, he can even be positively self-effacing at times.)" (KB to MC, January 14, 1951); and then about two weeks later: "Meanwhile, I continue with my me-and-Aristotle chapter which, after interruptions due to some fantastic ailments, is somewhere between 16 and 18 thousand words along the way" (February 1, 1951).

Of course Burke turned to Aristotle for reasons other than his health. He was, after all, in the midst of what he called "a Poetics," and as he writes in an essay published out of that effort, "I assume that such a project should be developed with Aristotle's *Poetics* in mind" ("On Catharsis, or Resolution" 337).[17] In the course of his "me-and-Aristotle thing," he took as his touchstone catharsis, the concept of transformation that anchors Aristotle's theory of tragedy. Catharsis (Greek *katharsis*), for Burke at least, evokes a kind of body-thinking and therefore binds bodies with ideas and language. This binding, though, takes multiple forms, all of which reorder the various ways bodies and language relate.

Bodies of Catharsis

Catharsis is not a simple term; its history is by no means meek. Historically medical and religious processes performed in its name range from leech-assisted bloodletting to orgiastic music to the ritual mingling of human blood with animal blood (Burkert 56–58). As Elizabeth Belfiore argues, Aristotelian *katharsis* is the pleasurable telos of tragedy's pain and destruction (258–59).[18] As such, and more generally, *katharsis* traverses domains of physicality, cognition, ethics, education, medicine, music, and religion (Belfiore 259).

More often than not, *katharsis* names an allopathic process, which is to say the separation or drawing out of blood or emotions is achieved by an other, foreign substance such as drugs or words. As Jonathan Lear points out, the dominant use of *katharsis* in Aristotle is biological; he uses the term most frequently to refer to menstrual discharge, though seminal discharge, micturition, and discharge at birth are not far behind (298n6). Stephen Halliwell, one of the most highly regarded and prolific commentators on Aristotle's *Poetics*, offers an account of ancient *katharsis* that joins it to "wider Greek ideas on the quasi-magical powers of music and language" (185). Such an observation brings Aristotle into close approximation with Gorgias, a point that Jeffrey Walker has pursued in his reading of *katharsis* as "a forcing-out" (78). For Halliwell and Walker, dramatic catharsis stems from a broader theory of poetics that depends on the magical properties of language. Burke's mystical methodology recognizes and values these same properties; words themselves, in both their clarifying and obfuscating capacities, participate in a cathartic economy.[19] And since catharsis is so inescapably somatic, it offers a rich conceptual staging ground for Burke to develop his bodily theories of language.

Because Burke is working in the realm of "symbolics," he attempts to bracket bodies in order to work out his theory of symbolics, but that attempt fails repeatedly.[20] After working most of the decade on a sprawling theory of poetics that was to form the core of his "Symbolic of Motives," Burke relents to a somatic theory of poetics. A pair of catharsis essays he published in 1959 and 1961 chronicles the stubborn persistence of bodies even as they toil away at their proclaimed mission: to fill in the promised discussion of catharsis missing from Aristotle.[21] In pursuing a "vocabulary of tragedy" ("On Catharsis" 338), Burke keeps bumping into bodies. He notices this tendency early on and observes, "The problem of *physicality* in tragedy will plague us throughout this essay" (342; emphasis in original).[22]

By my count Burke ends up confronting four bodies of catharsis.[23] Each of these categories can be traced back to his "Anaesthetic Revelation" story and into his most bodily essay, "The Thinking of the Body." The sections below will therefore discuss each of the four bodies of catharsis in turn in order first to consider more deeply the theoretical tangle Burke got himself in where bodies are concerned, and second to set up my later argument that he came to terms with this mess of bodies on the operating table.

Catharsis as Bodily Purge

Most discussions of the Greek term *katharsis* follow Aristotle by noting its beginnings as a concept in both music and medicine. As Burke's sometimes translation of the term as *purge* reveals, he is well cognizant of the conceptual overlap between the two domains, as he writes in "On Catharsis, or Resolution": "Also there are the body puns implicit in the very idea of Catharsis. Thus, in the *Politics*, Aristotle says that some people are as strongly affected by sacred melodies as though they had taken a purge in the purely medical sense of the term" (342). Burke goes even further, playing philological contortionist when he notes, "Nor should we forget that our word 'drastic,' which originally meant a strong laxative, comes from the same Greek root as the word 'drama'" (342). Here he seems to be suggesting just how close the association between catharsis and drama had become for a (distant) derivation to also pass on the purgative tones.[24] While some philologists, such as Lear, argue forcefully that dramatic and medical meanings of *katharsis* are decidedly distinct, it is nevertheless tempting to relate the two, as Burke did. Pursuing these bodily associations or "puns" of *catharsis*, he devotes an entire section of "On Catharsis, or Resolution" to its body-purging aspect. He begins by quoting a general discussion of bodily purging from the introduction to the Loeb translation of the *Poetics*: "The soul, like the body, needs an occasional purge. Pent-up emotion is apt to explode inconveniently. What the citizens need is an outlet such as dramatic poetry conveniently supplies. We must remember that the Athenian could not go to the theater every day. That would be emotional dysentery. He took his purge regularly twice a year" (Fyfe xvii; quoted in "On Catharsis" 354). No doubt Burke admires the line about a potential overdose on drama leading to "emotional dysentery." What remains less clear, as is evident from the next body of catharsis, is whether he buys the sharp distinction between soul and body and the subsequent seating of emotions in the soul or psyche rather than the body.

Opting instead for the less divisive language of "counterparts," Burke proceeds to extend his consideration of poetic purge, wondering about poetic language's ability to go beyond the usual on-and-off suspects—"laxatives, diuretics, aphrodisiacs, antaphrodisiacs, and anodynes or anaesthetics" (354). "Should not the language of poerty [sic]," Burke wonders,

> also somehow have its equivalents of emetics, sudorifics, astringents, expectorants, and sternutatories (with perhaps a special set for women: emmenagogues, arbortifacients [sic], oxytocics, lactifuges and galactagogues)? Imagery that somehow stood for *flatus* would belong here; and there would be the analogue of *crepitus ventris,* for which eructation would be a kind of euphemism. ("Respectable" translations of Aristophanes substitute terms for eructation in passages where the original vocabulary was frankly fecal, in accordance with modes proper to comic catharsis.) Coughing, sneezing, expectoration, even quick expulsion of breath, might be classed as attenuated variants of a cleansing operation; and the same would apply to any words that stood for them. Thus, persons sometimes sneeze at a remark they resent; or there is the cough of embarrassment, or a mere clearing of the throat, as a sign of disapproval. Fainting, and its milder form, dizziness, are doubtless on the outer edges of such responses (and might be secondarily indicated in the imagery of height, or speed)—though they might also, like horripilation, chills, fever, and cataleptic seizures, be classed rather as acute evidence that catharsis is needed. Hence they might be "pre-cathartic," if part of a process in which catharsis is consummated. (Consider, for instance, Dante's fainting in the circle of Hell where he encounters the dizziness of wind-driven Paolo and Francesca. It is "pre-cathartic," in the sense that it is on the road to Purgatory, by definition the *place of catharsis.*) ("On Catharsis" 354–55; emphasis in original)

Here Burke stocks his poetic pharmacy by running the gamut of physical conditions. These conditions range from expulsion and even (puzzlingly) suppression of bodily fluids and motions—from retching and sweating to sneezing and belching. Aside from reaffirming the connection between drugs and poetry that Burke notices as early as *Counter-Statement,* what exactly does this catalog of rather violent discharge accomplish with regard to a broad theory of catharsis?

The effect of this *accumulatio,* this "heaping up" of conditions and their remedies, is to fashion readers and viewers of poetic works as physical readers and viewers, readers and viewers with bodies. But even more than that, the various kinds of physicality presented here—goose bumps, chills, cataleptic seizures—make for a physically potent handlist of possible evocations. Such a list therefore functions inventively—as an accretion of the available kinds of cathartic responses—as much as it does constitutionally.

If the exhaustive list does not already demonstrate that Burke resists a biologically determined cathartic formula, he reins things in with this qualification:

> Please note that in pursuing such a line of thought we should *not* be deriving tragic catharsis from bodily processes. Our theory would be turned in exactly the opposite direction. We should be saying simply that, when catharsis attains its full poetic statement (as it must if it is to be thorough), its terminology may also be expected to re-enact some or other of these bodily analogues. That is: If the poet radically "gives body" to the idea of cleansing, besides such devices as cleansing by sacrifice, cleansing by the mimetics of the bath, and cleansing by association with things deemed ritually clean, there should be the equivalents of sheerly animal release (such "cleansing" as the body experiences when unburdening itself of its natural secretions, be they sexual or otherwise). (355–56)

And so Burke's drug theory of poetry—poetry as that which induces, expectorates, speeds up, or slows down—functions on a mimetic level. He then goes on to equate pity, fear, and pride—the *pharmaka* of dramatic catharsis—with the three "persons" of his demonic trinity: the erotic, the diuretic, and the excremental. This "giving body" of poetry therefore forms the center of Burke's theory of catharsis, what he will eventually publish as "The Thinking of the Body," an essay that has itself frequently functioned as an emetic for Burke scholars. The demonic trinity notwithstanding, however, cathartic excretion need not be confined to the lower body, as evidenced by the way Burke's catalog of conditions and remedies roves all over the body. Such range leads to the second body of catharsis: the body that laughs and cries.

Laughter, Tears

On the question of just who exactly is excreting and expelling—the characters? the audience? the author?—Burke is ambiguous at best, which suggests that the catharsis essays have gotten past his earlier allegiance to intrinsic criticism. Indeed the laughing and crying body—or the body that really interests Burke, the one that "laughs till it cries" (342)—noticeably resists his intrinsic poetics. In another section "plagued" by physicality, he writes, "Formally, Poetics deals with *poetry,* not *human bodies.* Yet tears and laughter can be almost convulsive in their physicality" (341). While Burke's later theories of poetics mightily try to stick with a kind of intrinsic physicality—with the bodies depicted in literature, for example—the discussion of laughter and tears inevitably is better suited to bodies in the audience (reader, listener viewer), the bodies that received much more attention in his earlier poetic theories, for example, in *Counter-Statement*.

Both the tearful body and the body racked with laughter present opportunities to consider the melding of at least three bodies: the body of the artist that "inspirits" the words; the purging bodies of dramatic characters (such as Prometheus); and the chuckling, sobbing bodies of readers. With Burke's dissolving categories as my guide, I would suggest that it is a mistake to isolate or to privilege any of these bodies over the others.[25] Literary criticism in the 1990s found the limits of bodies-as-represented, a move that frequently reaffirmed the tenets of social construction, but the more interesting possibility is the way bodies in literature leap right into readers' bodies in a physical process of transference. Such transference happens through words and what Burke calls in an earlier essay their "bountiful materiality."[26]

Poetic theories of transference—the spreading of body-thinking from body to body—work to complicate recent dismissals of body theory, the most notable one by Fredric Jameson, who believes that "the proliferation of theories of the body nowadays" depends on "a mechanical materialism descended from the eighteenth-century Enlightenment rather than a historical and social materialism of the type that emerged from Marx and from a properly historical (nineteenth-century) worldview" (713). And yet the process described by Burke is far from mechanistic. Indeed if the body-to-art-to-body transference were so predictable and regular, he likely would not have been so mired in its problems.[27]

When Burke considers, however briefly, the irreducible physicality of bodies that laugh and cry, he finds yet another vibrating node at which words and bodies meet. The work of laughter and tears to draw together physical lives and symbolic lives is a major focus in his second catharsis essay. Here he treats this version of physicality more thoroughly than the others, noting that "the striking thing about both these modes of release is their nature as *completions, fulfillments*. Weeping or laughing are *end-products*" (107; emphasis in original). He continues: "They have the finality of a ship coming into port. Also, although as responses to works of art they arise out of purely *symbolic* processes, at the same time they are both intensely *physical*. Thus, there is a sense in which they perfectly bridge the gap between man's nature as sheer animal and his nature as sheerly 'rational' or 'spiritual' (as symbol-user)" (108). Laughter and tears, for Burke, are precisely points where bodies greet language, given a work's ability to conjure such "intensely physical" responses. Importantly, however, in both catharsis articles, laughter and weeping raise one of the most confounding dualities of body-thinking: the individual versus collective, or the radical individuality of physical experience and language systems' dependency on more-than-one. Indeed this conundrum of individual versus collective is what distinguishes Burke's "first view" from his "second view" on catharsis.

Bodies in a Crowd: Individual versus Collective

One of the most formidable challenges of theorizing bodies is the temptation to assume that "body" always means an individual body, a discrete, knowable, and knowing subject. In such "a one body reference," "the body" simply becomes the new liberal subject, the stand-in for humanist principles, and therefore offers nothing new (Jameson 713).

And yet in "On Catharsis, or Resolution" Burke's poetics spills beyond the one-body model with two thought experiments, both inspired by crowds. Is there such a thing, Burke wants to know, as group purge? In the middle of that essay he invokes Euripides' *Trojan Women* in order to ground his discussion of political purges, or what he calls the "'civic emphasis'" in poetic works. According to Burke the play's focus on the fall of Troy takes the audience beyond the immediate issue—"the Athenians' disgraceful destruction of Melos, an act that split Athens in two"—and because of this poetic transference, Burke writes, "the entire audience, be they members of either the Peace Party or the War Party, could join in weeping together" (351). "And would that movement," he asks, "at least for the duration of the dramatic experience, be indeed a purging of the whole discordant city?" (351). Such a picture—"of eighteen thousand people being purged by weeping in unison"—once again, he observes, introduces the "question of 'physicality'" (352). To consider the question further he contrasts the physical space of the ancient theater with a more contemporary medium: "It is not inconceivable, for instance, that the dramatic effect of a situation in which many people are similarly moved would be greater if they were assembled in one gathering than if they were isolated from one another (if, say, they sat before eighteen thousand widely separated television screens, responding to the same play rather as 'individuals' than as parts of a single vibrant body)" (353–54).

The introduction of the "single vibrant body"—the body of the crowd—hearkens back to Burke's much earlier reflections on the live scene of music as much as it does to the mystical scene of Gurdjieffian dance performances. Curiously Burke departs from the scene of drama and turns to the world of nonhuman animals for the analogy he deems most apt: "I have in mind a response somewhat physically analogous to the uniform throb of insects on a warm night in early autumn" (354). He is noting a kind of life of the crowd, the "throb" of mobs, and his insect analogy marks a supersession of individual bodies, a mass joining-in of crowd bodies that can have a unifying effect, more so, he speculates in the above passage, than the same number of individuals watching the same drama in isolation and on a screen.

The mob-throb, or processes by which shared responses spread through a crowd, have enlivened the work of theorists in the late twentieth and early twenty-first centuries.[28] In Burke's brief discussion the use of insects demarcates crowd bodies as governed by something other than conscious, cognitive effort. The responsive effort is intensely physical, and Burke's noting of temperature—"a warm night"—seems significant as well, for heat is known to stir things up, and bodies pressed together in a crowd generate even more heat. The questions that haunt his treatment of groups are these: To what extent do physical, nonconscious factors such as temperature and noise level figure into the collective purge? At what point does a random gathering become a uniform crowd body?

At stake in this discussion is the question of the individuating effect of the body, and that question launches Burke's second catharsis essay. Here is the opening passage:

> In our first view of Catharsis, because we were working primarily with Greek models we stressed the *civic* nature of the "pollution" for which tragedy concocts a remedy. But there is a sense in which even elations or sorrows shared by us as members of a collectivity are experienced by us as *individuals*, quite as each person at a public banquet derives a particular gratification from the particular food that is eaten by him in particular. The centrality of the nervous system is a *principium individuationis* whereby, no matter how collective the nature of our symbol-systems and of the sociopolitical structures that go with them, our pleasures and pains are our own naturally inalienable private property. ("Catharsis—Second View" 107)

That physiological experiences—or feelings, as Rei Terada designates them—are at once inalienable and transmittable is what keeps bodies at the very edge of language, at the limn of communicability. Burke even goes so far as to note that laughter and tears demonstrate most visibly that "the body participates directly in the producing of catharsis by the organizing of symbol-systems" (107). The word *organizing* here suggests a kind of physiological distribution of meaning, one that follows the lead of endocrinology, which suggests through its engagement with hormones as transmitters that bodies participate directly in meaning-making processes.

This direct participation makes it very difficult indeed for Burke to limit his theory of poetics to the symbolic realm. His attempt to do so midway through the "Second View" essay reveals the futility of bracketing bodies for the sake of a pure theory of symbolism. His first attempt to isolate the symbolic ends with two exceptions: "Insofar as symbol-systems involve relationships and developments intrinsic to themselves and thus not strictly translatable into any kinds of bodily or social behavior, such purely symbolic sequences may possess modes of gratification or release not explainable by reference to physical hypotheses at all (except in the sense that the failure to solve a problem in physics or mathematics might impair a person's health, whereas success at finding a solution could have a good effect upon his attitude towards people and things in general)" (110).

In this paragraph the parentheses offer a distant and therefore subtle refutation of the suggestion that symbol systems may operate without reference to bodies.

But in the next paragraph—his second attempt—bodies become unavoidable: "When, in Poetics, we analyze the workings of a symbol-system, we require no reference to possible ways in which people might, by the complications of a plot, become in some sense physically charged and thus made ready to enjoy a corresponding physical state of discharge. Yet when asking about the possible relation between the symbol-using animal and his symbols, we do have to consider such 'hypotheses,' since the non-symbolic body is a necessary hypothesis of all symbol-systems" (110).

In other words, bodies are necessary but not sufficient for a theory of language. From here Burke continues to lay out guidelines for his poetics: "So we must keep too [sic] different considerations in mind here. We must be on the look-out for the possibilities of symbolic development that quietly 'transcend' the body (except insofar as physiological motions are a necessary ground of all empirical symbolic action). And we must be on the look-out for respects in which the body does figure, when we go from questions about comedy and tragedy as cathartic instruments to questions about laughter and tears as cathartic instruments" (110–11).

His final cautionary guideline is perhaps the most lucid statement on the relationship between what Burke would later call nonsymbolic motion and symbolic action: "And as we should guard against seeking for too close a correlation between the body and its symbol-systems, so we should guard against a tendency to ignore the points at which the two realms do significantly correlate" (111). In other words, critics should neither overemphasize nor underemphasize the constant back-and-forth, give-and-take relation between bodies and language. The catharsis essays therefore show Burke stuck in a labyrinth or two: "The 'cathartic' relation between articulate form and the inarticulate matter out of which such expression emerges I would call 'labyrinthine,' a pre-condition of the 'Daedalian' motive. It involves a maze in two senses: for not only is the inarticulate a tangle (at least, as viewed from the standpoint of the articulate); but also articulation itself is a tangle, since any symbol-system sets up an indeterminate range of 'implications' still to be explored" (364).

This pair of tangles, the articulate form of language and inarticulate matter (bodily impulses), forms a maze even more complex than the one fashioned by the cunning craftsman Daedalus to confine the Minotaur, in part because, as Burke notes, the maze of catharsis is double, involving on the one hand a whole heap of material—flesh, bile, tears—and the bounty of words (articulate matter) on the other. In Burke's tangled theory of poetic catharsis, the relation between the two is one of conversion, as he writes earlier: "Unquestionably the symbol-using animal experiences a certain kind of 'relief' in the mere act of converting any inarticulate muddle into the orderly terms of a symbol-system" (364).[29] And the movement between individual bodies and bodies of a crowd leads Burke to this overarching point.

Bodies and the Ecology of Their Cleansing

Despite Burke's attempt to move beyond the individual body problem, a focus on bodies and language might still seem to some a bit myopic, even apolitical. And yet the final body that emerges from his tangles with Aristotle sets him on what might be the most interesting, most fully developed, most politically relevant body discussed thus far: the body that is part of an ecology. An examination of the ecological body in Burke's writings provides a more legible, even more political framework for his cloacal criticism in "The Thinking of the Body."

Even though Burke's reflections in "On Catharsis, or Resolution" use the language of pollution,[30] the focus on ecology in relation to bodies begins to take hold in "Catharsis—Second View." Here he hits upon one of the basic lessons of what would later be termed ecocriticism, and it is a lesson that may be derived from the most basic tenets of his earliest writings: just as stressing a set of terms means destressing another set of terms, a "cleansing" or purifying usually entails a concomitant sullying.[31] Here is Burke: "If there is a cleansing, there must be persons or things that do the cleansing, and there must be the offscourings that result from the cleansing. Implicit here, in turn, is the idea of the need to dispose of the offscourings, or in some way to neutralize their bad effects" (123). As a remedy for pollution, catharsis enters into an infinite regress of cleansing, and this regress in turn leads Burke, however tacitly, to the Beauty Clinic. He continues, "We find implicit in the idea of offscourings the substitution or vicarage whereby one thing becomes unclean as a result of the process whereby another is cleansed. (Thus, if the purifying bath is one kind of 'fulfillment,' the impure bath-water is another.)" (123). The idea that purification is not, in the end, pure, captures Burke's attention, and he goes on to consider the wordy ecology that so many scholars have noticed:[32] "We refer to the fact that one can feel a whole universe of terms vibrant in the key term he chooses as his point of departure" (124). The notion of vibrant terms, however subtly, invokes the magical, material view of language set forth in the early poetics essays, and yet Burke does not stop there. Instead he moves back into the realm of material "offscourings," which is his translation of the Greek *katharmata*, those things which are "thrown away after cleansing" (Liddell, Scott, and Jones 850)—the dirty water, the corpse from an animal sacrifice, etc. This idea of residual pollution proves to be a most vexing paradox for Burke: "There is a sense in which the cleaning has led to the unclean. Or, otherwise put: the unclean is either displaced, or 'covered.' And this principle of removal introduces in effect the principle of substitution, or vicarage, since the cleansing of one place incidentally involves the polluting of another" (125). As a term *katharmata* thereby applies as equally to dirty bathwater as it does to dirty words, and dirty bodily processes covered over in what Burke calls the Beauty Clinic.

Burke's "me-and-Aristotle sort of thing," in the end, moves him through a theory of poetics to a decidedly physical, ecological perspective, a move that gets beyond the previously established confines of literature even as it surmounts the one-body problem. The reason for this decisive move to ecology may be read in the final line of his 1963 essay "The Thinking of the Body": "These pages are offered, not in the belief that the issue has been settled, but in the hopes that its relation to much more important matters has been indicated" (68). The referent of *its* here, though not entirely clear, is most likely "body-thinking," the hyphenated phrase that receives the most emphasis in the previous paragraph. It could also, however, refer back to the essay's subtitle—"Comments on the Imagery of Catharsis in Literature." Either way Burke's essay has labored to show how images of catharsis betray a body-thinking, a poetic act of "giving body" to ideas, as well as a decidedly physical account of reading (and weeping). The point here, though, is that body-thinking, catharsis, and *katharmata*, while rendered poetically as rain showers, as shackles, as mist, extend to "much more important matters," matters such as pollution and war, death and life. So much for the confines of literature.

This move—from intrinsic criticism early in the decade to ecology later in the decade—might well be credited to a revelation. Or perhaps two. Burke writes about one possible revelation toward the end of "The Thinking of the Body":

> Before closing, let's ask specifically just how the imagery of death as such might figure. As I write these words I am living on a Florida key, where I love to walk among the whole and broken shells (skeletons and parts of skeletons) that the waves toss up on the beach. Never for a moment do I cease to think of these things as the detritus of *death*, aspects of life's *offal*. I live with the thought that digestion and fertilization involve the life-giving properties of *corruption*, that life grows out of *rot*.
>
> Then, suddenly, an idea of this sort invaded me, when I was comparing and contrasting these natural forms with, say, the forms of sculpture. (65; emphasis in original)

Burke's invasive revelation is this: statues have no bones, and yet they are cast in such a way as to retain "the 'principle' of the skeleton beneath the flesh" (65–66). "By the same token, sheerly structural forms would be all skeleton, insofar as they are, however remotely, imitations of bodily articulations." He continues: "Insofar as they are not thus 'bodily' at all, presumably they are attempts to transcend death" (66). Sculptures of the human form, that is, exist at "a halfway stage between skeleton and skeleton transcended" (66); they are both body and not-body. Similarly "no-no" or cloacal language simultaneously invokes and "transcends" a "bowels of the earth" materiality: "All told, though the principle of the negative is often embodied in 'No no' kinds of imagery, it is itself neither 'life-affirming' nor 'life-denying.' It is a marvel of language, perhaps *the* marvel of language—and though 'Don't' can constrain us (thus to an extent, 'mortifying' our desires) it can also save us (when inducing us to guard against real danger)" (66).

In elaborating his seaside revelation, then, Burke hits upon a kind of "deathiness" as that which paradoxically binds and divides bodies and language: "The negative could in itself be 'deathy' only in the sense that, while man cannot properly use language at all unless he has a feel for the principle of the negative, all symbolism can be a mockery. That is, although symbolism may help us get food, as sheer bodies we live or die not by the words for food, but by the food. As a person we want another person, not just a symbol for that person. In this sense all such 'transcending' of the thing by its name is towards death. And in this sense, even the most 'vital' of language is intrinsically deathy'" (66).

Without bodies the realm of the symbolic is tantamount to death itself. Burke proceeds to clarify: language's realm "is a realm of 'essence' that, without the warm blood of live bodies to feed it, it cannot truly 'exist'" (66). And yet the next paragraph begins with a hedge: "But even if one concedes that symbolism is 'intrinsically deathy' in this ultimate sense, the fact remains that the great utility of language in helping men cooperate and prosper and praise and give thanks endows it with plenty of 'vital' associations" (66). In the John Crowe Ransom–inspired language of the catharsis essays, in relation to the world's body and the human body, language becomes deathy, slipping into a realm beyond the material, but in relation to the body politic—when individual bodies are seen as part of a collective—language fulfills its vital capacities. Burke's discussion of language's dependency on "warm blood of live bodies" provides one of the most clear formulations of what would become his perplexing "nonsymbolic motion / symbolic action" pair, a pair that so many scholars insist on reading as more divided than not. Instead, as Burke decided in "Catharsis—Second View," bodies—the realm of nonsymbolic motion—are necessary for the movement and life-giving properties of language.[33]

Crescendo: Ecopolitics

The end of "The Thinking of the Body" offers Burke's most startlingly clear formulation of an ecological view on literature. It is a view that would refuse to be confined to internal workings of a text, but that would always urge beyond, around the corner—toward humans' most stench-filled and "deathy" impulses. In allowing himself to be "plagued by the physical" and developing an ecological view of literature, Burke would also formulate what would become his "nonsymbolic motion / symbolic action" pair. All the more reason for Burkean critics to engage "The Thinking of the Body."

After the broad meditation on language and "deathiness," Burke then discusses the "subterfuges" by which images of catharsis are allowed in literature without violating "parlor 'propriety'" or formal "rules of the game" (67). Here he raises the scepter of gallantry, which corresponds directly to the Beauty Clinic—the critical impulse to overlook and thereby wipe clean any shit-smeared expression. Instead, and "in sum," Burke continues, "insofar as poets 'give body' to their thoughts, look for Aristophanes, Rabelais, Swift, and Company in the offing, however roundabout" (67).

Burke's next move is a quick one—from "Aristophanes . . . and Company" to "more important matters" (68)—and the speed with which he makes it intimates that the comic, satiric, and grotesque are also immanent in "all sorts of related paradoxical variations in our way of life, with its special stress upon hygiene as the modern equivalent for the ritually clean" (67). His "for instances" settle decisively on ecopolitical concerns, including "the ideal of floor wax that does not 'yellow,' when the floors are compulsively kept polished to the point where they become a major menace to life and limb"; "millions of dollars spent on detergents that add disgracefully to the pollution of our waters, and all for some slight extra edge of white in our fabrics that is wholly worthless except as the obedient response to a commercially stimulated idea of purely ritual cleanliness" (67). Here the pitch increases: "Precisely while loading up the world with murderous atomic wastes in the name of power and progress, or with dangerous chemicals that add some useless gloss or luster to the looks of a food, people have so 'disciplined' their critical faculties, they do not want to realize just what all, so far as 'body-thinking' is concerned, would be implied in the fact that we necessarily 'anthropomorphize' nature" (67–68).

Reading "The Thinking of the Body" in the context of the 1950s—especially in the context of Burke's Aristotle-inspired effort to cull a poetics with catharsis at its core—helps to show how Burke's poetics, his "Symbolic," expanded, much like a giant balloon, hovering, heavy and bloated, and then broke. The irrefutable importance of the body might be pinned to an operating table, to a rather traumatic hernia operation Burke underwent in 1956. His newly expanded aesthetics, it might be said, owes at least partly to anesthetics, and a major breakdown in hospital scheduling.

"A Very Bad Time with Bloatage"

Such a suggestion takes us back to the realm of body biography, where this chapter began. In late September 1956[34] Burke was placed under anesthesia for a routine hernia operation, and only after the anesthesia was administered did the hospital workers realize that the surgeon was not present. As Burke wrote to

William Carlos Williams after he had been discharged, "The operation, which was originally scheduled for 10:30, was moved ahead to somewhere around 8 or 8:30. And this caused a slip-up whereby, as I lay doped to the gills and all but ultimately out, on the operating table, everybody began asking where the hell the surgeon might be." As it turns out, the surgeon was "home having breakfast, nearly three-quarters of an hour away" (October 15, 1956; East 199). As Burke narrates it in the letter, "various things involved in this delay gradually worked me up into a fury, so that apparently I was squirting adrenalin during the operation. Anyhow, we know that I was in the operating room for two hours, for an operation that should have required much less time—so I had quite a batch of dope to get out of me afterwards" (East 199). In Burke's correspondence with Cowley, the operation ups the ante in their ongoing ailment competition: "As I was saying!" he exclaimed to Cowley from his hospital bed, "Concerning ailments. Bilateral inguinal hernia. And having a bad time with bloatage. A very bad time with bloatage" (October 1956). The marks of his suffering—"shots for this, that, and the other—including intravenous feeding"—are "all over" him, and his letter ends with a mournful whimper: "I am withered as an old man of ninety and feeble as a newborn baby. And not full of confidence, no. In fact, I'm going to crawl back to bed, a much beaten up piece of semi-human flesh." Burke's wife, Libbie, amended the letter, adding these details at the bottom for their friend's benefit:

Operation Sat. a.m.
Complications of alimentary canal terrific
Supposed to stay a week
Dr. (noted N.Y. surgeon!)
Lousy, and I mean lousy.

Burke had been drugged up, cut up, stitched up. He had been in effect broken down, and everyone around him was worried. Cowley's reply sympathizes, "That picture of KB lying anesthetized while his sawyer and seamster had breakfast twenty miles away is a frightening picture. Later I heard from Dutchie [Burke's eldest daughter, Elspeth], via Hannah, who met her on the street, that in the hospital you looked truly beat for the first time" (November 8, 1956).

As Burke indicates to Williams, though, the breakdown was only partly physical; the rest of his seething suffering came from the "wall of total silence" constructed about the hospital's error: "For me to so much as mention any of my experiences in the operating room was to say an unforgivably dirty word. One intern, at one point, growled that 'writers talk too much,' . . . so I lay there day after day, night after night, in stony steely vigil, following the hospital noises, in an anguish of unremitting wakefulness. I was not his patient, I was his prisoner—and the experience was something little short of terror" (October 15, 1956; East

199–200). If to speak of medical error is tantamount to uttering "an unforgivably dirty word," then Burke may have discovered the Beauty Clinic in the sterile halls and bright lights of the hospital. Indeed bright lights and sterile silence dominate the short story Burke wrote just following the experience, "The Anaesthetic Revelation of Herone Liddell."

Burke banged out "Anaesthetic Revelation" during an extended recuperative stay in Florida during the early months of 1957, the same trip where he revised "Thinking of the Body." In a letter to Cowley that begins with a meditation on shark's teeth, he includes a copy of "Anaesthetic" with this wry description, "I send you herewith my obviously fictitious story about a guy who had a hernia operation, and following it, took a trip south" (March 3, 1957).[35] Given that this visit to the shore is likely the same one during which Burke added the "revelatory" culminating paragraphs to "The Thinking of the Body," the winter of 1956–57 might be considered central for his return to ecology, and his botched anesthesia session figures prominently into that return. Indeed most scholars who write about Burke and ecology mention the story, but they do so only in passing, in order to mention the section title "Haunted by Ecology."[36] It is a seductive phrase, but simply calling up the phrase ignores the contours of the particular ecology about which Burke is writing and brushes past his most fervently ecological period, the period during which it all fell together, like a revelation.

Herone Liddell's Revelation

Left under anesthesia for hours longer than he should have been, the "little hero" of Burke's story notices how his body, its limbs "clamped tight" (508), formulates words and sentences that his mouth, frozen by anesthesia, could not fully articulate.[37] The description of Herone's predicament on the operating table is equal parts Aristotle, endocrinology, and gesture-speech theory:

> The Philosopher admonishes that anger drives out fear—and true to the book, Herone's fright turned to rage, almost rage in the absolute. For he was so confined that the only mode of fighting possible to him under the circumstances was limited to whatever kind of surgings could take place within his own guts. At least the physiological processes that might load his blood with his own adrenalin were not strapped down, so he freely seethed within. Outwardly, the resources of hating were reduced to mere cursing—but even that outlet in turn was reduced, by the aphasic conditions resulting from the amount of anaesthetics already in his system, to ineffectual words that somehow refused to come out right. Things were so set up that, if wanting to call someone a filthy bastard, he would at most hear himself, as though from within himself, shouting as though from outside himself, "oo lya snar!" This was especially vexing for a Word-man, in his ferocious but futile struggles against the "indifferent Powers" that had bound him. (508)

The easy movement from Aristotle's theory of pathos to the glandular outrage to the "ineffectual" "oo lya snar!" suggests that the trauma of such a procedural gaffe is capable of exciting all available resources of bodily expression. The word *snar,* not coincidentally, I think, appears in Paget's glossary of pantomimic roots as "twist, draw tight, entwine, make a noose" (*Human Speech* 152). That Herone is able to fight so determinedly even as he "lay, suspended in a state of helplessness and rage, just on the edge of extinction . . . a 'bruised bleeding maniac . . . made powerless by straps and pain and drugs'" (509), forms the basis for the questions driving the piece: "Had he fought even while wholly anaesthetized? Could the body, even in sheer mindless physicality, hate the instruments that prodded at its tissues; and might it thereby load the blood with the juices of sheerly physical strife?" (511). This pointed query arises from a pair of observations. The first names a particularly noticeable kind of body-thinking:

> Certain ideas that occurred to him (or came to ride him, rather) turned his diaphragm into a band of steel, stopped all unfolding, transformed the churning gases of his bowels into stony immobility. But other ideas, equally beyond his willpower, brought with them relaxation, and a corresponding flow of blessed flatulencies, until in the course of events things shifted again to associations of the rigidifying sort—and in a flash, the muscles of his stomach became hard knots, as clenched as a fist. In brief, he could shift (or, more accurately, he was shifted) between tense associations and relaxed ones, with the muscles of his bowels and stomach making a burlesqued behavioristic replica of the differences between the two attitudes. (510)

An associational tug-of-war plays out inside Herone's body, and the idea-motivated body has, by the end of the passage, all but won over, as evidenced by the explicit shift from active to passive voice ("he could shift" becomes "he was shifted"). Attitudes take hold in the title character's alimentary system, and the takeover is noticeable in part because the character has been forcibly rendered motionless: "Lying with distended bowels, a loathsome tube inserted through one nostril into his stomach . . . Herone was impressed first of all by the extreme *physicality* of his condition. He thought of himself as an item in a process, to be poked or jabbed at set stages along the way, in accordance with a pre-arranged schedule—and things would proceed as per schedule despite the fact (if it was a fact!) that something had gone radically wrong with the schedule at the very start—if he could trust the naggingly unforgettable though muddled memory of his impotent rage while lying strapped and waiting (a maniac in a straight jacket), under the inquisitorial glare of the floodlights, or whatever they were" (511; emphasis in original).

Perhaps the most striking thing about this passage is its uncertainty with regard to what exactly transpires while Herone is on the operating table. The character's groggy and drug-addled recollection is as tenuous as his sense that the hospital lights were roughly the same as those "used by police officers when questioning criminals or attempting to break the spirit of political prisoners" (509). The only certainty, in fact, is Herone's physicality, so that is where he begins to reconstruct the ordeal: "Had he fought even while wholly anaesthetized? Could the body, even in sheer mindless physicality, hate the instruments that prodded at its tissues; and might it thereby load the blood with the juices of sheerly physical strife?" These are not questions that Herone keeps to himself, and yet his queries receive the equivalent of a leg clamp: when "he had started to discuss them volubly with his room-mate, an intern who happened to be present made a sign indicating that Herone should shut up—and then severely murmured to himself for Herone's benefit, 'Writers talk too much'" (511). Finding himself "Under the Sign of the Quietus" (512)—a description that folds "hush hush" and "no no" in with death itself—Liddell has gotten doubly clamped, his wordy movements and bodily movements forcibly stilled. As he writes to a psychologist friend, "I feel as though I had had my connotations cut out" (527).

The hospital's censure preoccupies the main character, prompting him to reflect less on the schedule snafu and more on institutional taboo: "Ultimately, however, as always with a Word-man, the problem had developed into a problem of the Quietus. The ideal patient was expected simply to *believe in* the Routines, and no questions asked, whereas nothing was normal with Herone until it was talked about, if even then. But the surgeon had become so evanescent, Herone almost had to scheme to see him—and for quite understandable reasons, nurses and interns avoided all discussions like the plague. Everybody going about his or her business—and from the standpoint of a Word-man, it was as though some Dirty Deed had been done, with no one returning to the scene of the crime" (515).

On one level, the story, the metaphysical reflection, the "what is it" here offers a straightforward ideological critique of medical institutions. But that critique turns on the cloacal, here found in the phrase "Dirty Deed," which flattens beneath the clamp of the hush-hush.

The titular revelation, then, arrives in a mystical "fever-dream." "How could our hero hope to see around the corner of himself," the narrator asks, "if he could not catch himself dreaming?" (532). In the dream Liddell "had the conviction that he had watched the very essence of realism, through the very essence of criticism, become the very essence of idealism" (522). The revelatory dream features a light, a voice, and a drug. The light is emitted from a set of straight, glowing rods, splayed out yet connected "somewhat like the blades of a lawnmower" (520). "In this respect," Herone interprets, "there really would be a sense in which the different rods of light could be simultaneously one and many" (520). The voice, known in the dream to be "the Absolute Voice," in familiar dreamlike fashion both is and is not Herone's, and the dream voice "was giving a *rock-bottom explanation* of things, and with regard to the effects of 'proprio-nyl,' Herone's dream-name for his anaesthetic" (521).[38] While proprionyl does name an energy-releasing compound, in this context it more likely invokes the Latin combination of "not" (*nyl*) and "one's own." On this reading anesthesia evacuates any kind of self-control. In the dream's "Absolute Voice," then, "'proprio-nyl' was being praised not for its value as an anaesthetic, but for its contribution to the understanding of 'reality'" (521). That is, "the design of the glowing rods (in their ambiguous shift between oneness and plurality) . . . was intended to teach *exactly how* the universe is constructed. . . . it was intended not as a 'model,' not as a 'suggestive illustration,' but as a revelation of the literal basic fact" (521). And yet the revelation, interestingly, itself incorporates a narrative of breakdown: "The Voice explained how, on one occasion, something went wrong with the working of this fundamental educative device—and in the course of repairing it, an important new discovery was made" (521). At base the repair revealed that a one-to-one correspondence between the light rods and reality was not possible: "The rods could be seen from different angles of approach (that objects could be seen from many sides), so that the interpretation of reality became more complicated (we might say more 'perspectival,' though this word did not present itself during the dream)" (521).

At this point, perhaps to the relief of the story's readers, Herone wakes up. But when he does, he believes that the dream revealed realism and idealism as intricately mediated by interpretation: "Might his 'anaesthetic revelation' (or, more accurately, his 'post-anaesthetic revelation') be reducible ultimately to but the more pressing realization of a condition that he had realized long before he ever took his somewhat expensive punishment? Were there certain resources of language, driving us towards a purely linguistic fulfillment, as though towards the origin of everything? A terminology had certain logical conclusions implicit in it, certain possibilities of completion, or 'perfection'—and for a symbol-using species maybe these can form as real a kind of ultimate purpose as any congeries of material things and physical sensations" (530–31).

This section probes "the goad" from Burke's earliest poetics articles even as it urges toward the famous last line of Burke's definition of man, "rotten with perfection" ("Definition" 507). If Burke's ecological view holds that "life grows out of rot," then what results is an intricate, almost cyclical movement from body to language to motive, which then loops back around to body. Here is the formulation offered by Herone:

> First, there would be the sheer physicality of life, the human organism as simply one more species of alimentary canal with accessories.
> Second, there would be the miracle, or accident, or perhaps even morbidity, of language, in various ways helping this particular species of

alimentary canal to guide and protect itself in its task of grown, temporary individual survival, and reproduction.

Third, there would be the motives intrinsic to this special property, this miracle, or accident, or morbidity, of language—a plane of symbolism capable of pointing towards "perfections" intrinsic to itself. To live by these, in the sign of their sheer formality, would be to live by "real" ultimates, ultimates proper to the medium. However, in the light of sheer physicality, from the standpoint of the human species as digestive tract with trimmings, such a way of life would be but an "as if." (531)

Perhaps it goes without saying, but the dream that allows Herone to "see around the corner of himself," the dream that leaves him feeling "Ultimate and Beyondish" in the way that people often describe themselves as "peckish," hearkens back to the mystical modes of thought Burke encountered decades earlier and used as the bases for his methods (especially perspective by incongruity and grotesquing). And of course it all falls together in a section of the piece titled "Haunted by Ecology."[39]

"Convalescing," Herone "thought of that sanguine fellow, Benjamin Paul Blood, a protégé of William James, with avidity proclaiming the 'anaesthetic revelation' he had experienced in a dentist's chair" (537). "Surely," ruminates Herone, "at the bottom of [Blood] there was a happy simpleton that took delight in the sheer affinities of sound (along the lines of his thesis that 'icicle' is not a fit name for a 'tub'). Here was the symbol-using genius reduced to one perfect strand. Herone had this happy strand, too" (537). That "perfect," "happy" strand—the "sheer affinities" of sound, "the sheer jingle of words" (537)—marks a fascination with language's affinity for the stuff it relays and relates. The lessons of Sir Richard Paget's gesture-speech theory reverberate throughout the subsequent passages in which "Herone figured things out": "Once language has become re-enforced by a complex socio-political order (with its corresponding codes of 'reason' and 'imagination'), the *material* reality of the human body in physical association with other bodies human and non-human become submerged beneath the *ideality* of socio-political communities (which are saturated with the genius of language)" (539; emphasis in original).

Burke compresses several of the bodies of catharsis into the lengthy phrase "the *material* reality of the human body in physical association with other bodies human and non-human." The glowing light rods are separate but connected, layered with sociopolitical communities, which in turn are "saturated with the genius of language." The lively, noisy, and densely packed description launches a discussion of what Burke refers to elsewhere as cathartic imagery, and the falling together of multiple bodies: "Poetically, philosophically, the ideal world of the pun becomes at this stage available in all its reaches. Thus, if we speak of light as a stream, of ideas as part of a historical current, and of urine as flowing, then urine, light, and ideas can be secretly one (one with blood, with rivers, with the stream of consciousness and the flux of time). For underlying such similarities of usage, there are affinities linking the human body, the world's body, and the body politic" (539). In attempting to add yet another concept—this time that of attitude—to the mix, Herone grapples first with the language of unification and transcendence (attitude as "'transcendent' entitlement") and then opts for the language of music: "Suppose you are a musician—and of a sudden, a likely theme occurs to you. You awaken—and there it is. And somehow it is like an unopened bundle of possibilities. . . . Next you proceed to develop variations on your theme. Successively, you make it brisk, playful, plaintive, pensive, solemn, grandiose, nostalgic, muscularly ingenious, and the like" (540).

He writes of the effects of this fusing effort, the effort to bring bodily attitude in line with language, by following the happy, jingling sounds of words. The net effect is not just happy, fun game-playing but something far more serious, far more transformative: "You have had, in effect, an immediate vision of an ultimate oneness (thanks to symbolic manipulations that have brought many disparate things together). You have had the direct feeling of this principle. You have 'got the idea'" (541). Therefore dwelling on the jangly properties of language can also draw in its most magical properties. And yet the happy material properties may soon get swallowed by "the realm of 'gallantry,' of purely ideal gesturing" (542) that washes over sheer sound with the cleansing properties of terminological order. Here, Herone continues, "begins the drive towards a logic of completion, a cult of perfection, which shows up drastically alas! As a goad towards empire-building, while the ways of empire serve in turn to localize the terminologies of gallantry, with their increasingly minuscule code of courtliness" (543). The issue, for him, "will finally be settled by the extent to which the purely symbolic genius of perfection is allowed to fall out of line with the needs of the body as sheer body" (543). He continues, "For the world of gallantry . . . threatens at every point to disrupt the 'ecological balance' of the purely physical world. Man's 'dominion' over the 'lowlier' species that are put here for his 'use' threatens at every point to become manifest in a way whereby he destroys what he needs directly or indirectly for his own survival. The great 'as if' can be like a very delicate dance, at a gorgeous festival, atop a volcano that is about ready to blow. And often the dance isn't so delicate, or the festival so gorgeous, either" (543).

Herone's gallantry corresponds perfectly to Burke's Beauty Clinic, the point of which is that it has a dark, polluted underbelly. It comes as no surprise, then, that when "thinking along these lines, Herone began to feel 'haunted by ecology'" (543). And that haunting, "the very thoroughness of his concern with man's symbol-using genius," drives Herone "to think with new intensity of man as sheer animal" (543)—to return to physicality. "Anaesthetic Revelation" goes on to another section in which Herone announces this "formula": "Consider me a fairly well-stocked dictionary standing on the edge of the abyss, confronting the biological fatalities under the grim signs of geophysics and ecology, in a mood Ultimate and Beyondish" (545). Even though the characterization is followed with a swift and plunky "End of formula," the story proceeds to try more variations, including a dialectical dramatization, "a battle of Gallantry vs. Ecology," wherein "the principles of 'Gallantry' make for a tragically prideful inability to live a life modestly befitting a human animal, which is to say, a life that would permit us to be truly gallant with regard to the 'lowlier' species too" (557). Another variation combines music with ecology: "To think words by the seaside is like hearing music from a distance. . . . It is to be reminded that, though we think by symbols, we live or die by the demands imposed upon us physiologically, ecologically, geophysically" (557). And then the final variation is one of the sign, or rather of multiple signs: "Put me, motivationally, under the sign of Ailments, Ecology, Geophysics, and Symbolism. . . . I live by dodges, and so do my symptoms" (557). Just as for Burke in "The Thinking of the Body," where language depends on "the warm blood of bodies" for its variable movements, indeed its very existence, the lesson for Herone becomes one of minding the body: "Watching sunsets when shafts of golden sunlight shoot down from turbulent black and golden clouds, I would school the self to see these shafts as sheerly physically as possible" (557). In other words, to turn gallantly toward the sun would be to melt away into nothingness. Bodies—"huddling" and "loquacious"—are, simply put, the matter of life.

Conclusion | *Action in Motion*

> How many categories might we need, when discussing the problem of the relation between our bodies, as sheer physical objects, and their emergence into articulacy (that is, symbolicity)?
>
> Kenneth Burke, "Mind, Body, and the Unconscious"

> But where problems of terminology are concerned, we must always keep on the move.
>
> Kenneth Burke, "Mind, Body, and the Unconscious"

Consider the varieties of lively movement in a 1970s movie theater: the flickering, clapping motions of the film projector, the multisensory involvement enabled by the individual nervous system perched in each chair, the shifting bodies, their whispering chatter. In his 1978 essay "(Nonsymbolic) Motion / (Symbolic) Action" Burke offers such a scene as a way to think through the titular pair, the pair that perhaps best encapsulates the theories of bodies and language considered in this book. Burke's discussion of motion and action in cinema helps illustrate the interanimation of this "basic polarity" ("[Nonsymbolic] Motion" 809): "The sights and sounds of a motion picture are, in themselves, wholly in the realm of motion. But as interpreted by the audience they become a drama, in the realm of symbolic action. These sights and sounds reach the eyes and ears of the audience through the medium of motion. And the audience hears, sees, and interprets them through the motions of the bodily behavior under the control of the nervous structure without which we could not see the sights, hear the sounds, or interpret them as a 'story'" (833–34).

At base, nonsymbolic motion names strictly physical movement, human and nonhuman, while symbolic action names the interpretive, communicative activity of language, the story-ing of motion. And yet this quick description of the movie theater only gives part of the motion/action picture, as Burke observes: "Such purely physiological behavior on the part of the audience can figure in a totally different kind of 'communication'" (834). He then offers the theater's air conditioning system: "I have read that if a thriller is being played, this mechanism must work much harder than if the plot is of a milder sort because of the effects which the excitement of the audience has upon the conditions of the atmosphere in the theatre" (834). Burke dwells on the air conditioning system as a kind of response, its "'sensitivity'" restricted to "physical conditions produced by the sheer *bodies* of the audience in their responses to the motions of the film as a drama" (834; emphasis in original). The air conditioning is limited to the realm of motion; in contrast the crowd of human bodies possesses the dual capacity to respond in the realms of motion and action. The responses in both realms presumably shoot through or overlay each other, with interpretive action elevating symbolic motion and vice versa, prompting an automatic response from the cooling unit. As the villain stalks the hero, viewers translate motion into action; they also might themselves perspire or chill, and the climate control system whirs to motion.

Burke's terms *nonsymbolic motion* and *symbolic action* have caused a good deal of critical confusion. Critics frequently read a firm distinction between the terms and then locate Burke's allegiances on the side of symbolic action.[1] Symbolic action, after all, and not nonsymbolic motion appears in Burke's titles and writings with some frequency. Literary scholar Donald A. Pease, for example, profoundly misreads the terms as diametrically opposed when he claims that Burke "grounded this distinction on the conviction that a symbolic action could only properly originate with the motive to break free of the hold of animal immediacy, which he described as the realm of 'nonsymbolic motion.' This decisive distinction enabled Burke to differentiate symbolic actions from the senseless motions of bestial nature" (73). And yet nowhere in "(Nonsymbolic) Motion / (Symbolic) Action"—the article cited by Pease—does Burke claim that one should, or could, be liberated from bodily matters or that the realm of motion is "senseless," even bestial. If anything, motion is sense-full; for nonsymbolic motion names, among other things, the realm of sensory perception. Moreover, nonsymbolic motion—sheer physical movement—hovers at the edges of language, or symbolic action, neither juxtaposed nor mutually exclusive to it.

Bryan Crable's "Symbolizing Motion" offers the most nuanced reading of Burke's pair, but he also offers a "friendly amendment" to Burke's action and motion writings (121). Crable's amendment—that action or language is "already on the scene" of motion—effectively flips Burke's preferred order, which holds that there is no action without motion. When Crable concludes that "though action is founded in motion, action is already on the scene because it calls motion into existence" (128), he reveals his own faith in language's enormity, its always-and-everywhereness, language's necessity for knowledge.[2] Crable's amendment lends an epistemological emphasis that Burke's pair fundamentally resists in favor of an emphasis on movement.

Throughout this book I have tried to suspend a belief in language as always and only knowledge in order to shift the emphasis to language as action. Again, it is important to remember that for Burke action and knowledge are not necessarily mutually exclusive, but their difference does alter the degree of complexity with which bodies are approached by critics. In Crable's view, for example, motion, the realm of bodies and nature, remains insignificant—indeed nonexistent—until it is called into being by symbolic action or language. Burke is quite firm on this point, however: motion does not need action to keep moving. Burke makes this observation repeatedly in the writings in which the nonsymbolic motion / symbolic action pair figures prominently. As I have tried to show in this book, Burke's work in and around symbolic action often takes him to the edges of language and into the realm of motion, for the two categories overlap and intersect as often as they pull apart. Since nonsymbolic motion and symbolic action end up as Burke's last "words" on the matters of bodies and language—he uses them retrospectively and prospectively—they rightly provide an endpoint for a book on his most bodily theories.

"Words as Deeds": Burke Dramatizing Austin

Burke's 1975 review of the second edition of J. L. Austin's *How to Do Things with Words* is long and inspired, running nearly twenty pages and laying his own dramatism alongside Austin's speech-act theory, of which the most famous conceptual legacy is the performative, an utterance that—through saying—acts.[3] Burke's engagement with Austin begins by distinguishing knowledge and action, specifically vis-à-vis theories of language: "Theories of language involve two kinds of speculation that are quite different yet by no means mutually exclusive. One might be called 'scientistic' because it gravitates about language as a mode of *knowledge;* the other "dramatistic" because it approaches language in terms of *action*. . . . But I would confine the terms to a *terministic* emphasis" (147). Burke's reading of Austin underscores his insistence on the nonexclusivity of knowledge and action: "True," Burke writes, "[Austin's] theory of words as deeds is itself a contribution to knowledge. . . . But the systematic choice of a dramatistic approach to his subject implies that the pursuit of *knowledge* in such matters is best guided roundabout via speculations about language as a mode of *action*" (147). Worth emphasizing is the point about the nonexclusivity of action and knowledge. While action may very well entail certain kinds of knowledge, these are nevertheless different emphases. That emphasis merits further consideration for it makes an enormous difference in terms of how language gets theorized vis-à-vis bodies.[4] Knowledge and action graft onto guiding polarities—body/mind, motion/action—and each emphasis yields a distinctive theory of language. Burke's review of Austin helps him to formulate more precisely his stance vis-à-vis knowledge and action, and in doing so he invokes the nonsymbolic motion / symbolic action pair as both the inspiration for and the object of dramatistic inquiry.[5] In brief, nonsymbolic motion and symbolic action work together as an irreducible pair, contiguous but distinct. Reading the pair as the capstone of Burke's contributions places more stress on his earlier books (*Counter-Statement*, *Permanence and Change*, and *Attitudes toward History*) than his later books on motives. In those earlier books, and especially in his return to them via nonsymbolic motion / symbolic action in the 1970s—arguably the very beginning of the linguistic turn—Burke offers a potent critique of the dominance of language. That critique is buttressed by his transdisciplinary commitments.

(Dialectical) Distinction

Burke's encyclopedia entry on dramatism in the *International Encyclopedia of the Social Sciences* offers three propositions about motion and action that remain consistent as he "was working toward what the indications are" (KB to MC, March 7, 1978; Jay 413) in the 1970s.[6] They are

1. There can be no action without motion—that is, even the "symbolic action" of pure thought requires corresponding motions of the brain.
2. There can be motion without action (for instance, the motions of the tides, of sunlight, of growth and decay).
3. Action is not reducible to terms of motion. For instance, the "essence" or "meaning" of a sentence is not reducible to its sheer physical existence as sounds in the air or marks on the page, although material motions of some sort are necessary for the production, transmission, and reception of the sentence. (447)

Neither motion nor action is reducible to the other, and yet nonsymbolic motion not only precedes symbolic action, but its material movements also condition the possibility for symbolic action. As the chapters in this book have each demonstrated, language depends on motion to be developed, carried, and interpreted. Note that Burke counts as motion not just physical bodies but also brain waves, as well as the motions of writing and speaking that Paget helped him to theorize more thoroughly, and all manner of life-giving ecological activity discussed at the end of the last chapter. These add up to an infinity of possible motions.

Motion precedes action in at least two different ways. The first is the human body's motion on an ontogenetic or individual level. Here bodies precede words both developmentally and formatively. In "Questions and Answers" (1978), Burke invokes the etymology of *infancy*, from the Latin *infantia*, the inability to speak, in order to stress the transformation an individual organism undergoes when "emerging . . . into familiarity with some tribal idiom and cultural realm that symbolism makes possible" (330).[7] This passage helps credit Burke's motion/action with the final version of his famous definition of humans in the 1980s as "Bodies That Learn Language."[8] Beyond the physicality of language acquisition, language use depends upon immediate, individualized motions as well, as Burke points out in a discussion of the material motions that condition action in the

1983 afterword to *Attitudes toward History*: "Words as such could not be shaped by the speaker and sent through the air for the hearer or put on the page for the reader without a complicated 'infinite manifold' of *wordless* physiological motions" (383). Given that Paget's gesture-speech theory helped Burke to slow down and focus on the wordless motions—of laryngeal and mouth formations and chord vibrations—a large-scale evolutionary view is not far in the background.

Burke is quite fond of asserting the nonnecessity of symbolic action for motion in terms of the arrival and evolution of the human species in general, and he does so in a number of like observations. In his review of Austin he puts it this way: "Such nonverbal, nonconventional, nonsymbolic ground would be a realm of sheer MOTION in the sense that, if all <u>verbalizingly active</u> animals were erased from the world (as they in all likelihood some day will be) despite the absence of such speech acts there would still be the motions of the winds and tides, of the earth's revolutions about the sun, the processes of geology, astronomic unfolding in general, etc., all going their way without benefit of verbal clergy here on earth" ("Words as Deeds" 160; emphasis in original). And in "Questions and Answers" he is even more pithy: "Presumably the realm of nonsymbolic motion was all that prevailed on this earth before our kind of symbol-using organism evolved, and will go on sloshing about after we have gone" (334).[9]

Together these large-scale reflections on symbolic actions allow a rare but sure glimpse of Burke as something other than the humanist he is typically assumed to be (Blair 154); indeed, as with Nietzsche, Burke's focus on nonsymbolic motion subtly encourages a nonanthropomorphic view of the world since it places human bodies among the whole lot of sheer motion—the wind and trees, the sun and the universe, and the nonhuman animals that were effectively here first.[10]

As he writes in "Questions and Answers," "The realm of the word is tiny indeed, as compared with the vast extent of wordlessness through time and space" (330). Here is Burke, the scholar of symbolic action, returning to his mystical method by which the infinite and sprawling realm of nonsymbolic motion effectively dwarfs the realm of symbolic action, as it does through the image of the abyss at the end of *Permanence and Change*.

In the context of a whole universe of motion, the human body becomes a smaller-scale version of motion with its own motion principles. The first is what Burke calls the "principle of individuation," the notion that a body is more or less discrete, cut off from other bodies. That principle is for Burke empirical, private, and immanent. Notably he uses examples of pain and death to explain the principle of individuation. In his review of Austin, for example, after designating "a realm devoid of speech *acts* a realm of nonsymbolic *motion*" (160), Burke writes,

> Whatever the uncertainties of the metaphysical or grammatical "I" might be, such an out-and-out dramatistic statement of the case would give us a purely *empirical* principle of individuation to build from; namely: the human body in physiological *motion*, each with the centrality of its particular nervous system whereby, however its pleasures and pains might resemble the pleasures and pains of other such bodies, it *immediately* experiences only its own. Hence there would be a drastic qualitative difference between a state wherein *it* rather than some other physiological organism immediately experienced some particular pleasure or pain. And whatever may be the continuity between such organisms and the environment of which they are a part, the centrality of each one such particular organism's nervous system would be born and would die as that individual. (160–61)

The nonsymbolic motion / symbolic action pair therefore traverses a temporal, experiential rift. The temporal aspect of this "empirical principle" brings to light the body's radical immanence—the way its breathing rhythms, its pains and pleasures, its life persist only and always in the now. The immanence and singularity of nonsymbolic motion offers a pointed contrast to language, which rushes in to knit bodies together and to foster *inter*action, moving into what he calls at the end of the Austin review "the *collective* realm of 'culture'" (168). As he puts it in "Questions and Answers," "Symbolic action is public, social; but we live and die as individual bodies in the realm of nonsymbolic motion" (330). Burke reiterates this immanence point in "Words as Deeds" by distinguishing behavior in the nonsymbolic and the symbolic realms: "Given a performer's expertise in speech acts, for instance, his body may be 'behaving' in ways that are quite healthgiving, or maybe in the ways of a psychogenic illness. One dreamer's 'brain waves' may be all to the good, another's may be in bad need of repair. A citizen's behavior is one thing. His body's behavior is something else. In the speech department he may be anticipating and remembering. But with his nonsymbolic body, as with the dancer's symbolizing body, everything is NOW" (167). Here the "speech department" enables one to move across a range of temporalities by reaching into the past or projecting into the future, as opposed to dwelling with the sick or healthy body that inhabits only the present. Burke's use of the dancer's body is interesting, though, in that it combines motion and action. The temporality of the dancer hearkens back to Gurdjieff's dancing students, whose movements encourage the audience members to inhabit an equally physical now, and in doing so dancers dance at the very edges of language, at the place where the individual becomes part of a collective.

In "(Nonsymbolic) Motion / (Symbolic) Action," Burke uses "poor Keats, with his dying body," as an instance of a moment when motion and action are furthest apart. A letter Keats wrote on his deathbed "was concerned," according to Burke, "with a situation in which the sheer nonsymbolic realm of motion (the plight of his diseased body) was taking over; for such in essence is the unbridgeable 'polarity' between the social realm of 'symbolic action' and motion's 'principle of individuation' whereby the symptoms of *his* disease were the *immediate* sensations of *himself* and none other" (816–17; emphasis in original). The unbridgeability of this gap is evident only in certain situations, most notably in birth and death, leaving language to mingle with a body that is alive and moving.

Contiguity

And yet the polarity is not just a matter of distinction. While sensation demarcates motion from action in the context of the principle of individuation, it also provides Burke with a way to bind the two together. In his review of *How to Do Things with Words*, Burke seizes on Austin's distinction between phonetic, phatic, and rhetic sounds, which move the physicality of sound along a continuum of meaning. In Austin's scheme a phonetic act indicates sound units; a phatic act names the combination of phones to create words, and a rhetic act uses a string of words meaningfully—that is, "with a certain more or less definite 'sense' and a more or less definite 'reference'" (Austin 92–93). The sliding scale of meaning maps neatly onto the sliding scale of motion/action. Burke takes Austin's phonetic/phatic/rhetic distinction

> to be summing up the fact that the mere *sounds* of words, in their nature as mere sounds, are in the realm of *nonverbal motion*. Such sounds are in the realm of a speech act when interpreted as words, i.e. 'phatic.' Insofar as such words function with reference to contexts (either a context of situation or the text itself as a context) they become 'rhetic.' . . . And I particularly want to end by considering more closely the relation between the mere 'noises' of words (as 'phones') and their nature as 'phemes,' that is when their function in the proper symbol-system transforms them into the possibility of speech acts as 'rhemes.' For the mere noise of words (phones) is related to their role as speech acts (phatic, rhetic acts) as the realm of nonsymbolic motion is to the realm of symbolic action. (155)[11]

On the one hand Burke here reiterates the point that action entails motion, insofar as a meaningful utterance such as "I christen this boat *Johnny Cash*" combines physical sounds and relies on material conditions of air and vibrations (motions) to convey those sounds. As Burke puts it, "the 'act' of speaking (and of interpreting an utterance) is made possible only by its grounding in two aspects of *motion*; namely: (a) such physiological motions as the neural processes involved in speaking, hearing, interpreting, and the like; (b) such environmental motions as the vibrations in the air which carry the words from speaker to hearer" (164).[12] And yet in pursuing these distinctions to the end of Austin's book—a book that Burke aptly calls "one long ingeniously self-imposed *aporia*" (148)—he hits on a number of other, more precise ways that motion and action correlate. That is, motion and action may be mutually irreducible, and motion may entail action and not vice versa, and so the two do not strictly oppose each other but instead move in the same direction along parallel tracks, mediated by attitudes and sensations.

Correlation and Duplication

After citing nearly all the appearances of the word *attitude* in Austin's text, Burke threads it through Austin's main triad: the locutionary, the illocutionary, and the perlocutionary. The locutionary act is simply "the act of 'saying something' in this full normal sense," like the rhetic category. The illocutionary act, the act on which Austin's lectures "fasten" (Austin 103), names "the performance of the act *in* saying something" (99–100). Austin's examples are "informing, ordering, warning, undertaking" (109). The perlocutionary act, by subtle contrast, names the consequences of the act, "what we bring about or achieve *by* saying something, such as convincing, persuading, deterring, and even, say, surprising or misleading" (109). Despite Burke's claim that he is following Austin in limiting his considerations to the spoken word, he simply cannot omit bodily movement from his consideration.[13] Burke claims that he "must 'dramatistically' take it that all speech acts either as uttered or as responded to are *intrinsically* attitudinal" (160), and proceeds to equate parenthetically illocutionary force with attitudes (160, 164). Burke elaborates how attitudes work in Austin's scheme:

> The mere fact that I have a pronounced attitude towards something and want you to share it with me is no guaranty at all that my way of expressing the attitude will be the best way of getting you to share the attitude. But whatever differences between a one-way or a two-way kind of attitudinizing in my speech act, in either case my speech act involves correlative behavior in the realm of motion. Regardless of what attitude any speech act "symbolizes," it can be enacted only insofar as there are corresponding neural motions of the body (whatever they may be). And whatever attitude (response) such a "rhetic" structure of utterances (locutions) may evoke in a hearer, they will necessarily be paralleled somehow in the realm of wordless (nonconventional, non-symbolic) motion. (165)

This passage offers a different view of the relation between motion and action. Instead of operating in sequential distinction, they correlate or run parallel, with attitudes moving between them. In the very next passage Burke notes that "the distinction between the realms of action and motion is but a matter of *degree*, rather than a difference in kind" (165). In "summing up" his review of Austin, he emits his own illocutionary force, urging his readers to "think of these sample histories" (166). The "histories" number three, and they return Burke to his work at the Bureau of Social Hygiene. First, "A drug . . . introduced into the blood stream, produces physiological effects. The drug functions, let us say, as a kind of irritant . . . It makes me so irritable that my speech act reflects the attitude of irritation. By the same token, such would be the illocutionary force of my related utterances. Thereby a condition in the realm of physiological motion will have surfaced as a speech act which can have illocutionary force with hearers only insofar as the motions of their bodies and in the conditions of the environment make it possible for those familiar with the conventions of my utterance to receive it and interpret it as the kind of speech act (symbolic action) it is" (166).

The "surfacing" of a drug-induced condition in a speech act shows how Austin's category of the illocutionary act can encompass motion and action or, more precisely, how bodily conditions are capable of impeding or redirecting language. Burke quickly offers "another route," a second sample history: "Mine enemy referred to me in utterances (a rhetic act) the attitude, or illocutionary force, of which I found quite irritating. My response to his attitude had a physiological counterpart in the realm of motion by such 'behavior' as increased blood pressure, accelerated pulse beat, secretion of adrenalin, without which body symptoms his attitudinizing couldn't have had such illocutionary force so far as my response to his speech act was concerned" (166). Here, instead of a drug, the initial irritant is someone else's speech act. The response from the endocrine and nervous systems functions as a "counterpart" to the spoken response. The word *counterpart* designates an equivalency or complement. As he writes later in the piece, "dramatistic nomenclature sets the conditions for inquiries into the sheer *bodily* equivalents of the speech acts' attitudes" (167). Such equivalents, according to Burke, offer "a realm of *quantification* such as the corresponding *qualitative* nature of the speech act decidedly is *not*" (167). The equivalency or complementarity of motion and action, of course, depend in part on their differences.

Burke's third and final "history" is more general but moves in the other conversational direction: "Or I might address you in a way designed to build up in you an attitude of irritability that would induce you to sympathetically join with me against mine enemy. In any case, whether you went along with me or not (whether or not my illocutionary act attained the consequences that entitled it to be called a perlocutionary act) whatever your response was it necessarily involved physiological and environmental motions of one sort or another" (166). Utterances, that is, always transmit attitude and therefore involve a dual movement that breaks into something of a cycle—motion, action, motion, action, and so on, not unlike the example of the air conditioning in the movie theater with which this conclusion began. Burke designates these intervals of motions as "preformatives" (166), by which he means something like "pre-performative," or that force (motion) on which a successful performative depends.

The final way that motion and action interact is what Burke calls "duplication." A more tightly symmetrical version of equivalency, duplication names the way that motion and action complete each other: "the combination of bodily sensation with symbolic counterparts and corresponding analogical extensions" (821).[14] Again, attitude and sensation are the sources of duplication. As Burke describes the principle in the afterword to *Attitudes toward History*, attitudes are an organism's "built-in," wordless perspectives, and "human attitudes have an overall double provenience" (382). He explains further:

> I refer to a kind of duplication that arose when our primeval ancestors, by learning language, no longer experienced a sensation solely as a sensation. For instance, when they touched something that *felt hot*, their newfound ways with language enabled them to *duplicate* the *sensory* experience in the "transcendent" terms of a *nonsensory* medium such that our aforesaid primeval ancestors could say *"That feels hot."*
>
> And precisely at that time here on Earth the realm of *Story* entered the world. The taste of an orange *is a sensation*. The words "the taste of an orange" *tell a story*. And the story they tell is such that it must be a somewhat different story, depending on whether the hearer has or has not tasted an orange. Once such words have arisen as terms for *sensations*, their use can be extended *attitudinally* to encompass such steps as the one from "That feels warm" to "He, or she, is warm-hearted." (382–83; emphasis in original)

For Burke duplication works both to expand attitudes and complete sensations. In the subsequent, Nietzsche-inflected discussion in *Attitudes toward History*'s afterword, he observes that "words designed to duplicate the wordless aspect of our environment greatly expand the range of attitudes in keeping with the clutter of concordant and discordant *interests socially rife among us*" (384–85; emphasis in original). So while the realm of words is tiny compared to the gulf of motions, words also have the capacity to combine and recombine ad infinitum, thereby expanding the realm of action.

Such expansion enables what Burke calls "completion." As he writes in "(Nonsymbolic) Motion / (Symbolic) Action," "Whatever the possible range of incidental readjustments, DUPLICATION is so basic to the relation between motion and symbolicity, nothing of the moment seems quite complete unless we have rounded things out by translation into symbols of some sort, either scientific or aesthetic, practical or ritualistic. Sex is not complete without love lyrics, porn, and tracts on sexology. The nonsymbolic motions of springtime are completed in the symbolic action of a spring song" (822). Language therefore enables humans to press past the radical immanence of the body, to redouble motion and extend it outward.

Such is Burke's capacious, multidirectional theory of nonsymbolic motion and symbolic action. Bodies and language, then, are irreducibly distinct and yet parallel and complementary, mediated by sensation and attitude—at times undermining, at others duplicating each other, but often, if not always, in effect moving together. What we emphatically do not have in Burke's writings on bodies and language, however, is a notion of bodies as discursively constructed, or what Crable describes as "called into existence" by discourse ("Symbolizing Motion" 128). Here I want to insist that the absence of discursive bodies is not an oversight on Burke's part but instead helps us mark the importance of designating bodies and language as "the basic polarity." This shift from body/mind to motion/action is as crucial as it is difficult to register, in part because so many classical theoretical tensions have been guided by a body-mind polarity, and also because contemporary theory is still very much under the spell of discursive constructivism, a major legacy of the linguistic turn, which presumes that knowledge—including knowledge of bodies—is always and thoroughly language-dependent.[15]

At stake in the shift to motion/action from body/mind is an emphasis on moving rather than knowing. As with the title of this book, I use *moving* quite deliberately here, for I wish to preserve its broad sense of mobility and change—of moving and morphing—and also its more specific suasory force vis-à-vis traditional modes of rhetoric (for example, those of Cicero and St. Augustine), in which the three offices of rhetoric are to please, to instruct, and to move. The former sense of mobility and change, as Celeste M. Condit points out, is crucial for viewing materiality as not holding still even when stasis seems to prevail. Instead, as Condit puts it, motion figures the universe as "matter/energy in constant motion, taking on shifting forms through shifting relationships" ("Materiality" 332). The latter use of moving is closely related to aesthetic movement, which often centers on pathos, as in a "moving performance."

The linguistic turn depends on a body/mind polarity in this way: when theorized from a basic polarity of body/mind, language becomes an epistemological tool—if not *the* epistemological tool. Just as language in psychoanalysis is the means of producing self-understanding (and understanding of others), theories of discursive construction, too, tend to emphasize language's role in knowledge-production; as Foucault taught us, articulation is itself a form of knowing.[16] The relatively recent "linguistic turn" in the humanities and social sciences cinched language's centrality. What is more, when a theory of bodies is folded into an epistemological view of language, there is a tendency for bodies to become secondary to language, as evidenced by the theoretical perspectives that view bodies as discursively constructed or made legible through language, or those that stall at discussions of bodily representation.

In the afterword to the third edition of *Permanence and Change* (1983), Burke writes the motion/action pair back into his most bodily book. There he sums things up quite emphatically: "The body of the human individual is the point at which the realms of the physiological (nonsymbolic) motion and symbolic action meet" (309). In an effort to suss out the critical implications of such a simple statement, this book has examined the various perspectives that led Burke to that conviction. The result has been what the preface calls an "excursion" through and around his most salient and difficult writings on bodies and language. That excursion has moved across disciplines as well as decades, showing Burke's tendencies to work with available discourses of his moment while not abandoning those he has found useful in the past. Too often academic trends lead us to drop concepts prematurely, but Burke's persistent return to matters of bodies and language serves as an object lesson in cumulative refinement. He also usefully models the need to search for fresh perspectives that might augment and redirect rather than replace perspectives—in other words, to get perspectives to themselves move, to jar them a little. What Burke offers at both the beginning and end of his long career, then, is a sprawling amalgam of transdisciplinary perspectives, drawn together to help solve the "eternally unsolvable Enigma": bodies moving, at the edges of language.

NOTES

Introduction

1. Celeste M. Condit's discussion of the inadequacies of disciplinarity in the context of genetic research is useful here, for she focuses on "the failure to engage wisdom of an adequate breadth for addressing the subject at hand" ("The New Science" 234) and the resulting disengaged cacophony of interventions around reproductive technology.

2. And yet many of his criticisms seem on target, for reasons already enumerated by Julia Walker in her article "Why Performance? Why Now?" The overemphasis on language as the primary medium of performativity risks uttering bodies with all their kinetic materiality right back into the realm of the symbolic imaginary (170–71), where Jameson and Terry Eagleton can so easily wave them away.

3. For the term *nature* see Parrish (41–63); for ecocriticism see Buell and Heise; for a broad, applied cultural rhetorical perspective on the environment and bodies, see Pezzullo, *Toxic Tourism*, esp. 67–72; chapter 7 in this volume considers Burke's role in ecocritical studies.

4. An anonymous reader provided a list of such topics, including Wilhelm Reich's orgone box, the illness of Burke's wife, Libbie, and Mary Baker Eddy. While more could probably be done to augment Michael Feehan's work on Burke and Eddy vis-à-vis the body, I have chosen instead to focus on mysticism as the representative anecdote of spiritualism. The same might be said for the number of psychologists Burke cites and engages in *Permanence and Change* and elsewhere. William Marston, W. H. R. Rivers, and anthropologists such as Bronislaw Malinowski only receive cursory treatments here. This is because my research suggested that thinkers such as Ernst Kretschmer and Sir Richard Paget proved more integral to Burke's theories of how bodies and language relate, and—here is the important part—the theories of Kretschmer and Paget have a surprising resonance with contemporary work in the humanities.

Chapter 1. Bodies as Equipment for Moving

1. Burke's insomnia is well documented in his letters and interviews, and Burke discusses the "coronary spasm" in a letter to Malcolm Cowley on February 22, 1952, discussed below.

2. On November 16, 1950, Burke wrote to Cowley that he was "still avoiding doctors" and was "beginning to wonder whether my fantastic gulpo-gaggo-gaspo session of recent weeks may be not heart at all, but asthmatic" (Jay 301–2), and the diagnosis is shared a little over a year later: "'Coronary spasms,' resulting from tension" (February 22, 1952; Jay 303). Chapter 7 treats the gulpo-gaggo-gaspo in more detail.

3. Thanks to John Marsh for metrically confirming my arrhythmic reading.

4. See Wess, *Kenneth Burke*, esp. 53–54; Rueckert, *Kenneth Burke and the Drama of Human Relations* 8–33, esp. 31–33.

5. According to Gosling those most commonly diagnosed as neurasthenics include men in the professional class as well as elite women (10–11).

6. As Elizabeth Wilson contends, "neurasthenic symptoms are somatic or bodily rather than psychic in origin, and are not amenable to psychoanalytic intervention" (18).

7. The oxen's "colorlessness" is certainly worth contemplating in terms of racial differences, whiteness being the most status quo of all. Oxen, after all, can be brown or (more commonly) red.

8. The first entry begins as follows: "Decidedly, it is with misgivings. And one's resolve to learn docent is an inadequate apology to others. Nevertheless, Mr Rosenfeld having called for a sabbatical year and Mr Gilman having at the last found it impossible to take his place, we enter by a *non-sequitur*, though never for a moment forgetting our office as makeshift" (535).

Like so many of Burke's piecemeal jobs, he seems to have stumbled into this one as the music critic for the *Dial*. His first piece in this capacity ran in the December 1927 issue, and in the "Notes on Contributors," the editorial staff, then led by Marianne Moore, accounts for Burke's contribution: "In relinquishing the services of Mr. Lawrence Gilman who had expected to write the Musical Chronicle during Mr. Rosenfeld's absence from editorial duties this coming season, the editors are gratified to announce that the Musical Chronicle will be written this winter by Mr. Kenneth Burke" (unnumbered mast page). Burke was not only not the first choice, he wasn't even the second. And then in June 1928, the job became Burke's: "It is with profound regret that the Editors have accepted the resignation of Mr. Paul Rosenfeld. *The Dial* is to be congratulated, however, that Mr. Kenneth Burke has consented to assume officially the writing of the Musical Chronicle." And so were the circumstances in which Burke became the *Dial*'s music critic.

9. Burke shares the theories of music held by ancient Greeks, especially Plato and Aristotle, that music has the capacity to "move in" or, in Burke's word, irrupt (Hawhee, *Bodily Arts* 139ff.; see also chapter 3, on Burke's drug research).

10. From the essay "Trial Translation": the "'musicians attending'" "have played somewhat, encouraging you to rise and fall in *Einfühlung* with their melody, setting you so early into a mood of acquiescence. . . . In laying us open to clemency, music lays us open in general—and thus may also lay us open to inclemency, if there is inclemency about" (PLF 345).

11. Burke's interest in rhythm was shared by most of his critic and poet friends. One example will have to suffice. In a 1926 review of E. E. Cummings's poetry, Marianne Moore notes Cummings's debt to the Elizabethan poets: "we have, not a replica of the title, but a more potent thing, a replica of the rhythm—a kind of second tempo" (49).

12. Again this claim rubs against the accounts offered by Wess, Rueckert, and, to a smaller degree, Selzer, all of whom read Burke's aesthetic as having been worked out wholly in the context of literature.

Chapter 2. Burke's Mystical Method

1. The number of times this line is used as an epigraph (whether for a book or an article) or a major quote is especially remarkable in terms of disciplinary range. Here is just a sample of texts that have used as an epigraph or quoted the last line of *Permanence and Change*:

Epigraphs
Anthropology: Jennifer Cole, "The Work of Memory in Madagascar"; Clendinnen, *Aztecs: An Interpretation*; linguistics: Fishman, *Reversing Language Shift*; Wess, *Kenneth Burke: Rhetoric, Subjectivity, Postmodernism*.

Quoted
Rhetorical studies: Crable, "Rhetoric, Anxiety, and Character Armor: Burke's Interactional Rhetoric of Identity," 5; Lucaites, Caudill, Condit, eds., *Contemporary Rhetorical Theory: A Reader*, 546; O'Banion, *Reorienting Rhetoric*, 206; philosophy: Southwell, *Kenneth Burke and Martin Heidegger: With a Note against Deconstructionism*, 65; composition studies: Warnock, review of *The Writer's Mind*, 59; McPhail, *Zen in the Art of Rhetoric: An Inquiry into Coherence*, 189
English studies: Raymond, *English as a Discipline, or, Is There a Plot in This Play?*; communication studies: Trice and Beyer, "Writing Organizational Tales: The Cultures of Work Organizations," 227; Woolston, "Frontiers of Legal Aid Work," 153; advertising: Fillion, "Turning on: The Selling of the Present," 336; anthropology: Kluckhohn, "Myths and Rituals: A General Theory," 66; trade: Neumann, *On the Rim: Looking for the Grand Canyon*, 117.
Unattributed quote: Evans, "Foreign Aid for Agricultural Development: Philosophy and Implementation," 1402; misattributed to Edmund Burke in Philip Malcolm Waller Thody's *Don't Do It: A Dictionary of the Forbidden*, 9.

2. James Mark Baldwin's *Dictionary of Philosophy and Psychology*; Burke evidently consulted it frequently.

3. Burke mentions mysticism several times in his musical reviews; in one instance he notes that Kaminski is "tenuous in its mysticism" ("Musical Chronicle," February 1928: 174).

4. Burke himself sees these books as companions ("Afterword: In Retrospective Prospect," PC 3e 311; *Counter-Statement* 216). And Ann George and Jack Selzer have observed that *Permanence and Change* is the theory, *Attitudes toward History* the practice (George and Selzer, *Burke in the 1930s* 143). For Gunn's discussion, see, for starters, page 37. Later parts of the chapter will return to Gunn's spot-on analysis.

5. *Attitudes toward History* also offers Whitman and Emerson as mystics of a kind, but James dominates the opening section, and so this chapter will focus on him as Burke's model mystic.

6. Stanley Romaine Hopper begins his notes on a mysticism lecture by Burke with something of an understatement when he observes, "It is not easy to grasp Burke's views on mysticism" (Burke and Hopper 95).

7. The Arrow Collar man, a sensational creation of illustrator J. C. Leyendecker, according to fashion historian Carole Turbin, successfully thwarted the association of "comfortable cotton collars with unmanliness, even spinelessness" (471); Burke's letter appeared on the tail end of the Arrow man's reign, which spanned from 1907 to 1931.

8. In the retrospective afterword "Curriculum Criticum," Burke writes that *Permanence and Change* was written in 1932–33. The year 1933 is especially important for his engagement with mysticism; see the Tate letter discussed below.

9. The "offending" piece of Tate's, "Poetry and Politics," appeared in the *New Republic*, August 2, 1933, 308–10; the letter I am quoting from in this section can be found in the Allen Tate Papers, box 13, folder 61, Manuscript Division, Department of Rare Books and Special Collections, Princeton University Library.

10. I will return in chapter 5 to discuss Burke's use of the term *genius* in more detail.

11. Burke reiterated this view of mysticism in *A Grammar of Motives*, albeit with a much more reserved, academic tone. In the chapter on "Agency and Purpose" he writes:

> We may establish the connection between Mysticism and Purpose sociologically by noting that although individual mystics may arise at any period of history, mystical philosophies appear as a general social manifestation in times of great skepticism or confusion about the nature of human purpose. They are a mark of transition, flourishing when one set of public presuppositions about the *ends* of life has become weakened or disorganized, and no new public structure, of sufficient depth and scope to be satisfying, has yet taken its place. Thus precisely at such times of general hesitancy, the mystic can compensate for his own particular doubts about human purpose by submerging himself with some vision of a *universal,* or *absolute* or *transcendent* purpose, with which he would identify himself. (288)

When considered next to the letter to Tate from a decade earlier, the distant, reflective, philosophical tone of the passage more starkly sets off the howling, almost desperate tone of the letter to Tate, thus revealing the extent to which the letter was written both from and about a period of cultural and political upheaval, the very kind of moment Burke describes with such a staid, academic tone in the *Grammar* passage above.

12. Gunn parses this basic paradox of occultism with admirable thoroughness. See, especially, his treatment of obscure language in chapter 3 of *Modern Occult Rhetoric* (70–76).

13. I have already discussed Burke's regard for Yeats, and *Permanence and Change* features a prominently placed "qualified defense" of Lawrence (250–55).

14. For the difficulty of Gurdjieff, see Gunn's *Modern Occult Rhetoric* 272n39.

15. On January 9, 1924, upon Toomer's return, Crane wrote to Munson, "Jean's new hygiene for himself is very interesting to me. He seems to be able to keep himself solid and undismayed. Certain organic changes are occurring in us all, I think, but I believe that his is more steady and direct than I have been permitted" (Munson 207).

16. Anderson, it turns out, was intimately linked with Georgette Leblanc, one of Gurdjieff's pupils and dancers.

17. James Sibley Watson Jr., one of the *Dial*'s new owners, reviewed *Tertium Organum* in the *Dial* under the name W. C. Blum as early as September 1920.

18. Indeed, by overemphasizing the clairvoyant aspects of art, Munson, Crane, and their circle risked ignoring the important emphasis on the body in Gurdjieff's scheme, which Ouspensky pays careful attention to in his work on yoga. It is precisely the elements of yoga and Sanskrit, as indicated in Burke's letter to Williams quoted above, that most intrigued Burke. That Crane and Munson were exclusively interested in the implications Gurdjieff's system had for art is particularly evident in Munson's account of one of A. R. Orage's lectures (discussed below): "Orage talked about psychology but only incidentally about art, which disappointed this art group. Hart was silent throughout the meeting and expressed no views afterward" (210).

19. Toomer Collection, box 26, folder 45; reprinted in Byrd 70.

20. Ibid.

21. Such an emphasis on suspension of habit resonates with what Stephanie L. Hawkins locates in both Gertrude Stein's and William James's "science of superstition."

22. Toomer Collection, box 53, folder 26; reprinted in Byrd 69.

23. I have not been able to determine whether Burke attended Gurdjieff's dancers' performances, perhaps because participants in the Orage/Gurdjieff circles were discouraged from publishing anything explicit about the activities (Munson 262), and Burke may have been one of the few attendees to respect that discouragement. A selection of letters and published reviews suggest that Burke intimately knew the philosophy and the performances of Gurdjieff and his students. Burke's youngest son, Michael, recalled to me a time when Burke taught him Gurdjieff's philosophy by referencing a tree (author's discussion with Michael Burke, July 9, 2005).

Chapter 3. Burke on Drugs

1. In the course of presenting this research, I have found that scholars often want to invoke Burke as an addict himself. I simply haven't found enough evidence to corroborate theories that he was addicted to sleeping pills, though admittedly it has not been a focus of mine. Certainly he had a long-term addiction to alcohol, which chapter 7 discusses in more detail.

2. Jordynn Jack and I were working on this material independently but simultaneously as evidenced by our two articles published within months of each other. My "Burke on Drugs" appeared in the *Rhetoric Society Quarterly* in January 2004 and forms the basis of this chapter; Jack's "'The Piety of Degradation': Kenneth Burke, the Bureau of Social Hygiene, and *Permanence and Change*" appeared in the *Quarterly Journal of Speech* in November 2004. Jack and I arrive separately, through different tacks, at similar conclusions about piety, which I take to be a sign of happy confirmation. Jack has more recently published an article that examines Burke's criminology work in relation to his stance on social reform ("Kenneth Burke's Constabulatory Rhetoric").

3. According to Selzer (*Kenneth Burke in Greenwich Village* 241n2), letters to Matthew Josephson indicate Burke was at work on "Program" (formerly called "Manifesto") in August and November 1927, which corresponded precisely with the end of Burke's first stint with Rockefeller's Spelman Trust.

4. Burke's placing of the term *hypochondria* in quotation marks deserves consideration. As I will discuss in chapters 5 and 7, he preferred the term *hypochondriasis*, which

he viewed as a productive lingering on one's—and one's culture's—symptoms. Indeed, in Burke's corpus the term is often equated with the term *occupation*.

5. I am not the first to dwell on *efficiency* as one of Burke's goading terms. See, for example, Wolfe (69ff.) and Seigel (394–95). Both of these scholars, it should be noted, gravitate toward Burke's ecological writings, and his critique of efficiency, as they both demonstrate, figures prominently into his commitments to nature and ecology (Wolfe). I consider the ecological component in more detail in chapter 7.

6. In this way *efficiency* is a more specific formulation of *perspective*, a key term in the partner book to *Attitudes toward History*, *Permanence and Change*. Both of these terms together forecast *terministic screen*, the one that ultimately stuck.

7. In a futile attempt to save money to go to Europe, Burke spun the Wall Street roulette wheel. In December 1929 he wrote to Allen Tate: "The Dial Award, you must know, is in the strong hands of Wall Street. After showing great faith, and jumping in when the market was going smash, I am rewarded for my vision and fearlessness by being exactly two dollars ahead on a two thousand dollar investment" (December 19, 1929; Tate Papers, Princeton University Library).

8. Burke's ghostwriting stands as an interesting corollary to the fascinating article by Deborah Brandt that charts writing and power in the context of ghostwriting. For Brandt, "ghostwriting especially highlights power exchanges between writing and social structures and also illuminates assumptions about underlying reading and writing processes that enable such exchanges" (549). The writing is overlaid onto preconceived values and outcomes, because ghostwriters work in the shadows of the writing's authorizing structures (in this case Woods, the BSH, and the federal government). Brandt's interviews reveal a consistent effort on the part of ghostwriters to acquaint themselves with the values and beliefs of the authorizing figure or institution (556). And yet while Burke may have acquainted himself with the values of Woods and the BSH, that acquaintance repelled him, and that repulsion can be tracked in the ghostwritten book, as I demonstrate below. Brandt's study suggests that ghostwriters bring the authorizing force of writing and in the give-and-take of invention often create more than they follow. As the curious case study of Burke-as-ghostwriter suggests, the power structure can be tipped—the values of the ghostwriter can take over the writing, and in this case such a takeover results in a rhetorically incongruous piece of writing.

9. This epithet concludes a series of letters to Tate in which Burke indicates that Colonel Woods was talking of sending Burke to England. On March 15, 1929, he wrote to Tate in France that "there is a faintest chance that I may get to London for the Colonel within a few weeks." A month later he was still waiting for "fate and the Colonel [to] cast [Burke's] die" (April 13, 1929). Then finally in October he wrote, "No, Allen, I did not come to Europe. I changed my plans. I decided, instead, that I would not come. Also Colonel Woods, the Captain my Captain changed his plans" (October 17, 1929). Letters from the Allen Tate Papers, Princeton University Library.

10. Again, see Jack's "Kenneth Burke's Constabulary Rhetoric" for more on Woods's police work.

11. "Bureau of Social Hygiene Archives, 1911–1940"; quote excerpted from the archive Web site, available at www.rockefeller.edu/archive.ctr/bsh.html.

12. Here Burke appears to be following the ancient Greeks—both Plato and Aristotle believed that music "moved in" to the body and, as such, that the types of music should be carefully monitored. For a more thorough discussion of music and bodily rhythm as theorized by the ancients, see my "Bodily Pedagogies," as well as *Bodily Arts*, 135–41.

13. It is perhaps noteworthy that chapter 2, "The Alkaloids," is the only chapter in *Dangerous Drugs* that bears Burke's imprint so strongly. My hunch is that Woods, in the spirit of efficiency, placed Burke's co-ghostwriter, John D. Farnham (also, like Woods, a military man), in charge of writing the other, more policy-based, legalistic chapters, while leaving Burke to spin out the historical overview.

14. In a recent article, Bryan Crable claims that "Burke's thought about embodiment reaches maturity in *Permanence and Change*" ("Symbolizing Motion" 123). Such a claim fits in nicely with other scholars, such as Wess and Richard Thames, who have worked extensively on the concept of metabiology.

15. Thomas Rosteck and Michael Leff characterize Burke's move as "an ironic and potent realignment of terms" (327), specifically as a new alignment of piety with "propriety."

Chapter 4. From the Rhetoric of Science to the Science of Rhetoric

1. *Identification* (Isager and Just 249–50); *dramatism* (Gusfield, "Literary Rhetoric" 18–22; Weldon; Journet); *metonymy* (Gusfield, "Literary Rhetoric" 23); *form* (Halloran 82n16); *bureaucratization of the imaginative* (Wander and Jaehne 211); and *terministic screens* (Ceccarelli 94).

2. For a brilliant analysis of the knowledge effects of mixed metaphors in contemporary science, see Leah Ceccarelli's "Neither Confusing Cacophony nor Culinary Complements."

3. According to Medvei, Cannon was one of the "main pioneers" of neuroendocrinology, particularly the "concept of the chemical transmission of nerve impulses," which "faced great difficulties between 1910 and 1950 before it became accepted" (414).

4. Hoskins's contribution of the term *feedback* is seen by Jean Wilson (393) as on par with Starling's contribution of the term *hormone*, especially in terms of its "unifying" effects for the discipline of endocrinology.

5. Such an effort he refers to as "a kind of 'inverted Christian Science,'" and explains thus: "That is, whereas such projects of 'auto-suggestion' attempt to arrest physical ills by a 'transcendent' change in attitude (whereupon the body, as an actor, is invited to change its mimetic expression accordingly, shifting from physical illness to physical health as the 'artistic counterpart' of the change in attitude)" (323n). For an excellent study on Burke and Christian Science, see Feehan.

6. This according to data compiled by Malzberg. Pressman's *Last Resort* details Sakel's multiple visits to New York (172).

7. The number of articles on insulin therapy and schizophrenia is so high that the index to volume 12 (1938) includes a special index devoted to the topic (817–18).

8. The parenthetical explanation goes on to discuss the dancing of such attitudes through word selection, a phenomenon Burke derives from Sir Richard Paget, which will be discussed at length in chapter 6.

Chapter 5. Seeing "Deviance" as Inclination

1. The classics of feminist standpoint theory include Haraway, Hartsock, and Harding, *Whose Science*. See also *The Feminist Standpoint Theory Reader*, ed. Harding.

2. It is important to note too that this moment in Burke provides a rare opportunity to theorize disability in the vein of the thriving field of contemporary disability studies. See Bérubé, Kuppers, Siebers, Dolmage, and collections by Snyder and Mitchell and James C. Wilson and Cynthia Lewiecki-Wilson.

3. On Mead and constitution, see Banner. It was William Sheldon who adapted Kretschmer's types in the 1940s.

4. See Micale's collection *The Mind of Modernism*, especially his introduction, which delineates a number of responses to psychoanalysis. Malcolm Cowley's memoir makes a strong case for modernism as a panoply of "adjustments," of which "Freudianism is only one method" (61). Notably he also mentions a number of varieties of knowledge, including some espoused by Burke and treated in this book, namely Gurdjieff and endocrinology (61).

5. For a wonderful consideration of Rockefeller's support of synthetic medicine, see Pressman. For Burke's Rockefeller-funded research, see Hawhee, "Burke on Drugs," and Jordynn Jack, "'The Piety of Degradation.'" Fosdick's history of the various disciplinary (and interdisciplinary) formations at Rockefeller, especially the chapter "Medicine and Psychiatry" (123–55), offers a useful account of the synthetic mission as well.

6. Figures from *Bowker's Annual / Publishers Weekly*. Such a plum translating stint no doubt was owed to the success of Burke's well-regarded translation of Mann's *Death in Venice* for Knopf in 1925.

7. For a discussion of the late nineteenth century's "second-wave phrenology," especially in relation to physiognomy, in addition to Hartley, see Twine and Doyle (59ff.).

8. Chapter 7 will take this point about body biography in a new direction vis-à-vis Burke.

9. Kretschmer's typology entered into the mainstream in both Germany and America, and his name still appears in trade and reference books on personality as one of the first to develop a typology of the kind that has come to dominate in personality studies; cf. Corsini (212); Brunas-Wagstaff (19); Berens and Nardi; and Livesley (8).

10. See Heynick (423); and Gilman, *Smart Jews* (53). To be sure Kretschmer's system allowed people to make arguments about race and occupations alike; as Robert Proctor points out, Third Reich leader Fritz Lenz swiftly connected body types to races and from there theorized that particular races and ethnicities were more prone to tuberculosis; others believed that asthenics (tall, thin people) should not select occupations in medicine or nursing because of similar correlations found by Kretschmer (216).

11. The term *weltanschauung* itself occurs frequently in *Permanence and Change*, most notably in Burke's chapter on motives: "A motive is not some fixed thing, like a table, which one can go and look at. It is a term of interpretation, and being such it will naturally take its place within the framework of our *Weltanschauung* as a whole" (25). And in the "Retrospective Prospect" of *Attitudes toward History*, *weltanschauung* gets an appositive relationship to *attitude*: "Philosophically, with regard to a *Weltanschauung*, an ATTITUDE toward Life . . ." (415).

12. For a Bourdieu-inflected account of such correlations, see especially Dana Anderson, "Questioning."

13. I would be remiss not to remind readers of Burke's famous theory of five dogs in *Language as Symbolic Action* (73–74).

14. See also Burke's *Counter-Statement* 16–17, 36.

15. Here I am thinking of his discussion of hypochondriasis toward the end of *Grammar of Motives*: "To what extent can we confront the global situation with an attitude neither local nor imperialistic? Surely, all works of goodwill written in the next decades must aim somehow to avoid these two extremes, seeking a neoliberal, speculative attitude. To an extent, perhaps, it will be like an attitude of hypochondriasis: the attitude of a patient who makes peace with his symptoms by becoming interested in them" (442–43).

Chapter 6. Body Language

1. The question of where spoken language comes from is as intriguing as it is unanswerable. This may be why the question belongs to philosophers—and why linguists and other scientists have more often than not considered it taboo. For an accessible and compelling overview of the debates within linguistics around the questions of language's origins, see Kenneally.

2. The most recent resurgence of this theory is discussed in a 1999 issue of *American Scientist* that describes "manual gestures" as "'behavioral fossil' coupled to speech" (Corballis 138). Kennedy's treatment is interesting for its overt attempt to connect glossogenetics and even animal communication to Aristotelian categories of rhetoric. See also Kendon, esp. 35–61, for a review of glossogenetics from the point of view of gesture studies.

3. See "The Progress of Science: Voice and the Telephone. Mechanism of Speech," *Times*, September 13, 1926.

4. Thanks go to Burke's sons, Michael and Anthony, for allowing me the chance to visit Burke's study, which they have left intact since his death in 1992.

5. In the decade since scholars in rhetorical studies began to consider more intently how bodies figure into rhetorical theory and criticism, those in political rhetoric and performance studies have been confronting live bodies—activist bodies, minority bodies, disabled bodies, rhetorical bodies—in order to incorporate them and all their intensities, energies, and movements into rhetorical theory and criticism. Such work is often as difficult as it is groundbreaking. In his article on the use of bodies as performance and proof, Kevin DeLuca hints at the difficulty of developing a coherent theory of the body precisely because, as he puts it, "the body is a site of incoherence" (20). Similarly, as Gerard Hauser demonstrates, bodies are frequently antithetical to rhetoric's disciplinary touchstones: argument, persuasion, and reason (2). In his introduction to a two-part special issue of *Argumentation and Advocacy* on body argument, Hauser writes, "The body is an ambiguous form of signification. Arguments are warranted assertions. They are claims supported by evidence and reasoning. But the body, as a corporeal entity, is an organism; its biological status is not symbolic" (2).

According to Melissa Deem, emerging work on publics and counterpublics sustains that commitment through its allegiance to critical-rational discourse, oftentimes rendering bodies moot and even mute (450). Deem and DeLuca, along with Sharon Crowley, Phaedra Pezzullo ("Resisting"), and Mindy Fenske, have challenged rhetoric's unwavering commitment to reason, stressing instead the interrelated roles of affect, desire, movement, and bodily sensation in rhetorical practice and performance. For a sustained, productive emphasis on the body's capacity for movement and the resulting connections to life and energy, a major focus of the present chapter, see two articles by Fenske: "The Aesthetic of the Unfinished: Ethics and Performance" and "The Movement of Interpretation." Of course bodies are arguably not new to rhetoric, and this is where new theories and histories can productively converge. My book *Bodily Arts* in fact argues that rhetoric has long been intertwined with bodily matters; it's just that our Aristotelian commitments to thought and reason have historically produced trained incapacities, most notably our difficulty theorizing the body's relationship to rhetoric. See also Fredal.

6. See Jeff Bennett's review of an article on Burkean attitude, which phrases this "flatness" phenomenon aptly: "It is no small irony . . . that Burke's many writings are often utilized in pedagogy and research as a systematic approach to criticism, not as a rhetorical heuristic for inspiring invention."

7. Anderson: "the preparation for action that Burke signifies through *attitude* here refers to conscious preparation" ("Questioning" 261). This reading of course is fair enough, and much more understandable given the *Grammar* passage than the version attitude offered by Mahen-Hays and Aden, which I believe goes too far. O'Keefe's earlier piece is interesting because it grapples with the "troublesome" difficulties posed by Burke's formulation of dramatism (10) and hints that Burke may have gotten it wrong. Later writings by Burke—including Burke's "(Nonsymbolic) Motion / (Symbolic) Action," published in the same year as O'Keefe's article—corroborate O'Keefe's hunch.

8. Doing so helps distinguish between structuralist or poststructuralist theories of language, where Burke's theories are so frequently slotted (Condit, "Framing" 79), and his lively, robust, and, importantly, materialist theory of dramatism. What is more, in assuming the complete commensurability of dramatism, identification, and symbolic action with structuralist or even poststructuralist linguistics, rhetoric scholars commit an act of anachronism, an act that continues to ignore the body's importance for Burke's subsequent theories, as well as—more broadly—the body's crucial poetic role in communicative activity. For a structuralist Burke see Gusfield (introduction 2–3) and William Rueckert ("Kenneth Burke and Structuralism"). For poststructuralism see Nelson (156–58), Biesecker (2–23), and Wess (*Kenneth Burke: Rhetoric, Subjectivity, Postmodernism*). Wess's book actually links Burke to postmodernism, which I take to be distinct from and yet frequently commensurate with poststructural theories of language. Condit also bristles at attempts to characterize Burke as a poststructuralist—"The blending of human linguistic prowess with our animality is Burke's unique strength"— and warns that "effacing any material component . . . requires one to ignore the ties to history and physicality that are implicit in Burke's notions of 'familial' and 'geometric substance'" ("Framing" 79).

9. For a terrific model of such sorting that happens along the lines of neurology rather than glossogenetics, see Elizabeth A. Wilson's *Psychosomatic*, which follows the biological models of Darwin, Freud, and Sacks and ultimately offers biology as a

surprisingly productive venue for feminist theory. Celeste M. Condit's 2004 lecture "How Should We Study the Symbolizing Animal?" works through the risks and rewards of integrating biology into humanistic work (9), with frequent reference to Burke.

10. See also Vitanza's account of the reception of Kennedy's piece: "I had heard through the grapevine that Kennedy had written a 'wild,' perhaps savage, article. And indeed, he has" (ix).

11. It is a bit surprising that Kennedy's survey of glossogenetic theories does not include Paget's. Paget was not, after all, a little-known figure, though his development of the Paget-Gormon system of signed speech may have eclipsed his earlier work in glossogenetics. For a critique of neo-Cartesianism in regard to gesture studies, see Farnell, "Developments."

12. For more on Burke's counterrelation to abstraction, see Rueckert, who rightly observes that the separation between humans and biology occurs, in Burke's scheme, by dint of what Rueckert calls "a movement to abstraction" (*Encounters* 136). Celeste M. Condit's rejoinder to Phillip Tompkins and George Cheney offers Korzybski as a useful point of contrast in regard to the usefulness of abstraction ("Framing" 78).

13. The habit here of course happens on a phylogenetic rather than an individual scale, and this set of Darwin's theories closely approximates Lamarck. Paget's explicit crediting of Darwin with his insights about gesture, and Burke's subsequent engagement with Paget's theories, challenges Adam Kendon's view that "Darwin had little direct bearing on the development of gesture studies" until the latter half of the twentieth century (44).

14. It seems important to note that Paget's theories are not drawn exclusively from English or even Indo-European languages but from a variety of Eastern and ancient languages as well, with a strong leaning toward Polynesian languages.

15. The passage continues: "It is a curious, though perhaps an idle speculation, how early in the long line of our progenitors the various expressive movements, now exhibited by man, were successively acquired" (*Expression* 356).

16. It is worth noting, too, that Kennedy's theory of rhetoric as energy derives not from his extensive and monumental research on the history of rhetoric, nor from translating Aristotle, but from his observation of crows calling to each other on his campus in Chapel Hill (Vitanza ix)

17. This is also the section of Burke's copy of *Human Speech* that is the most marked up and worked over.

18. Chesebro (46) places the composition of "Auscultation" between 1930 and 1934, though since this piece precedes Burke's writing of *Permanence and Change*, which was happening in 1933 (cf. my "Burke on Drugs," 17), I would narrow Chesebro's estimation by a year.

19. It is also possible that Burke is responding to his own dog, Ping (whose brother's name was Pong), who gets an explicit reference earlier in "Auscultation," when Burke describes how Ping taught him an important lesson about anthropocentrism:

> gathering up the family, including the pup, who was small enough to be transported in a cardboard box with square holes cut here and there for ventilation, I started off on a slow train which—it being early spring—was heated both by

steam from the engine and by slanting sunlight. The pup . . . in his eagerness to see, would stick his nose into one of the holes, thus blocking his vision and leading me to realize that had he been less eager he would, by not pressing so tensely forward, have avoided plugging the hole with his nose, and so would have seen much better. I thought of calling the attention of all my daughters to this parabolic fact, but I was not quite sure of what it was parabolic, and insofar as dogs recognize by scent rather than vision, his nose was exactly where it should have been. (53–54)

20. Sociologists such as Joseph Gusfield (introduction 18) are particularly keen on identification's social, persuasive functions.

21. In *Counter-Statement*'s "Lexicon Rhetoricae," Burke writes, "The appeal of form as exemplified in rhythm enjoys a special advantage in that rhythm is more closely allied with 'bodily' processes. Systole and diastole, alternation of the feet in walking, inhalation and exhalation, up and down, in and out, back and forth, such are the types of distinctly motor experiences 'tapped' by rhythm." This passage is discussed in more detail in chapters 1 and 3.

22. Readers might recognize here the rudiments of speech act theory: "In names, there are implicit the act and the command (Piaget shows us the child picking up a block and saying: 'This is a boat.' The child next moves the block, commanding itself: 'Now, make the boat go across the ocean.' In time, name and command become inextricably intermingled, the command being implicit in the name.) To name various manifestations by the same name, is to organize a strategy with reference to these manifestations" (*ATH* 339).

23. *Philosophy of Literary Form* marks, as best as I can tell, the first time Burke uses the phrase *symbolic action,* and he of course uses the phrase in *Philosophy of Literary Form*'s subtitle, *Studies in Symbolic Action.* To be sure he is circling "symbolic action" in *Attitudes toward History* (1e 22; 2e 194) when he discusses symbolic kinship.

24. This is the date of his new preface for the second edition, which appeared in 1957 and so, I assume, roughly approximates the revisions he made.

25. It is telling that the conclusion of *Attitudes toward History,* so inflected by Paget's theories, as I demonstrate in *"Attitudes* I," above, can be left fully intact and unrevised for the second edition.

26. Though A. T. W.'s *Quarterly Journal of Speech* review foreshadows the possibility for poetic implications when he suggests that Paget's theory offers speech "as the basis of the arts of literature, poetry and song" (365).

27. At the very least this genealogy troubles the recent assertion of Mahen-Hays and Aden that Burkean attitude is "a strategy of interpretation and thus more of a cognitive activity that is then reflected in one's symbol use" (35). Mahen-Hays and Aden's error is their assumption that interpretation—especially Burkean interpretation—is necessarily and wholly cognitive. See my introduction.

28. In "Retrospective Prospect" in *Attitudes toward History* Burke writes: "But, whereas the *quo modo* of the medieval formula was originally treated as but a figurative variation on the theme of 'agency' ('he did the job with hammer and saw, with alacrity'), in time the strategic role of the term began to become apparent. For it designates the

point of *personal mediation* between the realm of nonsymbolic motion and symbolic action. Its 'how' refers to the role of the human individual as a physiological organism, with corresponding centrality of the nervous system, ATTITUDINIZING in the light of experience as marked by the powers of symbolicity (both in themselves and in the realm of the Counter-Nature that has developed as the results, intended and unintended, of those powers)" (*ATH* 3e 394).

29. These three articles are most useful for Burke's account of the negative, which is why I do not focus on them more here, despite their title, "A Dramatistic View of the Origins of Language." This series also ends up in his *Language as Symbolic Action*.

30. Consider, for example, Burke's rejoinder to Wayne Booth, "Dancing with Tears in My Eyes," and Booth's meditation in *Critical Understanding* called "The Dance as Cure" (124–26).

31. For more on this pair, see the conclusion.

Chapter 7. Welcome to the Beauty Clinic

1. Scholars except Ellen Quandahl, that is. See Quandahl's consideration of Burke and Freud, which acknowledges a certain indebtedness and yet allows that something decidedly different is going on. As this chapter shows, she is right.

2. The headnote to the *Psychoanalytic Review* version of "The Thinking of the Body" reads as follows: "The following pages are concerned with ways in which the functions of bodily excretion attain expression (sometimes direct, more often indirect) in works of the imagination. They were written in connection with a book I am writing on the subject of Poetics which, since the days of Aristotle's famous treatise, has variously concerned itself with processes of 'catharsis' in art" (25).

3. Later in the same essay Thames reconsiders his initial reaction: "But what if the stone that interpreters reject is the system's cornerstone?" He then offers this conclusion: "We should instead struggle with the strange. Wresting with rather than dismissing the anomalous, we may discern logical bearings for a different view. Willingly suspending disbelief, we may find our way to a new interpretation."

4. Just to be clear, when Rueckert mentions "Thinking of the Body" in the quote above, he is talking about a hundred-plus-page manuscript that formed part of the then recently discovered unfinished "Symbolic" manuscript, while Wess is talking about the article by the same title that appeared first in *Psychoanalytic Review* (1963) and was later reprinted in *Language as Symbolic Action*. According to Rueckert (2007), there was significant overlap between the unpublished section of the book and the published article.

5. Notable exceptions are Jack Selzer, whose account of Burke attends to all manners of Burke's life, and also Ross Wolin, whose reading of *Counter-Statement* begins with a mention of Burke's "near . . . nervous breakdown" in 1932 (37), and his account of Burke's books as attempts to "redo" *Counter-Statement* stands in stark contrast to most accounts of his career. Selzer devotes more space to dispelling notions of Burke as a *solitary* genius and portraying him as very much "among others."

6. I do not wish to fault Jay. Given the enormous load of letters these two exchanged over the course of seven decades, he had to make many editorial choices. My point is simply that reading the letters in their entirety is crucial if one is to get an accurate picture of Burke's engrossments.

7. Rueckert, for example, does not wish to include "The Thinking of the Body" in his past-imperfect, would-have-been version of the "Symbolic."

8. I have chosen to focus on Burke's relation to his own ailments as opposed to his relation to the ailments of others (for example, his mother and his wife, Libbie), mostly because, as this chapter suggests, Burke and his work were far more absorbed with his own immediate, accessible physical condition. In doing so I do not mean to discount the profound worry and sadness he experienced with his mother's ill health and especially Libbie's passing, which had an enormous impact on Burke's work in the 1970s, as he wrote to Cowley: "The thing is, Malcolm, since Libbie cleared out, I have quit putting out my books" (June 9, 1975; Jay 396).

9. See "Thinking of the Body" (25) and *Language as Symbolic Action* (308). Burke also uses the phrase in an undated six-page letter to John Crowe Ransom, most likely sent in late January or early February 1957. After a ranging discussion of the body in literature by Flannery O'Connor and Djuna Barnes, a meditation on the relation between excrement and creation, a long excerpt of his own work-in-progress, and a discussion of the way dirty jokes "back up the kind of connection between 'human body' and 'world's body'" he has "in mind here," a transitional paragraph begins, "So much for the Beauty Clinic at present" (Ransom Papers, Vanderbilt University).

10. The title of this section is the first line of a letter Burke sent to Cowley on June 23, 1960 (Jay 335).

11. Burke's ailments of decades past are neatly chronicled in a letter he wrote to William Carlos Williams in October 1945 seeking his professional advice about a "bony protuberance" in the roof of his mouth (October 12, 1945; East 80). Williams ultimately assisted with the lump's removal (WCW to KB, November 18, 1945; KB to WCW, November 23, 1945; East 88, 90). Here are Burke's reflections on "the thing":

> Whether accidents could have started the thing, I don't know. I am the proud possessor of a broken neck, as disclosed by X-ray photographs taken at a hospital some years ago. I had a bad fall when about three years old, and spent many years of my childhood in terror, a sense of being elsewhere, or dropping through the bottom. I guess the fall did its part in that. And I wonder whether it may also have got things to growing a bit wrong too, as my head sits awry. And then another time I had my front teeth batted out, an accident that might have dislocated the maxillary bones a bit. Anyhow, there is the egg, and I'm finding it more and more difficult to give priority rating to my other worries. So, if you had someone to suggest? (KB to WCW, October 12, 1945; East 80)

Thanks to Dana Anderson and an anonymous reader for directing me to this letter. East notes that "of the twenty letters that exchanged hands [between Burke and Williams] in 1945, eleven concern themselves with Burke's physical ailments" (xxii–xxiii).

12. Note that this process of engrossment deems hypochondria as neither unreal nor (therefore) dismissable, but posits the symptoms as quite real and quite important to one's way of doing things. While Burke's so-called hypochondria is well known, I fear that such a label risks being misunderstood without a constant reminder of what Burke himself meant by *hypochondriasis*. When East, for example, mentions his hypochondria (xxii), he does so only in passing and to account for the long lists of symptoms he sent

to his doctor friend Williams. And yet chalking this up to hypochondria without further discussion risks dismissing the symptom lists as (a) unreal and (b) unimportant to Burke's theory. My treatment of his symptoms resists such a move, and so I use the terms *hypochondria* and *hypochondriasis* sparingly, preferring instead such phrases as "intense interest" or obsessiveness.

13. The letters with citations not referring to Jay's volume are found in the Malcolm Cowley Papers at the Newberry Library. Of the teeth-pulling Cowley writes, "A plate in the mouth, with a sheet of pink plastic for the tongue to rest against instead of one's own palate, is an indignity offered to the human body" (February 13, 1953; Jay 317).

14. For more on the projected shape of the "Symbolic," see part 1 of Henderson and Williams's volume, especially Williams's "Toward Rounding out the *Motivorum Trilogy*," Burke's "'Glimpses into a Labyrinth of Interwoven Motives,'" and Rueckert's "Kenneth Burke's 'Symbolic of Motives.'" For Burke's correspondence with Cowley regarding his persistent symptoms, see his letters of November 16, 1950; January 6, 1951; January 14, 1951; March 2, 1951; September 6, 1952; and January 16, 1953 (Jay 313).

15. The mention of mud in such close proximity to the abyss subtly invokes the contact poetry of William Carlos Williams, who held that poetry should emerge from the gunk of real life, muddy shoes, wet wheelbarrows, peeling paint. John Crowe Ransom offers his version of a similar sort of poetics when in his 1938 book *The World's Body* he writes that poetry "recovers" "the world which is made of whole and indefeasible objects" (x–xi). This unfeeling material world marks a base materiality that Ransom designates as the "world's body," which Burke incorporates into his "Beauty Clinic." Ransom believes that the stuff of poetry lies not in conventional and cultivated beauty, for example, "the fragrance of roses," but rather "in the violence of return and regeneration." The world's body is therefore a world that exhibits its own "thickness" and "stubbornness." In this way Burke's cloacal criticism, his "symbolism as somnambulism," the point of which is to become alive to symbols' movements, owes as much to Williams and Ransom as to Freud. Thanks go to John Marsh, whose work on Williams's contact theory of poetry, especially in relation to poverty, brought to light the possible connections here. For more on connections between Burke and Williams, see Brian A. Bremen and David Blakesley.

16. Such a view stemmed from Nietzsche's own illnesses and his aphoristic axiom that "there is more reason in your body than in your best wisdom" (*Zarathustra* 146). For more on Nietzsche's philosophy of illness, see Blondel (218–34) and Kofman (52–53); for more on Burke's use of and relationship to Nietzsche, see Desilet and also my own "Burke and Nietzsche."

17. The article opens with this sentence: "This essay is part of a Poetics" (337).

18. Belfiore deduces this from the *Poetics* line 1449a34–37, where Aristotle remarks that tragedy and epic are distinct from comedy "which deals with what is not destructive or painful, but laughable" (259).

19. A similarly magical view of language can be found in a pair of essays published in the *Chicago Review* titled "The Language of Poetry, 'Dramatistically' Considered." Burke wrote these essays as part of a symbolism seminar conducted by the Institute for Religious and Social Studies in New York, 1952–53. The two-part intervention begins with a rather tidy theory that puts dramatism into relation with poetic language

and dissolves into an unwieldy account of poetic invention that is tantamount to magic.

20. The "Language of Poetry" essays cited in the previous footnote, with their focus on "intrinsic criticism"—restricted to the language within the poetry only—show Burke's early but firm commitment to symbolism. As my analysis of later work shows, however, he eventually gives up on isolating symbolic action in this way.

21. Aristotle promises in the *Politics* to say more about catharsis in the *Poetics*, but that section, like the discussion of comedy, is famously and frustratingly missing—and assumed lost.

22. That vocabulary, Burke writes, "like all vocabulary, has three non-empirical non-linguistic sources to draw on: the human body, the 'world's body' (the natural scene), and the body politic" ("On Catharsis" 338). These are categories he borrows from John Crowe Ransom's *World's Body*.

23. These are more specific than the world's body, human body, and body politic categories he borrows from Ransom. There are probably even more than four. For example, there is a spatial body lurking in Burke's discussion of the aim of poetics as a kind of proximity management—"Pity is said to be like a movement-towards; and fear (or 'terror') like a movement away-from" ("On Catharsis" 341). Burke discusses the resulting back-and-forth as a kind of dance, and he explicitly notes the "underlying 'physicalist' analogy" (341).

24. Such a reading is, even to my liberal philological eye, a stretch.

25. Indeed, Burke discourages such an exclusive focus when he ascribes stages of cleansing to the reader and work that closely correspond to the poet's.

26. The "bountiful materiality" line comes from the first installment of "The Language of Poetry, 'Dramatistically' Considered" (98).

27. This issue of transference directs our attention to affective response, a relatively new area of study for literary and rhetorical criticism. Eve Kosofsky Sedgwick's *Touching Feeling* offers that asking "new questions about phenomenology and affect" can dislodge the "recent fixation on epistemology" where theories of performativity are concerned (17). Sedgwick concerns herself with the irreducible phenomenology of touching and feeling (21). While theorists of what Jenny Rice calls "critical affect studies" do not respond directly to Jameson's charge of "mechanical materialism," the works together nevertheless stand as a strong refutation. Considerations of affect, emotion, touch, and feelings by Sedgwick, Teresa Brennan, Brian Massumi, Rei Terada, and Elias Canetti focus on an enlivening force of bodies that is far from mechanical, reductive, or deterministic. Indeed simply the way these scholars write about affect—with decidedly physical emphases of temperature, movement, and spatiality—refutes a mechanistic view of bodies. Massumi, as I discussed in the introduction, most explicitly directs our attention to the importance of movement where bodies are concerned. Sedgwick, in writing about affect, observes, "In writing this book, I've continually felt pressed against the limits of my stupidity, even as I've felt the promising closeness of transmissible gifts" (24); Terada and Brennan use the language of "transmission," though each focuses on different aspects of physicality—the face and voice (Terada 12) and pheromones and biochemical entrainment (Brennan 78–96).

28. Here I'm thinking of Elias Canetti's *Crowds and Power* and Lauren Berlant's discussion of how "unfeeling" spread in response to the 2004 presidential elections.

29. Dana Anderson's *Identity's Strategy*, a book-length exploration of Burkean conversion, is indispensable on this score.

30. For example "ideas of 'pollution' might be expressed in terms of nature or physiology (such as nausea or the plague)" (339); and "the purging of 'pollutions' in the body politic can be expressed directly or indirectly by the imagery of bodily purgation" (359).

31. See articles on ecocriticism by Robert Wess and Marika Seigel. Wess ("Ecocriticism") terms this way of thinking *ecological holism*, while Seigel (394–95) finds traces of ecological thinking in Burke's theories of efficiency. Indeed Burke's work on efficiency anchors most ecological readings of his work. See also Wolfe (69ff.), Blankenship ("Kenneth Burke on Ecology" 260), and Muir (36).

32. As Marika Seigel points out (388), this language-as-ecology point is one of the dominant strands in Burkean ecocriticism, and as her article shows by going in the opposite direction, the language-as-ecology interpretation misses its dependence on the science of ecology.

33. For an incisive account of Burke's nonsymbolic motion / symbolic action pair, see Crable, "Symbolizing Motion." See also this book's conclusion.

34. September 29, to be precise (this date deduced from Libbie's addendum to Burke's handwritten note to Cowley, discussed below).

35. The opening line of the letter is this: "Many more sharks' teeth have washed over the ridge since I wrote you a few days ago."

36. Representative here is Muir, who writes, "Burke has a deep and abiding concern with the general nature of such an 'ecological' balance. Burke's own fictional Herone Liddell (little hero) is 'haunted by ecology' and dismayed by the twisting and intensity of the human symbolism that he revels in" (37).

37. Burke answered a query from Ransom about an accent mark Burke had originally included over the last syllable of "Liddell"; Ransom had removed it and checked with Burke to see if that was okay: "As for the hickey-madoodle on Liddell: I have no strong feelings on the matter. So, since it's done this way, let's leave it so. Originally, I put it there because I heard somebody pronounce 'Liddell' on the first syllable—and I didn't know how prevalent this practice might be. So, just to be safe, I indicated the stress. . . . I also had in mind a remote pun on 'Little' (so that the name wd. have connotations of 'little hero')" (September 1, 1957; Ransom Papers, Vanderbilt Library).

38. The voice, according to the narrator, proceeds "not exactly either *ab intra* or *ab extra*, since it was too remote or impersonal to be his, yet too much in tune with his own thoughts for it to be someone else's" (521).

39. This is the section with which Cowley believed Burke should end: "Mightn't it be better to confine the ideas to a simple progression and end them with a clear note, like the contrast between Ecology and Gallantry?" (March 11, 1957).

Conclusion

1. Rhetorical scholars holding firm to nonsymbolic motion / symbolic action as a distinction include Dana Anderson ("Questioning" 259); and J. Clarke Rountree III. Robert Wess, too, reads Burke's essay as commentary on the "unbridgeable gap between

body and language" (*Kenneth Burke* 249). Bryan Crable ("Symbolizing Motion") offers an important reading of the two as a dialectical pair; I will engage his reading later.

2. As Crable himself notes, his reading is in line with Wess's, for which see *Kenneth Burke*, 134–35.

3. Burke treats this review "as a kind of 'work in progress'" (153) in which he will "see what might be done by a view of [Austin's notion of] 'illocutionary force' as a synonym for 'attitude'" (153). Attitude was the late addition to Burke's pentad, the crucial term that cinched language to bodies. Indeed Burke's work-in-progress eventually leads to a more precise formulation of the nonsymbolic motion / symbolic action pair, as evidenced in his observation later in the review that "only an out-and-out, formally dramatistic nomenclature sets the conditions for inquiries into the sheer bodily equivalents of the speech acts' attitudes" (167). The Austin review is to be reprinted in Rivers and Weber's *Equipment for Living*.

4. Burke later characterizes this shift in a little-known piece published in *College Composition and Communication* in 1978, the same year he named nonsymbolic motion / symbolic action "the basic polarity" in the pages of *Critical Inquiry*: "In the twenties, I began theorizing about the nature of literary form. Gradually such speculations developed into theories about the nature of language in general. I called these notions 'Dramatistic' because they viewed language primarily as a mode of *action* rather than as a mode of *knowledge*, though the two emphases are by no means mutually exclusive" ("Questions and Answers" 330). Again I would stress, with Burke, the nonexclusivity as much as the nonequivalence of knowledge and action.

5. Read in light of Burke's enduring terministic commitments—his favoring of action over knowledge, of bodies as much as language—it is no wonder that Jameson's attempt to read Burke's method as primarily ideological and therefore knowledge-centered stuck in Burke's critical craw. In his response to Jameson, "Methodological Repression and/or Strategies of Containment," Burke invokes the motion/action pair more than once in order to show how Jameson only tells part of the story about his work's implications (412). Burke's responses to Austin and Jameson might best be described respectively as "yes, and" and "no, but." In other words when placed next to one another, Burke's engagements with Jameson and Austin reveal a close association between dramatism and speech act theory and near repulsion from Jameson's "'historicist' ideology" (412), and Burke's account of the attraction and distinction sheds considerable light on the nonsymbolic motion / symbolic action pair. Jameson's initial piece ("The Symbolic Inference") appeared in the spring of 1978, in the issue just before "(Nonsymbolic) Motion / (Symbolic) Action." Burke's response and Jameson's rejoinder appeared together in the winter 1978 issue.

6. The letter cited here also shows Burke claiming that his nonsymbolic motion / symbolic action "routine" has effectively "sewed up" all his theory to date.

7. He also writes in that same piece that "though symbolism as such is a dimension that transcends the body, it is rooted in the body as a purely physiological organism, essentially as nonlinguistic as a fetus in the womb" (330).

8. This version of Burke's definition was, according to Richard Coe ("Defining" 39), first made public at the 1989 Conference on College Composition and Communication.

Burke uses the phrase "Bodies That Learn Language" in his 1983 afterword to the third edition of *Permanence and Change*, with the "proviso that the special human aptitude for *language* be understood to include the ability to behave with other such arbitrary, conventional symbol-systems as dance, music sculpture, painting, and architecture" (295; emphasis in original).

9. In "(Nonsymbolic) Motion / (Symbolic) Action" Burke writes that "the realm of nonsymbolic motion needs no realm of symbolic action; but there could be no symbolic action unless grounded in the realm of motion, the realm of motion having preceded the emergence of our symbol-using ancestors; and doubtless the time will come when motions go on after all our breed will have vanished" (811).

10. Indeed Burke's reply to Jameson literally trails off with a nonanthropomorphic aporia: "Without an appreciatively ironic view of specifically human strivings, my notions on the subject of 'anthropomorphization' . . . Well, I leave the sentence unfinished, for I don't know" ("Methodological" 416). Burke's insistence on the primacy of nonsymbolic motion gives his work on language an ecological, nonanthropomorphic cast, or at the very least the varying scales of motion—from the individual, ontogenetic level to the level of the universe and beyond—work to inject Burke's humanism with a solid hit of irony.

11. It is telling that Burke writes that he wants "to end" the review with this consideration and yet the review goes on for thirteen more pages.

12. Burke here notes that he is following Austin in "confining ourselves, for simplicity, to *spoken* utterance" and then adds, "Written words would depend on visual rather than auditory kinds of environmental motion, Braille on motions involved in touch" (164).

13. And nor, for that matter, can Austin. Burke cites nearly every instance when Austin mentions the movement of body parts, sometimes attached to weapons. He does not, however, mention the one that would make his point about attitude quite nicely: "It is characteristic of perlocutionary acts that the response achieved, or the sequel, can be achieved additionally or entirely by non-locutionary means: thus intimidation may be achieved by waving a stick or pointing a gun. . . . However this is not enough to distinguish illocutionary acts, since we can for example warn or order or appoint or give or protest or apologize by non-verbal means and these are illocutionary acts. Thus we may cock a snook or hurl a tomato by way of protest" (119).

14. Burke's notion of duplication is remarkably consonant with contemporary affect theories, which suggest that language doubles up on bodily force. In addition to Massumi (26–27), see Edbauer, "Executive Overspill" (6). See also Denise Riley's *Impersonal Passions*.

15. For more on the linguistic turn, see Rorty and Elizabeth A. Clark.

16. See Brenkman on Freud's devotion to stories and symbols, esp. 172–73, and Lacan, whose observation that "the unconscious is structured like a language" (20) gets taken beyond simple analogy. See also Grosz, *Jacques Lacan* 82–114. Foucault, I offer, would stop short at saying it is *the form* of knowing, or at the very least he honors material articulations, such as the gun with the soldier's body in *Discipline and Punish* (152–53). While Judith Butler's monumental theory of gender performativity

emphasizes movement through repetition (*Gender Trouble* 179), performativity also relies on internalized knowledge of coded behavioral norms that circulate within a matrix of intelligibility (*Bodies That Matter* 1–17). See Julia Walker, "Why Performance? Why Now?" for an extended critique of Butler's position.

WORKS CITED

Manuscripts and Archival Materials

Bureau of Social Hygiene. Archives, 1911–1940. Archive Web site, available at www.rockefeller.edu/archive.ctr/bsh.html (accessed September 18, 2008).

Kenneth Burke Papers. Paterno Special Collections Library, Penn State University.

Malcolm Cowley Papers. Midwest Manuscript Collection, Newberry Library, Chicago.

John Crowe Ransom Papers, Special Collections and University Archives, Jean and Alexander Heard Library, Vanderbilt University.

Allen Tate Papers, Manuscript Division, Department of Rare Books and Special Collections, Princeton University Library.

Published Sources

A. T. W. Review of *Human Speech* by Sir Richard Paget. *Quarterly Journal of Speech* 16 (June 1930): 364–68.

Anderson, Dana. *Identity's Strategy: Rhetorical Selves in Conversion*. Columbia: University of South Carolina Press, 2007.

———. "Questioning the Motives of Habituated Action: Burke and Bourdieu on *Practice*." *Philosophy and Rhetoric* 37 (2004): 255–74.

Anderson, Margaret. *The Unknowable Gurdjieff*. London: Arkana, 1991.

Arac, Jonathan. "Toward a Critical Genealogy of the U.S. Discourse of Identity: Invisible Man after Fifty Years." *boundary 2* 30 (Summer 2003): 195–216.

Austin, J. L. *How to Do Things with Words*. 2nd ed. Cambridge, Mass.: Harvard University Press, 1975.

Baldwin, James Mark, ed. *Dictionary of Philosophy and Psychology, Including many of the Principal Conceptions of Ethics, Logic, Aesthetics, Philosophy of Religion, Mental Pathology, Anthropology, Biology, Neurology, Physiology, Economics, Political and Social Philosophy, Philology, Physical Science, and Education*. 3 vols. New York: Macmillan, 1905.

Banner, Lois W. "Mannish Women, Passive Men, and Constitutional Types: Margaret Mead's *Sex and Temperament in Three Primitive Societies* as a Response to Ruth Benedict's *Patterns of Culture*." *Signs: Journal of Women in Culture and Society* 28 (2003): 851–58.

Barnard, G. William. *Exploring Unseen Worlds: William James and the Philosophy of Mysticism*. Albany: State University of New York Press, 1997.

Bechhofer, C. E. "The Forest Philosophers." *Century Magazine* 108 (May 1924): 66–78.

Belfiore, Elizabeth. *Tragic Pleasures: Aristotle on Plot and Emotion*. Princeton: Princeton University Press, 1992.

Benbow, Heather. "Ways in, Ways Out: Theorizing the Kantian Body." *Body and Society* 9 (2003): 57–72.

Bennett, Jane. "The Force of Things: Steps Toward an Ecology of Matter." *Political Theory* 32 (2004): 347–72.

Bennett, Jeff. Review of "Kenneth Burke's 'Attitude' at the Cross-roads of Rhetorical and Cultural Studies" by Sarah E. Mahen-Hays and Roger C. Aden. *KB Journal* 2 (2005). Available at kbjournal.org/node/48 (accessed September 18, 2008).

Berens, Linda V., and Dario Nardi, *The Sixteen Personality Types: Descriptions for Self-Discovery.* Hamilton Beach, Calif.: Telos, 1999.

Berlant, Lauren. "Unfeeling Kerry." *Theory and Event* 8 (2005). Available at muse.jhu.edu/journals/theory_and_event/v008/8.2berlant.html (accessed September 18, 2008).

Berman, Louis. *The Glands Regulating Personality: A Study of the Glands of Internal Secretion in Relation to the Types of Human Nature.* 2nd ed. New York: Macmillan, 1928.

Bérubé, Michael. *Life as We Know It: A Father, a Family, and an Exceptional Child.* New York: New York University Press, 1998.

Biesecker, Barbara. *Addressing Postmodernity: Kenneth Burke, Rhetoric, and a Theory of Social Change.* Tuscaloosa: University of Alabama Press, 1997.

Blair, Carole. "Symbolic Action and Discourse: The Convergent/Divergent Views of Kenneth Burke and Michel Foucault." In *Kenneth Burke and Contemporary European Thought*, ed. Bernard L. Brock, 119–65. Tuscaloosa: University of Alabama Press, 1995.

Blakesley, David. "William Carlos Williams's Influence on Kenneth Burke." Paper presented to the Modern Language Association, Toronto, December 1997. Available at http://www.cla.purdue.edu/dblakesley/burke/blake.html (accessed September 18, 2008).

Blankenship, Jane. "Kenneth Burke on Ecology: A Synthesis." In Chesebro, *Extensions of the Burkeian System*, 251–68.

———. "'Magic' and 'Mystery' in the Works of Kenneth Burke." In *The Legacy of Kenneth Burke*, ed. Herbert W. Simons and Trevor Melia, 246–76. Madison: University of Wisconsin Press, 1989.

Blondel, Eric. *Nietzsche: The Body and Culture: Philosophy as a Philological Genealogy.* Trans. Seán Hand. Stanford: Stanford University Press, 1991.

Blum, W. C. (James Sibley Watson Jr.). Review of *Tertium Organum* by P. D. Ouspensky. *Dial* 69 (September 1920): 308–12.

Bone, Robert. *The Negro Novel in America.* New Haven: Yale University Press, 1965.

Booth, Wayne. *Critical Understanding: The Powers and Limits of Pluralism.* Chicago: University of Chicago Press, 1979.

Bordo, Susan. *The Male Body: A New Look at Men in Public and in Private.* New York: Farrar, Straus & Giroux, 1999.

———. *Unbearable Weight: Feminism, Western Culture, and the Body.* Berkeley: University of California Press, 1993.

Bourne, Randolph S. "Mystic Turned Radical." In *Youth and Life*, 205–14. Boston: Houghton Mifflin, 1913.

Bragdon, Claude. "Introduction to the English Translation." In *Tertium Organum*, 1–6. New York: Knopf, 1951.
Brandt, Deborah. "'Who's the President?' Ghostwriting and Shifting Values in Literacy." *College English* 69 (July 2007): 549–71.
Bremen, Brian A. *William Carlos Williams and the Diagnostics of Culture*. New York: Oxford University Press, 1993.
Brenkman, John. "Freud the Modernist." In *The Mind of Modernism: Medicine, Psychology, and the Cultural Arts in Europe and America, 1880–1940*, ed. Mark S. Micale, 172–96. Stanford: Stanford University Press, 2004.
Brennan, Teresa. *The Transmission of Affect*. Ithaca: Cornell University Press, 2004.
Browne, Janet. "I Could Have Retched All Night: Charles Darwin and His Body." In *Science Incarnate: Historical Embodiments of Natural Knowledge*, ed. Steven and Christopher Lawrence Shapin, 240–87. Chicago: University of Chicago Press, 1998.
Brunas-Wagstaff, Jo. *Personality: A Cognitive Approach*. New York: Routledge, 1998.
Buell, Lawrence. *The Future of Environmental Criticism: Environmental Crisis and Literary Imagination*. Malden, Mass.: Blackwell, 2006.
Burke, Kenneth. "After Hours." *S4N*, third anniversary issue (November 1922): n.pag.
———. "The Anaesthetic Revelation of Herone Liddell." *Kenyon Review* 19 (1957): 505–59.
———. *Attitudes toward History*. 2 vols. New York: New Republic, 1937.
———. *Attitudes toward History*. 2nd ed. Los Altos, Calif.: Hermes, 1959.
———. *Attitudes toward History*. 3rd ed. Berkeley: University of California Press, 1984.
———. "Auscultation, Creation, and Revision: The Rout of the Esthetes Literature, Marxism, and Beyond." In Chesebro, *Extensions of the Burkeian System*, 42–185.
———. "The Book of Yul." *Secession* 2 (July 1922): 7–17.
———. "A Bright Evening, with Musicians." *Nation* 141 (January 1936): 27.
———. "Catharsis—Second View." *Centennial Review of Arts and Science* 5 (Spring 1961): 107–32.
———. *Counter-Statement*. 3rd ed. Berkeley: University of California Press, 1968.
———. "The Dance: The 'Problems' of the Ballet." *Nation* 140 (March 1935): 343–44.
———. "Dancing with Tears in My Eyes." *Critical Inquiry* 1 (September 1974): 1–31.
———. "David Wassermann." *Little Review* 8 (Autumn 1921): 24–37.
———. "Dramatism." In *International Encyclopedia of the Social Sciences*, ed. David L. Sills, 7:447–48. New York: Macmillan, 1968.
———. "A Dramatistic View of the Origin of Language." *Quarterly Journal of Speech* 37 (1952): 251–64, 446–60; 39 (1953): 79–92.
———. "Definition of Man." *Hudson Review* 16 (1963–64): 491–514.
———. "The End and Origin of a Movement." *Nation* 138 (April 1934): 422–24.
———. "The Excursion." *Dial* 69 (July 1920): 27–28.
———. "'Glimpses into a Labyrinth of Interwoven Motives': Selections from 'A Symbolic of Motives.'" in *Unending Conversations: New Writings by and about Kenneth Burke*, ed. Greig Henderson and David Cratis Williams, 81–98. Carbondale: Southern Illinois University Press, 2001.
———. *A Grammar of Motives*. California edition. Berkeley: University of California Press, 1969.

———. "Hindemith Does His Part." *Nation* 139 (October 1934): 487–88.

———. "In Quest of Olympus." *Secession* 4 (January 1923): 5–18.

———. "In Quest of the Way." Review of *A New Model of the Universe* by P. D. Ouspensky. *New Republic*, September 9, 1931, 104–6.

———. "Know Thyself." In *Collected Poems, 1915–1967*, 208. Berkeley: University of California Press, 1968.

———. *Language as Symbolic Action: Essays on Life, Literature, and Method*. Berkeley: University of California Press, 1966.

———. "The Language of Poetry, 'Dramatistically' Considered," part 1. *Chicago Review* 8 (Fall 1954): 88–102.

———. "The Language of Poetry, 'Dramatistically' Considered," part 2. *Chicago Review* 9 (Spring 1955): 40–72.

———. "Methodological Repression and/or Strategies of Containment." *Critical Inquiry* 5 (Winter 1978): 401–16.

———. "Mind, Body, and the Unconscious." In *Language as Symbolic Action*, 63–80.

———. "Mrs. Maecenas." *Dial* 68 (March 1920): 346–58.

———. "Musical Chronicle." *Dial* 83 (December 1927): 535–39.

———. "Musical Chronicle." *Dial* 84 (January 1928): 84–88.

———. "Musical Chronicle." *Dial* 84 (February 1928): 174–78.

———. "Musical Chronicle." *Dial* 84 (April 1928): 356–58.

———. "Musical Chronicle." *Dial* 84 (May 1928): 445–47.

———. "Musical Chronicle." *Dial* 85 (December 1928): 529–32.

———. "Musical Chronicle." *Dial* 86 (June 1929): 538–39.

———. "My Dear Mrs. Wurtelbach." *Broom* 4 (January 1923): 74–78.

———. "(Nonsymbolic) Motion / (Symbolic) Action." *Critical Inquiry* 4 (1978): 809–38.

———. "The Olympians." *Manuscripts* 1 (February 1922): 5–7.

———. "On Catharsis, or Resolution." *Kenyon Review* 21 (1959): 337–75.

———. *Permanence and Change: An Anatomy of Purpose*. New York: New Republic, 1935.

———. *Permanence and Change: An Anatomy of Purpose*. 3rd ed. Berkeley: University of California Press, 1984.

———. *The Philosophy of Literary Form: Studies in Symbolic Action*. 3rd ed. Berkeley: University of California Press, 1973.

———. "A Progression." *Secession* 7 (Winter 1923–24): 21–30.

———. "Questions and Answers about the Pentad." *College Composition and Communication* 29 (December 1978): 330–35.

———. *A Rhetoric of Motives*. Berkeley: University of California Press, 1950.

———. *The Rhetoric of Religion: Studies in Logology*. Berkeley: University of California Press, 1961.

———. "The Soul of Kajn Tafha." *Dial* 69 (July 1920): 29–32.

———. "The Thinking of the Body: Comments on the Imagery of Catharsis in Literature." *Psychoanalytic Review* 50 (1963): 25–68.

———. *Towards a Better Life: Being a Series of Epistles, or Declamations*. New York: Harcourt, Brace, 1932.

———. "'Watchful of Hermetics to Be Strong in Hermeneutics': Selections from 'Poetics, Dramatistically Considered.'" in *Unending Conversations: New Writings by and about Kenneth Burke*, ed. Greig Henderson and David Cratis Williams, 35–80. Carbondale: Southern Illinois University Press, 2001.

———. "The White Oxen." In *The White Oxen and Other Stories*, 3–62. New York: A. & C. Boni, 1924.

———. "William James: Superlative Master of the Comparative." Review of *The Thought and Character of William James* by Ralph Barton Perry. *Science and Society* 1 (Fall 1936): 122–25.

———. "Words as Deeds." Review of *How to Do Things with Words* by J. L. Austin. *Centrum* 3 (Fall 1975): 147–68.

Burke, Kenneth, and Stanley Romaine Hopper. "Mysticism as a Solution to the Poet's Dilemma." In *Spiritual Problems in Contemporary Literature: A Series of Addresses and Discussions*, ed. Stanley Romaine Hopper, 95–115. New York: Institute for Religious and Social Studies, 1952.

Burkert, Walter. *The Orientalizing Revolution: Near Eastern Influence on Greek Culture in the Early Archaic Age*. Cambridge, Mass.: Harvard University Press, 1992.

Butler, Judith. *Bodies That Matter: On the Discursive Limits of Sex*. New York: Routledge, 1993.

———. *Gender Trouble: Feminism and the Subversion of Identity*. New York: Routledge, 1990.

Byrd, Rudolph P. *Jean Toomer's Years with Gurdjieff: Portrait of an Artist, 1923–1936*. Athens: University of Georgia Press, 1990.

Canetti, Elias. *Crowds and Power*. Trans. Carol Stewart. New York: Noonday, 1998.

Cannon, Walter B. *Bodily Changes in Pain, Hunger, Fear, and Rage*. New York: Appleton, 1915.

———. "The James-Lange Theory of Emotions: A Critical Examination and the Alternative Theory." *American Journal of Psychology* 39 (December 1927): 106–24.

———. *The Wisdom of the Body*. New York: Norton, 1932.

Ceccarelli, Leah. "Neither Confusing Cacophony nor Culinary Complements: A Case Study of Mixed Metaphors for Genomic Science." *Written Communication* 21 (2004): 92–105.

Chesebro, James, ed. *Extensions of the Burkeian System*. Tuscaloosa: University of Alabama Press, 1993.

Clark, Elizabeth A. *History, Theory, Text: Historians and the Linguistic Turn*. Cambridge, Mass.: Harvard University Press, 2004.

Clark, Gregory. "Virtuosos and Ensembles: Rhetorical Lessons from Jazz." In *The Private, the Public, and the Published: Reconciling Private Lives and Public Rhetoric*, 31–46. Logan: Utah State University Press, 2004.

Clendinnen, Inga. *Aztecs: An Interpretation*. Cambridge: Cambridge University Press, 1991.

Cobb, Ivo Geikie. *The Glands of Destiny (A Study of Personality)*. London: Heinemann, 1927.

Coe, Richard. "Defining Rhetoric—and Us: A Meditation on Burke's Definitions." *Journal of Advanced Composition* 10 (1990): 39–52.

Cole, Jennifer. "The Work of Memory in Madagascar." *American Ethnologist* 25 (1998): 610–33.

Condit, Celeste M. "Framing Kenneth Burke: Sad Tragedy or Comic Dance?" *Quarterly Journal of Speech* 80 (1984): 77–82.
———. *How Should We Study the Symbolizing Animal?* Carroll C. Arnold Distinguished Lecture, 2004. Boston: Allyn & Bacon, 2006.
———. "The Materiality of Coding: Rhetoric, Genetics, and the Matter of Life." In *Rhetorical Bodies*, ed. Jack Selzer and Sharon Crowley, 326–56. Madison: University of Wisconsin Press, 1999.
———. "The New Science of Human Reproduction: A Reflection on the Inadequacy of 'Disciplines' for the Understanding of Human Life." *Quarterly Journal of Speech* 79 (1993): 232–65.
Connolly, William E. *Neuropolitics: Thinking, Culture, Speed*. Minneapolis: University of Minnesota Press, 2002.
Corballis, Michael. "The Gestural Origins of Language." *American Scientist* 87 (March–April 1999):138.
Corsini, Raymond J. *The Dictionary of Psychology*. New York: Routledge, 2002.
Coupe, Laurence. "Kenneth Burke: Pioneer of Ecocriticism." *Journal of American Studies* 35 (2001): 413–31.
Cowley, Malcolm. *Exile's Return: A Literary Odyssey of the 1920s*. New York: Penguin, 1994.
Crable, Bryan. "Ideology as 'Metabiology': Rereading Burke's *Permanence and Change*." *Quarterly Journal of Speech* 84 (1998): 303–19.
———. "Rhetoric, Anxiety, and Character Armor: Burke's Interactional Rhetoric of Identity." *Western Journal of Communication* 70 (2006): 1–22.
———. "Symbolizing Motion: Burke's Dialectic and Rhetoric of the Body." *Rhetoric Review* 22 (2003): 121–37.
Crane, Hart *The Letters of Hart Crane, 1916–1932*. Ed. Brom Weber. New York: Hermitage House, 1952.
Crowley, Sharon. *Toward a Civil Discourse: Rhetoric and Fundamentalism*. Pittsburgh: University of Pittsburgh Press, 2006.
Darwin, Charles. *The Descent of Man and Selection in Relation to Sex*. 2nd ed. New York: Appleton, 1897.
———. *The Expression of the Emotions in Man and Animals*. 3rd ed. Ed. Paul Ekman. New York: Oxford University Press, 1998.
Deem, Melissa. "Stranger Sociability, Public Hope, and the Limits of Political Transformation." *Quarterly Journal of Speech* 88 (November 2002): 444–54.
DeLuca, Kevin. "Unruly Arguments: The Body Rhetoric of Earth First!, Act Up, and Queer Nation." *Argumentation and Advocacy* 36 (Summer 1999): 9–21.
Derrida, Jacques. *Of Grammatology*. Trans. Gayatri Chakrovorty Spivak. Baltimore: Johns Hopkins University Press, 1976.
Desilet, Gregory. "Nietzsche Contra Burke: The Melodrama in Dramatism." *Quarterly Journal of Speech* 75 (1989): 65–83.
Dölling, Irene, and Sabine Hark. "She Who Speaks Shadow Speaks Truth: Transdisciplinarity in Women's and Gender Studies." *Signs: Women in Culture and Society* 25 (Summer 2000): 1195–98.

Dolmage, Jay. "Breathe upon Us an Even Flame: Hephaestus, History and the Body of Rhetoric." *Rhetoric Review* 25 (2006): 119–40.
Doyle, Laura. *Bordering on the Body: The Racial Matrix of Modern Fiction and Culture.* New York: Oxford University Press, 1994.
Eagleton, Terry. *After Theory.* New York: Basic Books, 2003.
———. *The Ideology of the Aesthetic.* Oxford: Blackwell, 1990.
East, James, ed. *The Humane Particulars: The Collected Letters of William Carlos Williams and Kenneth Burke.* Columbia: University of South Carolina Press, 2003.
Edbauer, Jenny. "Executive Overspill: Affective Bodies, Intensity, and Bush-in-Relation." *Postmodern Culture* 15 (2004). Available with subscription at http://muse.jhu.edu/login?url=/journals/postmodern_culture/v015/e15.1edbauer.html (accessed September 18, 2008).
Eliasberg, W. "Philosophy of Psychotherapy." *Philosophy of Science* 13 (July 1946): 203–14.
Elliott, Dyon. "The Physiology of Rapture and Female Spirituality." In *Medieval Theology and the Natural Body*, ed. Peter Biller and A. J. Minnis. 141–73. Rochester, N.Y.: York Medieval Press, 1997.
Evans, James Gilbert. "Foreign Aid for Agricultural Development: Philosophy and Implementation." *American Journal of Agricultural Economics* 51 (1969): 1402–12.
Farnell, Brenda. "Developments in the Study of 'Gesture' in Language." *Anthropological Linguistics* 46 (Spring 2004): 100–115.
———. *Do You See What I Mean? Plains Indian Sign Talk and the Embodiment of Action.* Austin: University of Texas Press, 1995.
Feehan, Michael. "Kenneth Burke and Mary Baker Eddy." In *Unending Conversations: New Writings by and about Kenneth Burke*, ed. Greig Henderson and David Cratis Williams, 206–24. Carbondale: Southern Illinois University Press, 2001.
Fenske, Mindy. "The Aesthetic of the Unfinished: Ethics and Performance." *Text and Performance Quarterly* 24 (January 2004): 1–19.
———. "The Movement of Interpretation: Conceptualizing Performative Encounters with Multimediated Performance." *Text and Performance Quarterly* 26 (April 2006): 138–61.
Fillion, Bryant. "Turning On: The Selling of the Present, 1970." *English Journal* 60 (1971): 333–38.
Fishman, Joshua A. *Reversing Language Shift: Theoretical and Empirical Foundations of Assistance to Threatened Languages.* Clevedon, U.K.: Multilingual Matters, 1991.
Fosdick, Raymond B. *The Story of the Rockefeller Foundation.* New York: Harper, 1952.
Foucault, Michel. *Discipline and Punish: The Birth of the Prison.* Trans. Alan Sheridan. New York: Vintage, 1979.
Foulkes, S. H. Review of *The Pharmacological Shock Treatment of Schizophrenia* by Manfred Sakel. *International Journal of Psycho-Analysis* 20 (January 1939): 97–99.
Frank, Waldo. *The Rediscovery of Man: A Memoir and a Methodology of Modern Life.* New York: Braziller, 1958.
Fredal, James. *Rhetorical Action in Ancient Athens: Persuasive Artistry from Solon to Demosthenes.* Carbondale: Southern Illinois University Press, 2006.

Fyfe, W. Hamilton. Introduction to *Aristotle, the Poetics; "Longinus," on the Sublime; Demetrius, on Style*. Trans. W. Hamilton Fyfe. Rev. ed. Cambridge, Mass.: Harvard University Press, 1932.

Gale, Richard M. *The Divided Self of William James*. Oxford: Cambridge University Press, 1999.

George, Ann, and Jack Selzer. *Burke in the 1930s*. Columbia: University of South Carolina Press, 2007.

———. "What Happened at the First American Writers' Congress? Kenneth Burke's 'Revolutionary Symbolism in America.'" *Rhetoric Society Quarterly* 33 (Spring 2003): 47–66.

Gigantes, Denise. *Taste: A Literary History*. New Haven: Yale University Press, 2005.

Gilman, Sander. *Picturing Health and Illness: Images of Identity and Difference*. Baltimore: Johns Hopkins University Press, 1995.

———. *Smart Jews: The Construction of the Image of Jewish Superior Intelligence*. Lincoln: University of Nebraska Press, 1996.

Gosling, F. G. *Before Freud: Neurasthenia and the American Medical Community, 1870–1910*. Urbana: University of Illinois Press, 1987.

Gralnick, Alexander. "A Seven Year Survey of Insulin Treatment in Schizophrenia." *American Journal of Psychiatry* 101 (January 1945): 449–52.

Grosz, Elizabeth. *Jacques Lacan: A Feminist Introduction*. New York: Routledge, 1990.

———. *The Nick of Time: Politics, Evolution, and the Untimely*. Durham, N.C.: Duke University Press, 2004.

———. *Volatile Bodies: Toward a Corporeal Feminism*. Bloomington: Indiana University Press, 1994.

Gunn, Joshua. *Modern Occult Rhetoric: Mass Media and the Drama of Secrecy in the Twentieth Century*. Tuscaloosa: University of Alabama Press, 2005.

———. "An Occult Poetics, or, the Secret Rhetoric of Religion." *Rhetoric Society Quarterly* 34 (Spring 2004): 29–54.

Gusfield, Joseph. Introduction to *Kenneth Burke on Symbols and Society*, 1–49. Chicago: University of Chicago Press, 1989.

———. "The Literary Rhetoric of Science: Comedy and Pathos in Drinking Driver Research." *American Sociological Review* 41 (February 1976): 16–34.

Halliwell, Stephen. *Aristotle's Poetics*. Chicago: University of Chicago Press, 1998.

Halloran, S. Michael. "The Birth of Molecular Biology: An Essay in the Rhetorical Criticism of Scientific Discourse." *Rhetoric Review* 3 (September 1984): 70–83.

Haraway, Donna. "Situated Knowledges: The Science Question in Feminism and the Privilege of Partial Perspective." *Feminist Studies* 14 (Fall 1988): 575–99.

Harding, Sandra, ed. *The Feminist Standpoint Theory Reader: Intellectual and Political Controversies*. New York: Routledge, 2004.

———. *Whose Science, Whose Knowledge? Thinking from Women's Lives*. Ithaca, N.Y.: Cornell University Press, 1991.

Harrower, Henry R. *Practical Endocrinology*. 2nd ed. Glendale, Calif.: Pioneer, 1932.

Hartley, Lucy. *Physiognomy and the Meaning of Expression in Nineteenth-Century Culture*. Cambridge: Cambridge University Press, 2001.

Hartsock, Nancy. "The Feminist Standpoint: Developing the Ground for a Specifically Feminist Historical Materialism." In *Discovering Reality: Feminist Perspectives on Epistemology, Metaphysics, Methodology, and Philosophy of Science*, ed. Sandra Harding and Merrill B. Hintikka, 283–310. Boston: Reidel, 1983.

Hau, Michael. *The Cult of Health and Beauty in Germany: A Social History, 1890–1930*. Chicago: University of Chicago Press, 2003.

Hauser, Gerard. "Incongruous Bodies: Arguments for Personal Sufficiency and Public Insufficiency." *Argumentation and Advocacy* 36 (Summer 1999): 1–8.

Hawhee, Debra. *Bodily Arts: Rhetoric and Athletics in Ancient Greece*. Austin: University of Texas Press, 2004.

———. "Bodily Pedagogies: Rhetoric, Athletics, and the Sophists' Three Rs." *College English* 65 (November 2002): 142–62.

———. "Burke and Nietzsche." *Quarterly Journal of Speech* 85 (1999): 129–45.

———. "Burke on Drugs." *Rhetoric Society Quarterly* 31 (2004): 5–28.

Hawkins, Stephanie L. "The Science of Superstition: Gertrude Stein, William James, and the Formation of Belief." *Modern Fiction Studies* 51 (Spring 2005): 60–87.

Heise, Ursula. "Greening English: Recent Introductions to Ecocriticism." *Contemporary Literature* 47 (Summer 2006): 289–98.

Henderson, Greig E. "Aesthetic and Practical Frames of Reference." In Chesebro, *Extensions of the Burkeian System*, 173–85.

Henderson, John. "Ernest Starling and 'Hormones': An Historical Commentary." *Journal of Endocrinology* 184 (2005): 5–10.

Heynick, Frank. *Jews and Medicine: An Epic Saga*. Hoboken, N.J.: KTAV, 2002.

Hoffman, Maud. "Taking the Life Cure in Gurdjieff's School." *New York Times*, February 10, 1924.

Hofstra, Marijke Gijswijt. Introduction to *Cultures of Neurasthenia from Beard to the First World War*, ed. Marijke Gijswijt Hofstra and Roy Porter, 1–30. New York: Rodopi, 2001.

Hoskins, R. G. *The Tides of Life: The Endocrine Glands in Bodily Adjustment*. New York: Norton, 1933.

Houck, Davis W., and Amos Kiewe. *FDR's Body Politics: The Rhetoric of Disability*. College Station: Texas A&M University Press, 2003.

Hunt, Edward E., Jr. "Human Constitution: An Appraisal." *American Journal of Physical Anthropology* 10 (1952): 55–74.

———. "The Old Physical Anthropology." *American Journal of Physical Anthropology* 56 (1981): 339–46.

Ingram, Richard A. "Beyond the Body Beautiful: The Uses and Dangers of Nietzsche's Rethinking of Health and Illness." In *Interdisciplinary Perspectives on Health, Illness, and Disease*, ed. Peter L. Twohig and Vera Kalitzkus, 21–34. Amsterdam: Rodopi, 2003.

Isager, Christine, and Sine Nørholm Just. "Rhetoricians Identified: A Call to Interdisciplinary Action and How it Resonated in the Field of Rhetoric." *Philosophy and Rhetoric* 38 (2005): 248–58.

Jack, Jordynn. "Kenneth Burke's Constabulary Rhetoric: Sociorhetorical Critique in *Attitudes toward History*." *Rhetoric Society Quarterly* 38 (Winter 2008): 66–81.

———. "'The Piety of Degradation': Kenneth Burke, the Bureau of Social Hygiene, and *Permanence and Change.*" *Quarterly Journal of Speech* 90 (2004): 446–68.
James, William. "On Some Hegelianisms." *Mind* 7 (April 1882): 186–208.
———. *The Varieties of Religious Experience* (1902). New York: Touchstone, 1997.
Jameson, Fredric. "The End of Temporality." *Critical Inquiry* 29 (2003): 695–715.
———. "The Symbolic Inference; or, Kenneth Burke and Ideological Analysis." *Critical Inquiry* 4 (1978): 507–23.
Jay, Paul, ed. *The Selected Correspondence of Kenneth Burke and Malcolm Cowley, 1915–1981.* Berkeley: University of California Press, 1988.
Johnson, Mark L., and Steve Larson. "'Something in the Way She Moves'—Metaphors of Musical Motion." *Metaphor and Symbol* 18 (2003): 63–84.
Jones, Amelia. *Irrational Modernism: A Neurasthenic History of New York Dada.* Cambridge, Mass.: MIT Press, 2004.
Journet, Debra. "Metaphor, Ambiguity, and Motive in Evolutionary Biology: W. D. Hamilton and the 'Gene's Point of View.'" *Written Communication* 22 (2005): 379–420.
Kendon, Adam. *Gesture: Visible Action as Utterance.* Cambridge: Cambridge University Press, 2004.
Kenneally, Christine. *The First Word: The Search for the Origins of Language.* New York: Viking, 2007.
Kennedy, George. *Comparative Rhetoric: An Historical and Cross-Cultural Introduction.* New York: Oxford University Press, 1998.
Kluckhohn, Clyde. "Myths and Rituals: A General Theory." *Harvard Theological Review* 35 (1942): 45–79.
Kofman, Sarah. *Nietzsche and Metaphor.* Trans. Duncan Large. Stanford, Calif.: Stanford University Press, 1993.
Kretschmer, Ernst. *Physique and Character: An Investigation of the Nature of Constitution and of the Theory of Temperament.* Trans. W. J. H. Sprott. New York: Harcourt, Brace, 1925.
———. *The Psychology of Men of Genius.* Trans. R. B. Cattell. New York: Harcourt Brace, 1931.
Kuppers, Petra. *Disability and Contemporary Performance: Bodies on Edge.* New York: Routledge, 2003.
Lacan, Jacques. *The Four Fundamental Concepts of Psychoanalysis: The Seminar of Jacques Lacan Book XI.* Ed. Jacques-Alain Miller, trans. Alan Sheridan. New York: Norton, 1981.
Larson, Theodore Hubert. *Why We Are What We Are: The Science and Art of Endocrine Physiology and Endocrine Therapy.* Chicago: American Endocrine Bureau, 1929.
Lawrence, Christopher. "Medical Holism: The Context." In *Greater Than the Parts: Holism in Biomedicine, 1920–1950,* ed. Christopher Lawrence and George Weisz, 1–22. New York: Oxford University Press, 1998.
Lawrence, Christopher, and George Weisz, eds. *Greater Than the Parts: Holism in Biomedicine, 1920–1950.* New York: Oxford University Press, 1998.
Lear, Jonathan. "Katharsis." *Phronesis* 33 (1988): 297–326.
Lefebvre, Henri. *Rhythmanalysis: Space, Time, and Everyday Life.* Trans. Gerald Moore.

London: Continuum, 2004.

Lentricchia, Frank. *Criticism and Social Change.* Chicago: University of Chicago Press, 1985.

Liddell, Henry George, Robert Scott, and Henry Stuart Jones. *A Greek-English Lexicon.* Oxford: Clarendon Press, 1996.

Livesley, W. John. *The DSM-IV Personality Disorders.* New York: Guilford, 1995.

Lucaites, John, Sally Caudill, and Celeste M. Condit, eds. *Contemporary Rhetorical Theory: A Reader.* New York: Guilford, 1999.

Ludwig, Emil. *Bismarck: The Story of a Fighter.* Trans. Eden and Cedar Paul. Boston: Little, Brown, 1927.

———. *Cleopatra: The Story of a Queen.* Trans. Bernard Miall. New York: Viking, 1937.

———. *Genius and Character.* Trans. Kenneth Burke. New York: Harcourt, Brace, 1927.

———. *Goethe: The History of a Man, 1749–1832.* New York: Putnam, 1928.

———. *Napoleon.* Trans. Eden and Cedar Paul. New York: Boni & Liveright, 1926.

———. *Son of Man: The Story of Jesus.* Trans. by Eden and Cedar Paul. New York: Boni & Liveright, 1928.

Mahen-Hays, Sarah E., and Roger C. Aden. "Kenneth Burke's 'Attitude' at the Crossroads of Rhetorical and Cultural Studies: A Proposal and Case Study Illustration." *Western Journal of Communication* 67 (Winter 2003): 32–55.

Malzberg, Benjamin. "Outcome of Insulin Treatment of One Thousand Patients with Dementia Praecox." *Psychiatric Quarterly* 12 (July 1938): 528–53.

Marett, R. R. *Tylor.* New York: Wiley, 1936.

Marsh, John. "'Thinking / of the Freezing Poor' William Carlos Williams's Poetry of Poverty." *William Carlos Williams Review* 27, no. 2:1–21.

Massumi, Brian. *Parables for the Virtual: Movement, Affect, Sensation.* Durham, N.C.: Duke University Press, 2002.

Max-Neef, Manfred A. "Foundations of Transdisciplinarity." *Ecological Economics* 53 (2005): 5–16.

Mccrae, Niall. "'A Violent Thunderstorm': Cardiazol Treatment in British Mental Hospitals." *History of Psychiatry* 17 (2006): 67–90.

McPhail, Mark Lawrence. *Zen in the Art of Rhetoric: An Inquiry into Coherence.* Albany: State University of New York Press, 1996.

Medvei, V. C. *A History of Endocrinology.* Lancaster, England: MTP, 1982.

Micale, Mark S. "The Modernist Mind: A Map." In *The Mind of Modernism: Medicine, Psychology, and the Cultural Arts in Europe and America, 1880–1940,* ed. Mark S. Micale, 1–19. Stanford: Stanford University Press, 2004.

Moore, Marianne. "People Stare Carefully." *Dial* 80 (January–June 1926): 49–53.

Muir, Star A. "Toward an Ecology of Language." In *Kenneth Burke in the Twenty-first Century,* ed. Bernard L. Brock, 35–69. Albany: State University of New York Press, 1999.

Munson, Gorham. *The Awakening Twenties: A Memoir-History of a Literary Period.* Baton Rouge: Louisiana State University Press, 1985.

Nelson, Cary. "Writing as the Accomplice of Language: Kenneth Burke and Poststructuralism." In *The Legacy of Kenneth Burke,* ed. H. W. Simons and Trevor Melia, 156–73. Madison: University of Wisconsin Press, 1989.

Neumann, Mark. *On the Rim: Looking for the Grand Canyon.* Minneapolis: University of Minnesota Press, 1999.

Nicolescu, Basarab. *Manifesto of Transdisciplinarity.* Trans. Karen-Claire Foss. Albany: State University of New York Press, 2002.

Nietzsche, Friedrich. *Thus Spake Zarathustra.* Trans. Walter Kaufman. New York: Modern Library, 1954.

O'Banion, John D. *Reorienting Rhetoric.* University Park: Pennsylvania State University Press, 1992.

O'Keefe, Daniel J. "Burke's Dramatism and Action Theory." *Rhetoric Society Quarterly* 8 (1978): 8–15.

Orage, A. R. "Life as Gymnastics" (1930). In *Psychological Exercises and Essays,* 117–21. London: Janus, 1968.

"Origin of Human Speech: Combination of Two Arts. Sir R. Paget's Theory." *Times* (London), September 7, 1928.

Oudshoorn, Nelly. *Beyond the Natural Body: An Archeology of Sex Hormones.* New York: Routledge, 1994.

Ouspensky, P. D. *A New Model of the Universe: Principles of the Psychological Method in Its Application to Problems of Science, Religion and Art.* Trans. R. R. Merton. New York: Knopf, 1931.

———. *Tertium Organum: The Third Canon of Thought, a Key to the Enigmas of the World.* Trans. Nicholas Bessaraboff and Claude Bragdon. Rochester, N.Y.: Manas, 1920.

Paget, Sir Richard. *Human Speech: Some Observations, Experiments, and Conclusions as to the Nature, Origin, Purpose and Possible Improvement of Human Speech.* London: Routledge & Kegan Paul, 1930.

———. *This English.* London: Kegan Paul, Trench, Trübner, 1935.

Parrish, Susan Scott. *American Curiosity: Cultures of Natural History in the Colonial British Atlantic World.* Chapel Hill: University of North Carolina Press, 2006.

Paulson, William. "For a Cosmopolitan Philology: Lessons from Science Studies." *SubStance* 30 (2001): 101–19.

Pease, Donald A. "Ralph Ellison and Kenneth Burke: The Nonsymbolizable (Trans)-Action." *boundary 2* 30 (2003): 65–96.

Perry, Ralph Barton. *The Thought and Character of William James.* Boston: Little, Brown, 1935.

Pezzullo, Phaedra. "Resisting 'National Breast Cancer Awareness Month': The Rhetoric of Counterpublics and Their Cultural Performances." *Quarterly Journal of Speech* 89 (November 2003): 345–65.

———. *Toxic Tourism: Rhetorics of Pollution, Travel, and Environmental Justice.* Tuscaloosa: University of Alabama Press, 2007.

Pressman, Jack D. "Human Understanding: Psychosomatic Medicine and the Mission of the Rockefeller Foundation." In Lawrence and Weisz, *Greater Than the Parts,* 189–208.

———. *Last Resort: Psychosurgery and the Limits of Medicine.* Cambridge: Cambridge University Press, 1998.

Proctor, Robert. *Racial Hygiene: Medicine under the Nazis.* Cambridge, Mass.: Harvard University Press, 1988.

"The Progress of Science: Voice and the Telephone. Mechanism of Speech." *Times* (London), September 13, 1926.

Quandahl, Ellen. "'More Than Lessons in How to Read': Burke, Freud, and the Resources of Symbolic Transformation." *College English* 63 (2001): 633–54.

Ransom, John Crowe. *The World's Body.* New York: Scribners, 1938.

Raymond, James C., ed. *English as a Discipline, or, Is There a Plot in This Play?* Tuscaloosa: University of Alabama Press, 1996.

Rice, Jenny. "The New New: Making a Case for Critical Affect Studies." *Quarterly Journal of Speech* 94, no. 2 (2008): 200–212.

Riley, Denise. *Impersonal Passions: Language as Affect.* Durham, N.C.: Duke University Press, 2005.

Rivers, Nathaniel, and Ryan Weber. *Equipment for Living: The Literary Reviews of Kenneth Burke.* West Lafayette, Ind.: Parlor Press, 2008.

Rorty, Richard. *The Linguistic Turn: Essays in Philosophical Method.* Chicago: University of Chicago Press, 1992.

Rosteck, Thomas, and Michael Leff. "Piety, Propriety, and Perspective: An Interpretation and Application of Key Terms in Kenneth Burke's *Permanence and Change.*" *Western Journal of Speech Communication* 53 (Fall 1989): 327–41.

Rountree, J. Clarke, III, "'Coming to Terms' with Kenneth Burke's Pentad." *ACJournal* 1 (1998). Available at http://acjournal.org/holdings/vol1/iss3/burke/rountree.html (accessed September 18. 2008)

Rueckert, William. *Encounters with Kenneth Burke.* Urbana: University of Illinois Press, 1994.

———. "Kenneth Burke and Structuralism." *Shenandoah* 21 (Autumn 1969): 19–28.

———. *Kenneth Burke and the Drama of Human Relations.* 2nd ed. Berkeley: University of California Press, 1982.

———. "Kenneth Burke's 'Symbolic of Motives' and 'Poetics, Dramatistically Considered.'" In *Unending Conversations: New Writings by and about Kenneth Burke,* ed. Greig Henderson and David Cratis Williams, 99–124. Carbondale: Southern Illinois University Press, 2001.

Rueckert, William, ed. *Essays toward a Symbolic of Motives.* West Lafayette, Ind.: Parlor, 2007.

Sakel, Manfred. "The Methodical Use of Hypoglycemia in the Treatment of Psychoses." *American Journal of Psychiatry* 94 (July 1937): 111–29.

———. *The Pharmacological Shock Treatment of Schizophrenia.* New York: Nervous and Mental Disease, 1938.

Saussure, Ferdinand de. *Course in General Linguistics.* Ed. Charles Bally and Albert Sechehaye in collaboration with Albert Riedlinger, trans., with an introduction and notes, by Wade Baskin. New York: McGraw-Hill, 1966.

Schiebinger, Londa. *Nature's Body: Gender and the Making of Modern Science.* New Brunswick, N.J.: Rutgers University Press, 1993.

Schlapp, Max G., and Edward H. Smith. *The New Criminology: A Consideration of the Chemical Causation of Abnormal Behavior.* New York: Boni & Liveright, 1928.

Scott, Joan Wallach. *Gender and the Politics of History.* New York: Columbia University Press, 1988.

Sedgwick, Eve Kosofsky. *Touching Feeling: Affect, Pedagogy, Performativity.* Durham, N.C.: Duke University Press, 2003.

Seigel, Marika. "'One Little Fellow Named Ecology': Ecological Rhetoric in Kenneth Burke's *Attitudes toward History.*" *Rhetoric Review* 23 (2004): 388–404.

Selzer, Jack. "Kenneth Burke among the Moderns: *Counter-Statement* as Counter-Statement." *Rhetoric Society Quarterly* 26, no. 2 (1996): 19–49.

———. *Kenneth Burke in Greenwich Village: Conversing with the Moderns, 1915–1931.* Madison: University of Wisconsin Press, 1996.

Shapin, Steven, and Christopher Lawrence. Introduction to *Science Incarnate: Historical Embodiments of Natural Knowledge*, ed. Steven Shapin and Christopher Lawrence, 1–20. Chicago: University of Chicago Press, 1998.

Siebers, Tobin. "Disability Aesthetics." *Journal for Cultural and Religious Theory* 7 (2006): 63–73.

———. "Disability and the Right to Have Rights." *Disability Studies Quarterly* 27, no.1–2 (2007). Available with subscription at http://www.dsg-sds-archives.org/login.asp?referer=/articles_html/2007/winter/stebers_right-to-rights.asp (accessed September 18, 2008).

Skodnick, Roy. "Counter-Gridlock: An Interview with Kenneth Burke." *All-Area* 2 (1983): 4–32.

Snyder, Sharon L., and David T. Mitchell. *Cultural Locations of Disability.* Chicago: University of Chicago Press, 2006.

Southwell, Samuel B. *Kenneth Burke and Martin Heidegger: With a Note against Deconstructionism.* Gainesville: University of Florida Press, 1987.

Starling, Ernest. "Croonian Lecture: On the Chemical Correlation of the Functions of the Body." *Lancet* 166, no. 4275 (1905): 339–41.

Stockard, Charles R. *The Physical Basis of Personality.* New York: Norton, 1931.

Tate, Allen. "Poetry and Politics." *New Republic*, August 2, 1933, 308–10.

Taylor, Paul Beekman. *Gurdjieff and Orage: Brothers in Elysium.* York Beach, Maine: Weiser, 2001.

Terada, Rei. *Feeling in Theory: Emotion after the "Death of the Subject."* Cambridge, Mass.: Harvard University Press, 2001.

Terry, Jennifer. *An American Obsession: Science, Medicine, and Homosexuality in Modern Society.* Chicago: University of Chicago Press, 1999.

Thames, Richard H. "The Gordian Not: Untangling the Motivorum." *KB Journal* 3 (2007). Available at http://www.kbjournal.org/thames1 (accessed September 18, 2008).

———. "Nature's Physician: The Metabiology of Kenneth Burke." In *Kenneth Burke and the Twenty-first Century*, ed. Bernard L. Brock, 19–34. Albany: State University of New York Press, 1999.

Thiele, Leslie Paul. *The Heart of Judgment: Practical Wisdom, Neuroscience, and Narrative.* New York: Cambridge University Press, 2006.

Thody, Philip Malcolm Waller. *Don't Do It: A Dictionary of the Forbidden.* New York: St. Martin's Press, 1997.

Thompson, Christina. "Editorial." *Harvard Review* 27 (2004): 5.

Thorndike, E. L. "The Origin of Language." *Science*, July 2, 1943, 1, 3.

Tracy, Sarah W. "An Evolving Science of Man: The Transformation and Demise of American Constitutional Medicine, 1920–1950." In Lawrence and Weisz, *Greater Than the Parts*, 161–88.
Trice, Harrison M., and Janice M. Beyer. "Writing Organizational Tales: The Cultures of Work Organizations." *Organization Science* 6 (1995): 226–28.
Tucker, W. B., and Lessa, W. A. "Man: A Constitutional Investigation." *Quarterly Review of Biology* 15 (1940): 265–89, 411–55.
Turbin, Carole. "Fashioning the American Man: The Arrow Collar Man, 1907–1931." *Gender and History* 14 (November 2002): 470–91.
Twine, Richard. "Physiognomy, Phrenology and the Temporality of the Body." *Body and Society* 8 (2002): 67–88.
Unterecker, John. *Voyager: A Life of Hart Crane*. New York: Farrar, Straus, and Giroux. 1969.
Viswanathan, Gauri. "The Ordinary Business of Occultism." *Critical Inquiry* 27 (Autumn 2000): 1–20.
Vitanza, Victor. Editor's preface in *Writing Histories of Rhetoric*, vii–xii. Carbondale: Southern Illinois University Press, 1994.
Walker, Jeffrey. "*Pathos* and *Katharsis* in 'Aristotelian' Rhetoric: Some Implications." In *Rereading Aristotle's Rhetoric*, ed. Alan G. Gross and Arthur E. Walzer, 74–92. Carbondale: Southern Illinois University Press, 2000.
Walker, Julia. "Why Performance? Why Now? Textuality and the Rearticulation of Human Presence." *Yale Journal of Criticism* 16 (2003): 149–75.
Wander, P. C., and Dennis Jaehne. "Prospects for 'A Rhetoric of Science.'" *Social Epistemology* 14 (April 2000): 211–33.
Warnock, Tilly. Review of *The Writer's Mind: Writing as a Mode of Thinking*, ed. Janice N. Hays, et al. *ADE Bulletin* 79 (1984): 56–59.
Welch, Louise. *Orage with Gurdjieff in America*. Boston: Routledge and Kegan Paul, 1982.
Weldon, Rebecca. "The Rhetorical Construction of the Predatorial Virus: A Burkian Analysis of Nonfiction Accounts of the Ebola Virus." *Qualitative Health Research* 11, no. 1 (2001): 5–25.
Wess, Robert. "Ecocriticism and Kenneth Burke: An Introduction." *KB Journal* 2 (Spring 2006). Available at http://www.kbjournal.org/wess2 (accessed September 18, 2008)
———. *Kenneth Burke: Rhetoric, Subjectivity, Postmodernism*. Cambridge: Cambridge University Press, 1996.
———. "Looking for the Figure in the Carpet of the Symbolic of Motives." *KB Journal* 3 (Spring 2007). Available at http://www.kbjournal.org/spring2007wess (accessed September 18, 2008)
Williams, David Cratis. "Toward Rounding out the *Motivorum Trilogy*: A Textual Introduction." In *Unending Conversations: New Writings by and about Kenneth Burke*, ed. Greig Henderson and David Cratis Williams, 3–34. Carbondale: Southern Illinois University Press, 2001.
Wilson, Elizabeth A. *Psychosomatic: Feminism and the Neurological Body*. Durham, N.C.: Duke University Press, 2004.

Wilson, James C., and Cynthia Lewiecki-Wilson. *Embodied Rhetorics: Disability in Language and Culture*. Carbondale: Southern Illinois University Press, 2001.

Wilson, Jean D. "The Evolution of Endocrinology." *Clinical Endocrinology* 62 (2005): 389–96.

Wolfe, Cary. "Nature as Critical Concept: Kenneth Burke, the Frankfurt School, and 'Metabiology.'" *Cultural Critique* 18 (Spring 1991): 65–96.

Wolin, Ross. *The Rhetorical Imagination of Kenneth Burke*. Columbia: University of South Carolina Press, 2001.

Woods, Colonel Arthur. *Crime Prevention*. Princeton: Princeton University Press, 1918.

———. *Dangerous Drugs: The World Fight against Illicit Traffic in Narcotics*. New Haven: Yale University Press, 1931.

———. *Police and Public*. New Haven: Yale University Press, 1919.

Woolston, Howard. Review of *Frontiers of Legal Aid Work*, ed. John S. Bradway. *Annals of the American Academy of Political and Social Science* 205 (1939): 153–54.

Yoshioka, Kumiko. "The Body in the Thought of Kenneth Burke: A Reading of 'The Philosophy of Literary Form.'" *Angelaki: Journal of the Theoretical Humanities* 5 (December 2000): 31–38.

INDEX

action, 11, 26, 39, 40, 46, 48, 72–73, 87, 92, 93, 96, 99, 101, 102, 103, 108, 110, 112, 113–15, 117–18, 120, 121, 122, 123, 156–67, 178n7, 186n4, 186n5; pure, 45–46; symbolic, 48, 106, 108, 109, 112–13, 115, 119, 120, 122, 123, 124, 128, 143, 146–47, 156–66, 178n8, 180n23, 180–81n28, 184n20, 185n33, 185n1, 186n3, 186n4, 186n5, 186n6, 187n9. *See also* motion; movement

Aden, Roger C., 108, 178n7, 180n27

adrenaline, 5, 78, 79, 82–83, 85, 90, 148, 149, 164

aesthetics, 13–14, 21, 23, 25, 26–28, 35, 39, 57, 60, 74, 97, 147, 165, 166, 170n12, 178n5; humanism, 13; literary, 27; rhetorical, 13, 14, 23

affect, 5, 7, 8, 11, 47, 62, 67, 68, 70, 80, 82–83, 83–86, 90, 91, 102–3, 110, 111, 178n5, 184n27, 187n14

"After Hours" (Burke), 15

alcohol, 50, 62, 66, 128, 135, 173n1; and artists, 16

alienation, 34–35

"Anaesthetic Revelation of Herone Liddell, The" (Burke), 10, 137, 149–55

Anderson, Dana, 108, 177n12, 178n7, 182n11, 185n29, 185n1

Anderson, Margaret, 37, 38, 172n16

anesthesia. *See under* Burke

animals, 6, 20, 109, 136, 141, 144, 157, 160; communication, 109, 111–14, 177n2, 178n8; human, 139, 140, 143, 154–55, 160, 178n8

antics of refusal, 33, 42

Aristophanes, 138, 147

Aristotle, 16, 35, 135–36, 136–37, 144–45, 147, 149, 150, 170n9, 175n12, 179n16, 181n2, 183n18, 184n21

arrhythmia. *See under* Burke. *See also* rhythm

art, 1, 12–13, 15–16, 19, 20, 26, 27, 43, 44–45, 56, 57–58, 59–60, 66, 86, 93, 97, 101, 103, 104, 111, 113, 117, 122, 173n18, 180n26, 181n2; connection to the body, 12, 14, 15, 19, 20, 22, 113, 140; as disruptive and arrhythmic, 12, 14, 16; and efficiency, 57–60; in Gurjieffian mysticism, 35–39, 42, 48, 53; as rhetorical, 13, 26, 27

artistic temperament, 1; and ill health, 15–17, 18–20

artists, 1, 13, 14, 15–18, 19–20, 21, 22, 24, 27, 28, 37, 57–58, 59–60, 73, 95, 140

attitude, 11, 32, 36, 39, 48, 72–73, 84, 86–91, 100, 108, 112–14, 114–24, 150, 150, 154, 163–66, 175n5, 176n11, 177n15, 178n6, 178n7, 180n27, 186n3, 187n13; animal, 112–14; aptitude, substitute for, 122; bodily, 86, 87, 112, 113, 119, 122, 123–24, 154, 175n5; danced, 119, 123, 175n8; and insulin, 86–91; interpretive, 4; and language, 114, 121–22; mystic, 33, 47–54; Pagetian genealogy, 115–18, 121, 123; rhythm, 117

Attitudes toward History (Burke), 30, 31, 32, 47–49, 51–52, 53, 56, 57, 58, 59, 62, 64, 69, 86–91, 106, 115, 117, 118, 119, 121–22, 126, 159, 160, 165, 171n4, 171n5, 174n6, 176n11, 180n23, 180n25, 180n28

audience, 14, 23–25, 27, 37, 110, 139, 141, 156; bodies of, 13, 14, 23–24, 25, 28, 43–44, 140, 157; Burke's turn to, 14, 22–29; for dance, 35, 43–44, 161; and music performance, 22–27; and rhetoric, 14, 27. *See also* collective; crowd

"Auscultation, Creation, and Revision" (Burke), 70, 71, 114, 115, 118, 179n18, 179n19
Austin, J. L., 11, 158, 160–61, 162–64, 186n3, 186n5, 187n12, 187n13

Bacon, Francis, 35
Baudelaire, Charles, 16, 17
Beard, G. M., 18
Beauty Clinic, 10, 128, 129, 144, 145, 147, 149, 154, 182n9, 183n15
Belfiore, Elizabeth, 136, 183n18
belief, 3, 20, 21, 22, 34, 40, 42, 45, 49, 66–67, 68, 70, 72, 77, 92, 132, 174n8, 181n3
Bennett, Jane, 2, 7, 8
Bennett, Jeff, 178n6
Bergson, Henri, 36
biology, 3, 5, 7, 8, 76, 84, 91, 92, 93, 94–97, 97, 101, 109, 112, 114, 117, 118, 121, 136, 139, 155, 177n5, 178–79n9, 179n12, 184n27; metabiology, 8, 75, 175n14; reductionism, 92
Blavatsky, Helena Petrovna, 34
Blood, Benjamin Paul, 50, 55
body, 2, 4, 5–11, 66–68, 92, 108, 125, 141–44, 144–46, 147, 153–54, 169n4, 177n5, 178n8, 182n9, 183n13, 184n22, 186n7, 187n13; and art 12, 13, 14, 20; of artist, 17; attitude, 121, 124, 175n5; and belief, 21; Burke's, 12, 15, 128, 129–36, 147–49; and catharsis, 137–41, 185n30; and communication, 5, 56, 79, 91, 107, 114; and criminality, 78; of dancers, 38–45, 161; and drugs, 55, 65, 68–74; and efficiency, 58, 62, 66, 77; and endocrinology, 77–86, 90, 91, 93, 164; genius of, 33, 42, 76–77, 99–103, 105; healthy, 161; as inclination, 29, 94, 99–101; individual, 141–44, 153–54, 160, 167; and language, 2, 106, 109–15, 118, 124, 128, 146, 152, 186n1; and meaning making, 2, 14, 28–29, 75, 77, 90–91; movement/motion of, 20, 22, 29, 122, 126, 128, 159, 160–61, 163, 166; and music, 2–28, 175n12; and mysticism, 31, 32, 33–35, 35–38, 38–45, 45–46, 47, 51, 56, 173n18; nonsymbolic, 143, 161; and occupation, 93; and poetics, 83, 118–22, 124; productive, 45, 105; and psychoanalysis, 18, 75, 83, 91, 105; sick/unhealthy, 17, 18, 19, 21, 161–62, 183n16; symbolic action, 119, 143; transdisciplinary view of, 14; types, 94, 95, 96, 97–98, 103, 105, 176n10. *See also* attitude; biology; hypochondriasis; machines; movement
body biography, 11, 128–36, 147–55, 176n8
body thinking, 126, 136, 145, 147, 150
body-mind, 45, 68, 84, 85, 87–89, 90, 98, 101, 105, 108, 109, 122–23, 126, 158, 166; body and mind (or mind and body), 53, 96, 117, 119, 122, 124; mimetics, 75, 86
"Book of Yul, The" (Burke), 15
Bordo, Susan, 6, 92
Bourne, Randolph S., 54
Brandt, Deborah, 174n8
breakdown, 128, 129, 133, 147, 148, 152
breathing, 28, 45, 66, 107, 128, 129–36, 138, 161; gaspo-gaggo-gulpo, 12, 129–36, 169n2 (ch. 1)
Brennan, Teresa, 7, 8, 184n27
Buddhist philosophy, 35
Bureau of Social Hygiene (BSH), 54, 55–74, 75, 78, 80, 88, 164, 173n2, 174n8, 174n11
bureaucratization of the imaginative, 59, 75, 175n1
Burke: anesthesia, 147, 149; arrhythmia, 12, 133; body, 12, 15, 129, 134–35; coronary spasms, 23, 133, 169n1 (ch. 1), 169ch1n2; diagnoses, 42, 129, 169n2 (ch. 1); short fiction, 9, 10, 12, 13, 14–22, 26, 76, 149–55, 185n36; gaspo-gaggo-gulpo, 12, 129–36, 169n2 (ch. 1); hernia operation, 131, 147–49; illness, 127; method, 4–5, 9, 31, 33, 48, 54, 56–61, 64, 66, 74, 76–77, 86, 92–93, 104, 106, 116, 121, 123, 124, 133, 136, 153, 160, 186n5; music criticism, 9, 12, 13–14, 22–29, 68, 170n8

Burkean terms. *See* attitude; bureaucratization of the imaginative; clustering; constitutions; dramatism; form; identification; metonymy; occupation; orientation; pentad; perspective by incongruity; piety; substance; symbolic action; synecdoche; terministic screens
Butler, Judith, 6, 92, 187n16

Cannon, Walter B., 77, 78, 80–83, 84, 85, 87, 175n3
Carlyle, Thomas, 103
Cartesianism: Burke's anti-Cartesianism, 2; neo-Cartesianism, 109, 179n11
catharsis, 126, 128, 135–36, 136–47, 153, 181n2, 184n21
"Catharsis—Second View" (Burke), 140, 142, 144, 146
Clark, Gregory, 13
cleanliness, 10, 139, 144–47
cloacal criticism, 125–55, 183n15; diuretic, 138, 139; erotic, 125, 139; excremental, 10, 125, 128, 139, 182n9; introduced, 10; urinary, 125, 154–55
clustering, 5, 11, 22, 27, 48, 52, 93, 116, 118; and transdisciplinarity, 5–11
Coleridge, Samuel Taylor, 19, 56, 119
collective, 52, 54, 110, 114, 140, 141–44, 146,161. *See also* audience; crowd
Committee on Research in Problems of Sex, 78, 80
communicability, 72–73, 110–12
communication, 1, 2, 8, 9, 14, 21, 28, 29, 45, 46, 56, 60, 72, 77, 91, 104, 106, 107, 112, 113–14, 114–15, 124, 127, 156–57, 178n8; connection with body and mysticism, 33, 38–39, 40, 41, 44, 45–47; and endocrinology, 79–83, 86; as life, 93. *See also* animals; body
Condillac, Etienne, 107
Condit, Celeste M., 7, 8, 166, 169n1 (intro.), 171n1, 178n8, 179n9, 179n12
Connolly, William E., 7
consciousness, 2, 36, 37, 38, 40, 41, 49, 50–51, 55, 77, 99, 108, 109, 110–11, 128, 142, 154, 187n16

constitutional analysis, 95–96, 97–98, 99, 101, 134
constitutional medicine, 5, 10, 74, 96, 106
constitutional morphology, 7, 106
constitutional types, 94, 94–97, 97–98
constitutionality, 139
constitutions, 94–97; artistic, 16–17; social, 7
constructivism, 7, 166
contagiousness. *See* communicability
counter-efficient method, 64, 74
Counter-Statement (Burke), 1, 13, 20, 24, 26, 27, 33, 56, 57, 58, 59, 60, 66, 68, 71–74, 106, 116, 117, 138, 140, 159, 171n4, 177n14, 180n21, 181n5
Cowley, Malcolm, letters to and from, 15, 26, 31–32, 38, 42, 56, 59, 61, 116, 127, 129–36, 148, 149, 169n1 (ch. 1), 169n2 (ch. 1), 176n4, 182n8, 182n10, 183n13, 183n14, 185n39
Crable, Bryan, 75, 157–58, 166, 171n2, 175n14, 185n33, 186n1, 186n2
Crane, Hart, 31, 37, 38, 41, 47, 55, 172n15, 173n18
criticism, 1, 4, 5, 8, 11, 21–22, 31, 33, 57, 64, 69, 74, 76, 85, 91, 121, 124, 128, 133, 139, 143, 145, 147, 151, 178n6, 184n20; cloacal, 10, 125, 132, 144, 183n15; cluster approach to, 5; dance, 43; literary, 140, 184n27; music, 9, 12, 13–14, 22–29, 68, 170n8; rhetorical, 129, 177n5, 184n27. *See also* ecocriticism
crowd, 28, 43, 141–44, 157; mob-throb, 141. *See also* audience; collective
Crowley, Sharon, 178n5
culture, 8, 13, 17, 30, 35, 41, 43, 47, 48, 52, 54, 56–57, 58, 70, 98, 159, 161, 173–74n4

dadaism, 18
dance, 6, 38–45, 86, 119, 122, 123, 154, 184n23, 186–87n8; language of / linguistic, 117–18, 122, 124, 161; and mysticism, 9, 35, 38–42, 43, 47, 49, 67, 141, 161, 173n23; religion, 86; stop movements, 38–42, 44, 45, 52. *See also* movement

"Dance: The 'Problems' of the Ballet, The" (Burke), 42, 43
"Dancing with Tears in My Eyes" (Burke), 181n30
Dangerous Drugs (Wood), 61, 62, 63–64, 67, 68, 69, 70, 71, 175n13
Darwin, Charles, 107, 109–10, 111–12, 129, 178–79n9, 179n13
Darwinism, 35, 108–12, 113, 120, 123, 124
"David Wassermann" (Burke), 14, 15, 17–19, 21, 76
"Death of Tragedy, The" (Burke), 15
Deem, Melissa, 177–78
"Definition of Man" (Burke), 152
DeLuca, Kevin, 177n5, 178n5
Derrida, Jacques, 108
deviance, 10, 69, 78, 92–105
Dewey, John, 53, 59, 76, 100
Dial, 1, 22, 26, 27, 38, 170n8, 172n17; *Dial* Award, 59, 174n7
discourse, 7, 9, 10, 11, 13, 29, 47, 95, 118, 166, 167, 177–78n5; of endocrinology, 84–85; of mysticism, 33, 34; scientific, 7, 9, 10, 29, 56, 74, 75, 86, 90, 93
disease, 19, 21, 63, 73, 86, 87, 89, 93, 104–5, 129, 162; and occupation, 101, 103–4
dispositions, 14, 17, 26, 114–15; bodily, 77, 115, 122; dispositional effects/changes, 26, 62
Dostoyevsky, Fyodor, 36
Doyle, Laura, 95, 176n7
dramatism, 11, 75, 106, 107–8, 121–22, 123–24, 126, 127, 158, 159, 161, 163, 164, 178n7, 178n8, 183n19, 186n3, 186n4, 186n5
"Dramatism" (Burke), *International Encyclopedia of the Social Sciences*, 159
"Dramatistic View of the Origin of Language, A" (Burke), 124, 181n29
dreams, 27, 40–41, 131, 151–53, 161
drug fiend, 69, 105
drugs, 7, 55–74, 78, 79–80, 90, 106, 136, 148, 150–51, 164; and endocrinology, 79–80, 83, 84–85;; and mystical states, 50, 55; and poetry, 67, 138–39; research, 10, 56, 57, 58, 68, 74, 78, 88, 94, 106, 170n9; as transformative substances, 67; use, 55, 62, 63, 64, 67, 68–69, 70, 71, 74, 79, 85, 88, 135
duplication, 163–66, 187n14

Eagleton, Terry, 11, 13, 28, 169n2 (intro.)
ecocriticism, 8–9, 10, 144, 169n3, 185n31, 185n32
ecology, 10, 59, 73, 128, 135, 144–46, 146–47, 149, 152, 154–55, 159, 174n5, 185n31, 185n32, 185n36, 185n39, 187n10. *See also* catharsis
Edbauer, Jenny. *See* Rice, Jenny Edbauer
effects, 5, 142; on audience, 14, 23–26, 28, 141, 156; as definitive of rhetoric, 13; of drugs, 63, 64, 65, 67, 79, 152, 164; and effort, 154; and mysticism, 40, 47
efficiency, 17, 56, 57–61, 62, 63–66, 67, 69, 70, 73, 74, 93, 102, 174n5, 174n6, 185n31; and aesthetics, 57; counter-efficient method, 64–65, 74, 76–77; inefficiency, 57, 59, 61, 62, 104; journalism as example of, 59
Emerson, Ralph Waldo, 48, 171n5
"End and Origin of a Movement, The" (Burke), 6
endocrinology, 5, 8, 9, 10, 74, 75–91, 93, 106, 142, 149, 175n4, 176n4; and meaning making, 75–91
energy, 2, 28, 29, 39, 65, 77, 86, 96, 106, 107, 109, 112, 113, 115, 152, 166, 178n5, 179n16
entrainment, 5, 184n27
equivalency. *See* duplication
essentialism, 7–9, 10, 66
Euripides, 141
everydayness, 46–47, 53–54; and mysticism, 36, 40, 44, 47, 53–54; rhythms, 14
evolution, 7, 10, 37, 106, 107, 112, 114, 115, 127, 160
excrement, 10, 125, 128, 139, 182n9; turds, 125, 126, 131–32. *See also* shit
"Excursion, The" (Burke), 1–2, 15, 28

facial morphology, 95, 109
feedback, 82, 85, 87, 104, 175n4

feminist theory, 3, 6, 92–93, 129, 176n1, 178–79n9
Fenske, Mindy, 178n5
fiction. *See* short fiction (Burke)
Flaubert, Gustave, 27, 125
form, 26–27, 75, 84, 104, 143, 145, 180n21, 186n4; appeal of, 66; artistic, 14; as eloquence, 27; and music, 24, 26; poetic, 66, 72
Foucault, Michel, 6, 166, 187n16
frames: of acceptance and rejection, 48, 50; of causality, 92–93; comic, 116; cultural, 52; interpretive, 4; logical, 52
Frank, Waldo, 31, 32, 33, 37, 38, 47
Freud, Sigmund, 100, 125, 178–79n9, 181n1, 183n15, 187n16

gagging, 115–18, 121, 130, 131–34
gallantry, 147, 154; and ecological imbalance, 154–55, 185n39
genius, 15, 16, 22, 76, 93, 94, 96, 97, 99–103, 103–5, 153, 154, 181n5; of the body, 33, 42, 76–77, 99–103, 105; Burke's, 126–27, 128–29, 181n5; of the machine, 33, 42
George, Ann, 106, 171n4
gesture, 5, 10, 28, 38, 44, 45, 106–24, 177n2, 179n11, 179n13
gesture-speech theory, 106–24, 149, 153, 160; and dramatism, 107, 122, 124, 127; as expression of attitude, 114–15, 124; introduced, 10
Gide, André, 19–21, 116
Gilman, Sander, 20
"'Glimpses into a Labyrinth of Interwoven Motives': Selections from 'A Symbolic of Motives'" (Burke), 183n14
Grammar of Motives, A (Burke), 30, 46, 52, 108, 122–23, 124, 125, 129, 172n11, 177n15, 178n7
Grosz, Elizabeth, 6, 7, 92, 187n16
grotesque, 52–53, 54, 126, 147, 153
Gunn, Joshua, 31, 34–35, 40, 52, 54, 171n4, 172n12, 172n14
Gurdjieff, G. I., 9, 30–47, 48, 51, 52, 54, 55, 161, 172n14, 172n16, 173n18, 173n23, 176n4

Gurdjieffian mysticism, 9, 33, 35–38, 45, 47; and dance, 9, 35, 38–42, 43, 47, 49, 67, 141, 161, 173n23; stop exercises, 38–42, 44, 45, 52

habit, 5, 44, 47, 58, 67, 68–74, 110, 173n21, 179n13; and drugs, 67–68, 68–74, 83, 90; as mechanical, 40–42, 52
Halliwell, Steven, 136
Hartley, Lucy, 95, 176n7
Hau, Michael, 96, 100
Hauser, Gerard, 177n5
Hawhee, Debra, 9, 170n9, 173n2, 175n12, 176n5, 177–78n5, 179n18, 183n16
Hazlitt, William, 119
health, 104, 133, 142, 175n5; as suspect, 14–22, 57. *See also* illness
Heap, Jane, 37
Hegel, Georg W., 50, 52
hormones, 7, 78, 79–80, 82, 83, 86, 142; coining of term, 79–80, 175n4
Hoskins, R. G., 79, 80, 82, 87, 175n4
humanism, 7, 8, 11, 13, 58, 141, 160, 178–79n9, 187n10
humanities, 8, 10, 11, 166, 169n4; and transdisciplinarity, 3, 4, 6
Huxley, Julian, 112
hypochondria, 57, 104, 173–74n4, 182–83n12
hypochondriasis, 103–5, 130, 173–74n4, 177n15, 182–83n12

identification, 75, 106, 108, 116–18, 178n8, 180n20; gestures as component of, 117; somatic notion of, 108
identity, 52, 73, 117, 131; practices, 72; production, 56
illness, 5, 10, 20, 86–89, 103–105, 117, 134, 161, 169n4, 175n5, 183n16; Burke's illness, 10, 127, 129–36; in short-fiction characters, 14–21; transformative power of, 134
illocution, 163–64, 186n3, 187n13
imbalance, 73, 78; and efficiency, 58, 61
imitation, 110, 111, 118, 120, 145

immorality. *See* morality
"In Quest of Olympus" (Burke), 15
"In Quest of the Way" (Burke), 36, 55
inclination, 10, 14, 19, 22, 29, 93–94, 96, 99–101, 103, 105
incongruity, 3–5, 51–52, 53, 63–66, 153; incongruous naming, 76; method of, 48, 86; reading incongruously, 126. *See also* perspective by incongruity
individual: bodies, 8, 93, 100, 156, 159, 160–162, 167, 180–81n28, 187n10; and body types, 96, 100; and the collective, 100, 104, 140, 141–44, 146, 161; and the endocrine system, 82; and gesture-speech, 114, 179n13; in Gurdjieffian mysticism, 37; and hypochondria, 104; and language, 114, 153, 187n10
individuation, 22, 160–62
inefficiency. *See* efficiency
information, 26–27, 45–46, 80
innovation, 17, 57, 58
insomnia, 83, 85–86, 90, 105; Burke's, 12, 128, 134, 169n1 (ch. 1)
Institute for Religious and Social Studies, 183n19
Institute for the Harmonious Development of Man, 35, 39, 40, 42
Institute of Physics, 107
insulin, 79; shock therapy, 88–90, 175n7
intensities, 7, 45, 47, 55, 63, 71, 82, 177n5
interaction, 7, 70, 161
interpretation, 4, 76, 83–85, 86, 90, 91, 152, 156–57, 159, 162, 176n11, 180n27; bodily, 78, 85
invention, 129, 133, 139, 174n8, 178n6, 183–84n19

Jack, Jordynn, 55, 173n2, 174n10, 176n5
James, William, 31, 33, 36, 47–54, 55, 82–83, 153, 171n5, 173n21
Jameson, Fredric, 6–7, 8, 11, 140, 141, 169n2 (intro.), 186n5, 187n10
Jay, Paul, 127, 131, 181n6, 183n13
Johnson, Mark, 28
Jones, Amelia, 18
journalism, 59, 132

Kant, Immanuel, 36, 129
Keats, John, 19, 129, 161–62
Kennedy, George, 107, 109, 177n2, 179n10, 179n11, 179n16
"Know Thyself" (Burke), 12
Kretschmer, Ernst, 92–105; Burke's use of his theories, 99–103; explanation of his theories, 97–98; on genius, 103–5

language, 14, 143–44, 146, 152–55, 156–58, 159; and bodies as discursively constructed, 166; and catharsis, 128, 136, 142, 144; and dancing, 44–45; as drug, 73–74; and efficiency, 63, 69; and endocrinology, 77; epistemological view of, 11, 157, 166; evolutionary theories of, 106–24; as knowledge, 157–58; and laughter/tears, 140; magical view of, 183n19; and mysticism, 48–49, 51–52; in nonsymbolic motion / symbolic action, 122, 156–67; Paget's theories of, 106–24; and poetic purge, 138; poststructural theories of, 109, 178n8; as rhythmic, 27, 28; structural theories of, 109, 178n8
Language as Symbolic Action: Essays on Life, Literature, and Method (Burke), 109
"Language of Poetry, 'Dramatistically' Considered, The" (Burke), 183n19, 184n26
Larson, Steve, 28
laryngeal posture, 109, 110, 113, 115, 117, 160
laughter, 50–51, 52, 96, 111–12, 139–40, 142–43
Laura Spelman Rockefeller Memorial Trust, 55, 57, 173n3
Lawrence, Christopher, 127
Lawrence, D. H., 35, 46–47
Lear, Jonathan, 136
Lefebvre, Henri, 14, 28
Leff, Michael, 175n15
Lenin, Vladimir, 96
Little Review, 37
Ludwig, Emil, 94–97, 100, 101–3, 134

machines, 33; bodies as, 40–43, 58; university as, 16
magic, 37, 43–44, 52, 101–2, 136, 144, 154, 183–84n19
Mahen-Hays, Sarah E., 108, 178n7, 180n27
Malinowski, Branislaw, 100, 169n4
Mann, Thomas, 19–20, 21, 52, 104, 116, 176n6
Marañon, Gregorio, 82–83, 85
Martin, Randy, 6
Marxism, 92–93, 140
Massumi, Brian, 6–8, 184n27, 187n14
materiality, 1–2, 5–6, 9, 11, 14, 124, 140, 146, 166, 169n2 (intro.), 183n15
matter, force of, 2
Max-Neef, Manfred, 6
meaning making, 3–4, 8, 28–29, 75–91, 103, 106; and affect, 103; body's role in, 2, 14, 28–29, 75, 77, 90–91; and endocrinology, 75–91
mental illness, 87–90. *See also* insulin, shock therapy; neurasthenia; psychosis; schizophrenia
metabiology, 8–9, 75, 175n14
"Methodological Repression and/or Strategies of Containment" (Burke), 186n5, 187n10
methodology: of the book, 4–5, 9; Burke's, 4–5, 9, 31, 33, 48, 56–61, 64, 66, 74, 76–77, 86, 92–93, 104, 106, 116, 121, 123, 124, 133, 136, 153, 160, 186n5; development of Burke's at BSH, 55–74; counter-efficient, 64–65, 74, 76–77; and endocrinology, 77; Kretschmer's, 97–98, 100; mystical, 30–54, 136; as theory of drama, 121
metonymy, 75
micturition, 125, 136
mimesis, 43–44, 45–47, 88, 117, 119, 120
mimetics, 44, 45, 47, 83, 109–11, 113–14, 115–16, 117–18, 120, 139, 175n5; body-mind, 75, 86–88, 90
mind-body. *See* body-mind
mobility, 1, 6, 7, 119, 166
modernism, 1–2, 13, 18, 24, 31, 176n4

morality, 21, 34, 57, 63–66, 68, 69–73, 90, 95–97
morphine, 61, 63, 65–66, 69, 89
morphology, 7, 9, 11, 79; body, 100; facial, 95, 109
morpho-psychological approach, 94
motion, 111, 156–67, 187n12; and attitude, 123; of the body, 122, 138, 143; and hormones, 80; motion/action pair, 123, 124, 128, 143–44, 146–47, 156–67, 180–81n28, 185n33, 185n1, 186n3, 186n4, 186n5, 186n6, 187n9; motionlessness, 150. *See also* dance; movement
motives, 10, 91, 92–93, 102
movement, 1–2, 5, 7–8, 11, 20, 21–22, 25, 28–29, 32, 35–37, 45–47, 54, 66–68, 110, 112, 130, 144, 152, 156–67, 177–78n5, 184n23, 184n27, 187n13, 187–88n16; Gurdjieffian, 38–45; and hormones, 80; and language, 106–108, 110–12, 113, 115, 117, 118–21, 146, 151, 155, 183n15. *See also* dance; motion
"Mrs. Maecenas" (Burke), 14, 15–17, 19, 20–21
Munson, Gorham, 31, 35, 37–39, 41, 47, 172n15, 173n18, 173n23
music, 2, 11, 15, 28, 67, 86, 154, 155, 186–87n8; Burke's criticism, 9, 12, 13–14, 22–29, 68, 170n8; and catharsis, 136, 137, 141, 170n9; and mysticism, 22, 23, 39, 41, 56, 171n3; and rhetoric, 24–25; and rhythm, 13, 33, 66, 117, 175n12
"Musical Chronicle" (Burke), 22–29, 170n8, 171n3. See also *Dial*
musicians, 13, 15, 21, 23, 26, 154, 170n10
"My Dear Mrs. Wurtelbach" (Burke), 15
mysticism, 5, 7, 9, 11, 30–54, 55, 56, 58, 67, 77, 126, 141, 151, 169n4, 171n5, 171n6, 172n8, 172n11; and attitude, 33; and drugs, 55; and the grotesque, 52–54, 126, 153; as method, 31, 76–77, 86, 104, 136, 153, 160; and music, 22, 23 171n3; secular, 22, 31

National Committee for Mental Hygiene, 88
nature, 9, 147, 157, 158, 169n3, 174n5
neurasthenia, 15, 17–19, 170n5, 170n6
New Age, 35, 37
New Republic, 36, 172n9
Nicolescu, Basarab, 3
Nietzsche, Friedrich, 30, 37, 107, 129, 134, 160, 165, 183n16
nonsymbolic motion, 123, 124, 128, 143–44, 146–47, 156–67, 180–81n28, 185n33, 185n1, 186n3, 186n4, 186n5, 186n6, 187n9, 187n10
"(Nonsymbolic) Motion / (Symbolic) Action" (Burke), 156, 157, 161, 165, 178n7, 186n5, 187n9
Nordau, Max, 103
nosology, 129–30

occultism, 31, 34, 37, 54, 172n12
occupation, 46, 93, 99–105, 130–31, 134, 135, 173–74n4; as inclination, 99–100
O'Keefe, Daniel, 108, 178n7
"Olympians, The" (Burke), 15
"On Catharsis, or Resolution" (Burke), 136, 137–38, 141, 144, 184n22, 184n23
opium, 55, 56, 63, 64–65, 70–71
Orage, A. R., 33, 35, 37–42, 44, 45, 173n18, 173n23
orientation, 46, 49, 83, 86, 89, 91, 100
Ouspensky, P. D., 31, 32, 33, 35–38, 40, 42, 55, 173n18

Paget, Richard, 106–24, 125, 150, 153, 159, 160, 169n4, 175n8, 179n11, 179n13, 179n14, 180n25, 180n26
Paulson, William, 8
Pease, Donald A., 157
pentad, 30, 106, 107–8, 114, 122, 123, 124, 134, 186n3
perception, 24, 36, 55, 82, 157
performance, 5, 13, 22–25, 43, 120, 163, 166, 177–78n5; Gurdjieffian, 9, 35, 38, 39–41, 42, 44, 141. *See also* dance; movement
performativity, 5, 11 165, 169n2 (intro.), 184n27, 187–88n16

Permanence and Change: An Anatomy of Purpose (Burke), 4, 7, 30–31, 32, 34, 45–47, 51, 56, 59, 62, 68–69, 70–71, 72, 73, 76–77, 83–86, 90–91, 92, 93, 100–101, 102–3, 104–5, 106, 116, 159, 160, 167, 169n4, 171n1, 171n4, 172n8, 172n13, 173n2, 174n6, 175n14, 176n11, 179n18, 186–87n8
Perry, Ralph Barton, 48–51, 53
perspective by incongruity, 4, 48, 51–52, 153
Pezzullo, Phaedra, 169n3, 177–78n5
phenomenology, 8, 14, 53, 184n27
philology, 107, 109, 111, 119, 122, 137
philosophy, 40, 42, 52, 129, 171n1, 183n16; Western, 36, 92; Eastern, 35, 36
Philosophy of Literary Form, The (Burke), 5, 25–26, 56, 106, 118–20, 121, 122, 123, 130, 180n23
phrenology, 95–96, 176n7
Physical Society of London, 107
physiognomy, 95–96, 97, 98, 176n7
physiology, 5, 46, 63, 64, 67, 68, 70, 71, 77, 78–79, 82–83, 89, 112, 122–23, 124, 126, 142, 143, 155, 156, 160–61, 162, 164, 167, 180–81n28, 185n30, 186n7
piety, 56, 62, 68–74, 75, 86–87, 173n2, 175n15; definition of, 69
poetics, 71, 77, 122, 125–126, 129, 131, 135–37, 139–40, 141, 142–47, 152, 181n2, 184n23; bodily, 83, 118–22, 124; dramatistic theory of, 127; occult, 31
poetry, 45, 46, 47, 52, 66–67, 71–72, 76, 85, 102, 115–16, 117, 119, 123, 126–27, 137–39, 141, 147, 153, 170n11, 178n8, 180n26, 183n15, 183–84n19, 184n20; and drugs, 67; and laughter/tears, 139; poetic force, 60; and rhythm, 27–28
politics, 10, 47, 53–54, 104, 132, 141, 144, 146–47, 172n11, 177n5; and "antics of refusal," 33; and culture, 35; drug, 61, 63, 74; in mystic action, 46–47
pollution, 10, 142, 144–45, 147, 185n30
posture, 36, 39–40, 44, 45, 67, 100, 107, 110, 111, 113, 115, 117, 120, 121, 122

Pound, Ezra, 37
prayer, 45, 86–87, 90
preoccupation, 20, 46, 93, 100, 102–5
"Progression, A" (Burke), 15
psychiatry, 5, 77, 79, 86, 88–91
psychic disturbances. *See* insulin, shock therapy; mental illness; neurasthenia; psychosis; schizophrenia
psychoanalysis, 10, 27, 75–76, 79, 83–84, 86, 87, 89–91, 92–93, 94, 100–101, 105, 166, 176n4; in "David Wassermann" (Burke), 17, 18–19
psychogenic illness, 73, 86–87, 90–91, 161
psychology, 8, 26, 53, 63, 68, 90, 92, 94, 95, 97–98, 101, 104, 117, 118, 173n18
"Psychology and Form" (Burke), 26, 27
psychosis, 76–77, 94, 97–98, 100, 104; body as starting point of, 101; occupational, 76, 134
purge. *See* catharsis
purification. *See* catharsis
purpose, 4, 30, 45, 46, 93, 107, 112–14, 115, 123, 124, 172n11

"Questions and Answers about the Pentad" (Burke), 159, 160, 161, 186n4
Quietus, 151

race, 98, 176n10
Ransom, John Crowe, 146, 182n9, 183n15, 184n22, 184n23, 185n37
receptivity, 14, 28, 50, 67
refusal through rearticulation, 57, 60, 70, 97, 99, 100
religion, 9, 49, 92, 136; and music, 22; and mysticism, 32, 36, 39, 45–46, 49
responsive sympathy. *See* imitation
Rhetoric of Motives, A (Burke), 30, 55, 126, 129
Rhetoric of Religion: Studies in Logology, The (Burke), 31
rhetoric of science, 9, 75–91
rhetorical force, 27, 77, 124
rhythm, 2, 5, 11, 14, 22–29, 66–68, 71–72, 123, 134, 170n11; and arrhythmia, 12, 14, 21, 26, 130, 133; and attitude, 117–118; bodily, 9, 12, 28, 31, 33, 67–68, 161, 175n12; and Burke's ailments, 12; and Burke's short fiction, 21; and change, 22; expressive, 120–21; and form, 27–28, 180n21; and Gurdjieff, 33, 39; and music, 13, 27; and mysticism, 31; quotidian, 14, 17; as rhetorical appeal, 24, 25; routinized, of healthy bodies, 21
Rice, Jenny Edbauer, 184n27, 187n14
Richards, I. A., 46
ritual, 28, 39, 44, 67, 70, 72, 121, 136, 139, 147, 165
Rivers, William H. R., 101, 104, 130, 169n4
Rockefeller Foundation (John D. Rockefeller), 55, 61, 75, 78, 79, 88–89, 94
Rosteck, Thomas, 175n15
Rueckert, William, 9, 13, 126–27, 170n12, 178n8, 179n12, 181n4, 182n7, 183n14

Sakel, Manfred, 89, 175n6
Saussure, Ferdinand de, 109, 110
Schiebinger, Londa, 6
schizophrenia, 78, 88, 89, 98, 105, 175n7
science, 9, 10, 56–57, 74, 96, 97, 106, 107, 127, 175n2, 185n32; as disembodied theory, 127, 129; and mysticism, 51, 53, 54; and rhetoric, 75–91; studies, 74, 92
Science and Society, 48
Scott, Joan, 6
Sedgwick, Eve Kosofsky, 5, 184n27
Seigel, Marika, 174n5, 185n31, 185n32
Selzer, Jack, 1, 13, 14–15, 17, 18, 19, 21, 27, 55–56, 106, 170n12, 171n4, 173n3, 181n5
sensation, 5, 19, 36, 39, 68, 152, 162, 163, 165–166, 177–78n5
Shapin, Steven, 127
shit, 125, 147. *See also* excrement
short fiction (Burke), 9, 12, 13, 14–22, 26
signifier/signified, 109
signs, 84–85, 96, 111, 151, 153, 155
social construction, 10, 140
"Soul of Kajn Tafha, The" (Burke), 15

speaking, 74, 129, 162; and writing, 130–31, 134, 159,
speech, 106–24, 177n2, 179n11, 180n26
speech-act theory, 11, 158, 160–64, 180n22, 186n3, 186n5
Spelman Fund of New York. *See* Laura Spelman Rockefeller Memorial Trust
spiritualism, 35, 169n4
spirituality, 31, 54, 99, 140
Starling, E. H., 79, 80, 175n4
Stravinsky, Igor, 24
Stein, Gertrude, 50, 173n21
style, 72–74, 100
subjectivism, 38, 55
substance, 67, 68, 73–74, 80, 118, 178n8
supernatural, 31
symbol use, 8, 44, 131, 140, 143, 152, 153, 154, 180n27, 187n9
symbolic, 8, 9, 22, 28, 43, 112, 125, 128, 131, 136, 140, 142, 143, 154, 165, 169n2 (intro.), 177n5; realm, 142, 146, 161
symbolic action, 48, 106, 108, 109, 112–13, 115, 119–20, 122, 123, 124, 128, 143, 146–47, 156–67, 178n8, 180n23, 180–81n28, 184n20, 185n33, 185n1, 186n3, 186n4, 186n5, 186n6, 187n9
"Symbolic of Motives" (Burke), 10, 125–155, 181n4, 182n7, 183n14
synecdoche, 5–6

Tate, Allen, 31, 33–35, 42, 45, 46, 52, 53, 58, 61, 77, 172n9, 172n11, 174n7, 174n9
tears, 82, 139–44
terministic screens, 75, 174n6
texture, 4, 5, 24, 69, 71, 72
Thames, Richard, 75, 126–27, 175n14, 181n3
theosophy, 34–35
Thiele, Leslie Paul, 7, 8
thing power, 2
"Thinking of the Body, The" (Burke), 125–27, 137, 139, 144–47, 149, 155, 181n2, 181n4, 182n7, 182n9
Thorndike, E. L., 111

thought, 1–2, 4, 40, 86, 101, 153, 159, 177–78n5
tonality, 45, 118, 119–20
Toomer, Jean, 37–38, 39, 40, 41, 172n15
touch, 5, 25, 184n27, 187n12
Towards a Better Life (Burke), 63, 131–32
transdisciplinarity, 2, 3–6, 8, 14, 51, 56, 75, 88–89, 92, 94, 97, 106, 159, 167; and interdisciplinarity, 3; and the methodology of the book, 9
transference, 140, 141, 184n27
transformation, 7, 9, 33, 46, 47, 74, 118, 159; and catharsis, 136; in mystical dance, 41, 42, 44; rhythmic, 13

Veblen, Thorstein, 76
Vesey, W. T., 80
vision, 36, 70, 76, 78, 90, 94, 100, 105, 142, 179–80n19. *See also* ways of seeing
Viswanathan, Gauri, 34–35
vocation, 93

Wagner, Richard, 23, 25
Walker, Jeffrey, 136
Walker, Julia, 6, 169n2 (intro.), 187–88n16
ways of seeing, 34, 97. *See also* vision
Weber, Max, 34
Welch, Louise, 35, 38, 39, 40–41
weltanschauung, 100, 176n11
Wess, Robert, 7, 13, 66, 126, 170n12, 175n14, 178n8, 181n4, 185n31, 185–86n1
Western philosophy, 92; versus Eastern, 36, 45
"White Oxen, The" (Burke), 14, 15, 20–21, 131
Whitman, Walt, 47–48, 53–54, 171n5
"William James: Superlative Master of the Comparative" (Burke), 50, 51
Williams, William Carlos, 32, 148, 173n18, 182–83n12, 183n15
Wilson, Elizabeth A., 7, 8, 92, 170n6, 178n9
Winchell, Walter, 120
Woolf, Virginia, 125, 128, 134
Wolfe, Cary, 8, 75, 174n5, 185n31

Woods, Colonel Arthur, 55, 56, 57, 60–61, 61–62, 63–64, 65, 68–69, 70, 71, 74, 89, 174n8, 174n9, 175n13
words, 28, 51, 77, 86, 106, 107, 111–12, 113, 115–18, 119–20, 126, 128, 130, 136, 140, 143, 145–46, 153–54, 158–62, 165, 187n12
"Words as Deeds" (Burke), 158–62

world view. *See* orientation; weltanschauung
writing, 26, 53, 73, 106, 110, 128, 129, 130–36, 159, 184n27; ghostwriting, 60–61, 64–66, 67, 68, 174n8, 175n13

Yeats, W. B., 32, 33, 35, 49, 54
Yoshioka, Kumiko, 66

ABOUT THE AUTHOR

DEBRA HAWHEE is associate professor of English and of communication at the University of Illinois at Urbana–Champaign, where she teaches courses in history of rhetoric, rhetorical theory, bodies, and gesture. She is the author of *Bodily Arts: Rhetoric and Athletics in Ancient Greece* and coauthor with Sharon Crowley of *Ancient Rhetorics for Contemporary Students*.

www.ingramcontent.com/pod-product-compliance
Lightning Source LLC
Chambersburg PA
CBHW030650230426
43665CB00011B/1022